The New
CAMBRIDGE
English Course

PRACTICE

1

■ *mit Lösungsschlüssel*

**MICHAEL SWAN
CATHERINE WALTER**

Cambridge University Press

Ernst Klett Verlag
Stuttgart Düsseldorf Leipzig

Inhalt

Acknowledgements

The authors and publishers are grateful to the following copyright owners for permission to reproduce photographs, illustrations, texts and music. Every endeavour has been made to contact copyright owners and apologies are expressed for any omissions.

page 5: Reproduced by permission of *Punch*.   page 6: Reproduced by permission of *Punch*.   page 10: *b* From *Weekend Book of Jokes 22* courtesy of Weekend.   page 14: *b* Reproduced by permission of *Punch*.   page 23: From *Weekend Book of Jokes 22* courtesy of Weekend.   page 24: *b* Reproduced by permission of British Telecom. ® The British Telecom logo is a registered trade mark of British Telecommunications public limited company.   page 25: *b* Reproduced by permission of *Punch*.   page 26: From *Weekend Book of Jokes 22* courtesy of Weekend.   page 31: Chart from THE F-PLAN CALORIE AND FIBRE CHART by Audrey Eyton (Penguin Books 1982), copyright © Audrey Eyton, 1982, pp 76–7.   page 37: *t* Reproduced by permission of the IFL Penfriend Service; *br* Reproduced by permission of The Post Office (International Letters) and Union Postale Universelle (Bureau International).   page 38: Reproduced by permission of *Punch*.   page 39: Reproduced by permission of *Punch*.   page 40: Reprinted by permission of Johnny Hart and Creators Syndicate, Inc. page 43: *bl* Reproduced by permission of *Punch*.   page 47: Courtesy of Hilton International, London. page 49: Reproduced by permission of *Punch*.   page 50: Reproduced by permission of *Punch*.   page 53: *b* Excerpt from 'Hello, Britain' text reprinted courtesy of the British Tourist Authority; London Regional Transport trade mark by permission of the London Transport Museum; British Rail logo by permission of the British Railways Board.   page 59: Reproduced by permission of Dover Publications, Inc., New York. page 62: Reproduced by permission of *Punch*.   page 63: From *Weekend Book of Jokes 22* courtesy of Weekend.   page 65: Reprinted by permission of The Putnam Publishing Group from THE SPY WHO CAME IN FROM THE COLD by John Le Carré. Copyright © 1963 by Victor Gollancz. Also by permission of David Higham Associates Ltd and Le Carré Productions. page 66: From *The Guinness Book of Records* © Guinness Publications Ltd by permission of Guinness Publishing Ltd.   page 68: © Express Newspapers plc. page 69: *bl* and *br* Reproduced by permission of *Punch*. page 72: Reproduced by permission of *Punch*.   page 77: *t* From *Adolescent Boys of East London* by Peter Wilmott, reprinted by permission of Routledge & Kegan Paul; *bl* and *br* Reproduced by permission of *Punch*. page 79: *bl* and *br* Reproduced by permission of *Punch*. page 86: *b* Reproduced by permission of *Punch*.   page 87: Adapted from *Love and War in the Apennines* by Eric Newby, reprinted by permission of Collins.   page 88: Cartoon by SAX reproduced by permission of Mail Newspapers plc.   page 89: Reproduced by permission of *Punch*.   page 90: *b* From *Weekend Book of Jokes 22* courtesy of Weekend.   page 92: *tl* Adapted from *How to be an Alien* by George Mikes © André Deutsch 1984; *tr* Cartoon by Artemas Cole (Manuel Gonzalez); *br* Reproduced by permission of *Reveille* and

Syndication International (1986) Ltd.   page 97: *r* From *Weekend Book of Jokes 23* courtesy of Weekend.   page 98: *b* Reproduced by permission of *Punch*.   page 99: Adapted from *Baby and Child Care*. Copyright © 1945, 1946, © 1957, 1968, 1976 by Dr Benjamin Spock. Reprinted by permission of Pocket Books, a division of Simon & Schuster, Inc.   page 100: *tr* From PHYSICAL FITNESS developed by the Royal Canadian Air Force (Penguin Books, 1964), Crown copyright © Queen's Printer, Canada, 1958, 1960: reprinted by permission of the Ministry of Supply and Services, Canada, Penguin Books Ltd, UK, and the Government Printing Office, New Zealand; *bl* and *br* Reproduced by permission of *Punch*.   page 105: Abridged from *The Guinness Book of Answers* © Guinness Superlatives Ltd and Norris McWhirter, by permission of Guinness Publishing Ltd.   page 106: *t* Reproduced by permission of the Consumers' Association; *cl* and *br* Reproduced by permission of *Punch*.   page 108: Courtesy of Rolls-Royce Motor Cars Ltd.

Artist Partners: Tony Graham, pages 13, 21 *r*, 37 *bl*, 42 *b*; Robin Harris, page 99; Biz Hull, page 11 *l*. B. L. Kearley: Tony Kenyon, pages 4 *b*, 5, 7 *r*, 8 *b*, 9 *b*, 11 *tr*, 12 *b*, 14, 16 *t*, 20 *bl*, 23, 24, 25 *t*, 53, 100; Barry Wilkinson, page 74.   Maggie Mundy: Hemesh Alles, page 97 *l*; Maggie Brand, page 96 *t*; Ann Johns, pages 11 *br*, 15, 20 *t*, 25 *c*, 29 *b*, 33, 39 *b*, 44, 48, 51, 56, 57, 61, 67, 71, 75, 81, 86 *t*, 90 *t*, 94, 98 *t*, 103, 107, 110.   Young Artists: Sarah John, pages 22 *b*, 34, 52, 65.

Nancy Anderson, pages 76, 80.   John Blackman, pages 42 *t*, 58, 69 *t*, 101.   Joe McEwan, pages 18, 21 *l*, 22, 36, 38.   Rodney Sutton, pages 6, 7 *l*, 8, 10 *t*, 12 *t*, 16 *b*, 27, 30, 32, 39 *t*, 43 *r*, 45, 55 *t*, 66, 96 *b*.

Darren Marsh, pages 4 *tc*, *c* and *cr*, 9 *t* and *c*, 29 *c*. Ken Weedon, page 47.   The Image Bank, pages 4 *tl*, and *cl*, 10 *c*, 19.

(*t* = top *b* = bottom *c* = centre *r* = right *l* = left)

Vorwort

Liebe/r Lerner/in

Dieses *Practice Book* mit zahlreichen Übungen zum Wortschatz, zur Grammatik, aber auch zur Aussprache und zur Entwicklung von Lese-, Hör- und Schreibfertigkeiten, bietet Ihnen die Möglichkeit, das im Unterricht Gelernte zu wiederholen, zu vertiefen und zu festigen.

Das *Practice Book* enthält darüber hinaus eine Kurzgrammatik, einen Schlüssel zur Selbstkorrektur sowie Arbeitsanweisungen in deutscher Sprache. Sie können daher parallel zum Unterricht unabhängig zu Hause arbeiten, was für Ihre Bemühungen, die englische Sprache zu lernen, von Vorteil sein wird.

Auch wenn Sie einmal nicht zum Unterricht erscheinen können, kann Ihnen das *Practice Book* – zusammen mit dem *Student's Book* und den *Student's Cassettes* – helfen, das versäumte Wissen selbständig zu Hause aufzuarbeiten.

Der Unitaufbau im *Practice Book* entspricht der Reihenfolge der Units im *Student's Book*.

Neben Wiederholungs- und Festigungsübungen, die sich in ihren thematischen und strukturellen Schwerpunkten auf die jeweiligen Units im *Student's Book* beziehen, enthält das *Practice Book* auch eine Reihe von Lese- und Hörverständnisübungen, die Ihnen helfen, von Anfang an Ihre Hör- und Lesefertigkeiten systematisch zu trainieren. Wenn Sie die Übungen zum Hörverständnis bearbeiten möchten, brauchen Sie die *Student's Cassettes*. Diese enthalten unter anderem eine Auswahl aus dem Hörmaterial, das Ihr/e Kursleiter/in im Unterricht einsetzt. Die Lösungen zu den Höraufgaben finden Sie entweder im *Student's Book* oder im Schlüssel zum *Practice Book*.

Außer Hörverständnisübungen gibt es im *Practice Book* auch eine Anzahl von Übungen zum Leseverständnis. Hierbei handelt es sich um Aufgaben, zu deren Lösung Sie nicht den gesamten Text verstehen müssen. Lesen Sie die Arbeitsanweisungen zunächst sorgfältig durch und tun sie genau das, was sie Ihnen aufgeben. Erst nachdem Sie die Aufgabe gelöst haben, sollten sie – wenn Sie möchten – den Text mit Hilfe Ihres Wörterbuchs intensiver bearbeiten.

Eine besondere Komponente der Leseübungen ist *IT'S A LONG STORY*, eine episodenhafte Geschichte, die ab Unit 2, dem jeweiligen Lernstadium entsprechend, in den Folgeunits fortgesetzt wird. Eine Aufnahme der einzelnen Episoden befindet sich auch auf den *Student's Cassettes* als zusätzliches Angebot zum Hörverständnistraining.

Im Anhang zum *Practice Book* finden sie einen ausführlichen Lösungsschlüssel zu allen geschlossenen Übungstypen. Sie können also Ihre Lösungen zu den Aufgaben jederzeit überprüfen und sich nur in Zweifelsfällen an Ihre/n Kursleiter/in wenden.

Nicht zuletzt hilft Ihnen auch die Kurzgrammatik, wenn Sie bei der Arbeit mit dem *Practice Book* auf eine Schwierigkeit stoßen. Ein übersichtliches Inhaltsverzeichnis sorgt für eine schnelle und gezielte Orientierung. Die Grammatik bietet in deutscher Fassung eine leicht verständliche Darstellung der wichtigsten sprachlichen Strukturen für diese Lernstufe und enthält viele Beispiele mit deutschen Übersetzungen, an denen wichtige Unterschiede zwischen den beiden Sprachen verdeutlicht werden. Schließlich ist noch auf die Zusammenstellung von nützlichen Ausdrücken und Redewendungen der englischen Alltagssprache am Ende der Grammatik hinzuweisen.

Wir sind überzeugt, daß sie mit dem *Practice Book* für ihre selbständige Arbeit parallel zum Unterricht bestens ausgerüstet sind und wünschen Ihnen viel Freude beim Englischlernen mit dem *New Cambridge English Course*.

Autoren und Redaktion

Unit **1** **Hello**

1A What's your name?

1 Schreiben Sie die Sätze.

1. What's your name?

2. Carmen. What's _my name?_

3. Is _My own name_ Joe?

4. No, _it isn't._ It's _Mark._

5. _Is_ your name Lucy?

6. Yes, it _is._

7. Is _your name_ Sally?

8. Yes, _it is._

9. Hello. _My nam name is_ Anne.

10. _What's your name?_

2 Schreiben Sie die unverkürzten Formen.

1. No, it _isn't._ _No, it is not._
2. _What's_ your name? _What is your name?_
3. My _name's_ Judy. _My name is Judy._
4. _It's_ Mary. _It is Mary_

3 Schreiben Sie die Antworten.

1. One + one = _two_
2. Three − two = _Five_
3. Two + one = _Three_
4. Three − one = _Four_
5. One + two = _Three_

4 Üben Sie die Aussprache.

isn't   it isn't   No, it isn't.
name   your name   What's your name?
is   it is   Yes, it is.

5 Übersetzen Sie ins Deutsche.

1. Hello. My name's Mary Lake.
2. Hello. Yes, room three one two, Mrs Lake.
3. Thank you.

4. What's your name?
5. Catherine.
6. What's _your_ name?
7. John.

8. Is your name Mark Perkins?
9. No, it isn't. It's Harry Brown.

6 Wenn Sie _Student's Cassette A_ haben, suchen Sie _Unit 1, Lesson A, Exercise 1._ Hören Sie sich die Gespräche an und versuchen Sie, sie aufzuschreiben. Benutzen Sie _Student's Book, Exercise 1_ zur Kontrolle. Üben Sie die Aussprache.

1   2

1B His name's James Wharton

1 Setzen Sie *my* oder *your* ein.

1. What's _your_ name?
2. Hello. _My_ name's Bond – James Bond.
3. 'Is _your_ name Anne?' 'Yes, that's right.'
4. '_My_ name's Robert, isn't it?' 'No, it's Mike.'

2 Setzen Sie *his* oder *her* ein.

1. _Her_ name's Brigitte.
2. _His_ name's James.
3. 'Her name's Anne.' 'What's _her_ surname?'
4. '_His_ name's Lee.' 'Is that his first name or his surname?'

3 *First name* oder *surname*?

1. Denise _first name_
2. Gavin _first name_
3. Quinton _surname_
4. Wharton _surname_
5. Dorrington _surname_
6. Gillian _first name_
7. Jowitt _surname_
8. James _first name_

4 Übersetzen Sie ins Deutsche.

1. Her name. _Ihr name_
2. His name. _Sein name_
3. Her surname is Quinton. _Ihr Nachmame is Quinton._
4. His first name is James. _Sein Vorname ist James._ *
5. I don't know. _Ich weiss nicht_
6. Yes, that's right. _Ja, das ist richtig._
7. No, it isn't. _Nein, ist es nicht._

5 Ein Kreuzworträtsel.

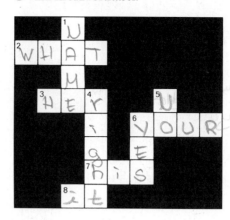

ACROSS

2. _What_'s your name?
3. _Her_ name's Jacqueline Onassis.
6. 'Is _your_ name Paul?' 'Yes, it is.'
7. Not *her*.
8. Yes, _it_ is.

DOWN

1. What's your _name_?
4. Yes, that's _right_
5. Not *yes*.
6. Not *no*.

6 Wenn Sie *Student's Cassette A* haben, suchen Sie *Unit 1, Lesson B, Exercise 5*. Hören Sie zu und sprechen Sie nach.

1   2

"Right! What's your name?"

5

1C How are you?

1 Schreiben Sie die Antworten.

1. 'Hello.' 'Hello .'
2. 'How are you?' 'I'm , fine .'
3. 'What's your name?' 'James Quinton ', Fine,
4. 'How do you do?' 'How do you do ?'

2 Vervollständigen Sie die Gespräche.

'Excuse me . Is your name Alice Stevens?'
'No, I'm sorry. It's Alice Carter.'

* * *

'Excuse me. Are you Bill Wallace?'
'Yes , I am .'
'Hello, Bill. My name's Jane Marks.'

3 Schreiben Sie die Antworten.

1. Six ÷ three = two
2. Six ÷ two = three
3. Three + two = five
4. Five − one = four
5. Five − three = two
6. One × five = five
7. One + one + two = four
8. (Two + three + one) ÷ two = three
9. Four − three = one
10. Four − two + four = six

4 *Excuse me* oder *I'm sorry?*

1

2

3

4

5

5 Übersetzen Sie ins Deutsche.

1. Hello.
2. How are you?
3. How do you do?
4. Fine, thanks.
5. Excuse me.
6. I'm sorry.

1D Where are you from?

1 Achten Sie auf die richtige Betonung beim Aussprechen folgender Wörter:

Australia	Australian
Germany	German
England	English
Britain	British
Italy	Italian
China	Chinese
Japan	Japanese

2 Schreiben Sie die unverkürzten Formen.

1. *I'm* English. I am English
2. No, it *isn't.* No, it is not
3. *He's* from Tanzania. He is from Tanzania
4. *She's* American. She is American
5. *I'm* from Oxford. I am from Oxford
6. *Where's* she from? Where is she from?

STOWELL

3 Welches Eigenschaftswort paßt zu welchem Bild?

Thai	French	Japanese
Cuban	Swiss	British
Egyptian	Chinese	Greek
German		

1. Swiss chocolate

2. a Thai dancer

3. an Egyptian pyramid

4. a Japanese camera

5. a Greek statue

6. a German car

7. a British car

8. French perfume

9. a Cuban cigar

10. a Chinese plate

4 Übersetzen Sie ins Deutsche.

1. Where are you from?
2. She's from India.
3. He's Chinese.
4. Helena's from Greece.
5. Andrew's Scottish.

Wo kommst du her
Sie ist aus Indien
Er ist Chinese Griechenland
Helena ist aus
Andrew ist Schotte

5 Wenn Sie *Student's Cassette A* haben, suchen Sie *Unit 1, Lesson D, Exercise 4.* Üben Sie die Aussprache der Wörter aus *Student's Book, Exercise 4.* Benutzen Sie die Cassette zur Kontrolle Ihrer Aussprache.

1

2

6 Ein Kreuzworträtsel.

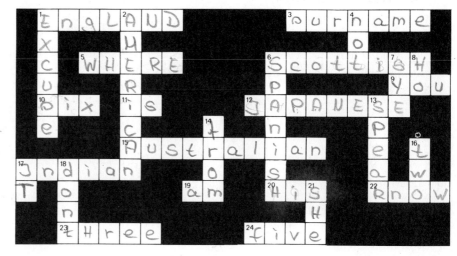

ACROSS ⇒

1. She's English. She's from ....
3. 'What's your ....?'   'Jowitt.'
5. .... are you from?
6. Andrew is .... He's from Scotland.
9. She's French. .... name's Isabelle.
10. 6.
11. 'Is your name Catherine?'   'Yes, it ....'
12. Yumiko is from Tokyo. She's ....
15. Tony's from Australia. He's ....
17. She's from India. She's ....
19. 'Are you American?'   'Yes, I ....'
20. He's from England. .... name's Mark Perkins.
22. 'Where is Anne from?'   'I don't ....'
23. 3.
24. 5.

DOWN ⇓

1. .... me. Are you Gavin Jowitt?
2. Sharon's from the United States. She's ....
4. *isn't = is* ....
6. Carlos is from Madrid. He's ....
7. Colette's Swiss. .... is from Zurich.
8. Erik's German. ....is from Germany.
13. I .... Spanish, French, and a little English.
14. Where are you ....?
16. 2.
17. 'Is his surname Hayashi?'   'Yes, ... is.'
18. 'What's her name?'   'I'm sorry, I .... know.'
21. 'Is Carla from Rome?'   'Yes, ... is.'

7

Unit 2 You

2A   What do you do?

1 Setzen Sie ein: *I, you, he, she, it, my, your, his* oder *her.*

1. 'Are _you_ Mary Lewis?' 'Yes, _I_ am.'
2. She's from Spain. _Her_ name's Carmen.
3. _He_'s from Japan. His name's Mr Watanabe.
4. 'Are _you_ Italian?' 'No, I'm Greek.'
5. 'Is your name John Collett?' 'No, _it_ isn't.'
6. _My_ name's Alice Stephens. I'm a dentist.

2 Achten Sie auf die richtige Betonung beim Aussprechen folgender Wörter:

artist	dentist	United
electrician	surname	Excuse me
engineer	Hello	Chinese
architect	Goodbye	British

3 Tragen Sie weitere Wörter in die Listen ein.

A	AN
a doctor	an electrician

4 Vervollständigen Sie die Gespräche.

A: What's your name?
B: It's Smith.
A: ...., Mr Smith? *What's your first name?*
B: James.
A: ....? *What do you do?*
B: I'm an electrician.

A: *Are you a* .... photographer?
B: No, *I'm an* .... accountant.
A: Oh!

A: *Is she a* doctor?
B: No, *she's an* actress.

A: *Is he a* pilot?
B: Yes, *he is.*

5 Übersetzen Sie ins Deutsche.

1. What do you do?
2. How do you do?
3. How are you?
4. I'm an engineer.
5. She's an engineer.
6. He's an engineer.
7. Is she a doctor?
8. Yes, she is.
9. No, she isn't.

6 Wenn Sie *Student's Cassette A* haben, suchen Sie *Unit 2, Lesson A, Exercise 5.* Üben Sie die Aussprache der Wörter aus *Student's Book, Exercise 5.* Benutzen Sie die Cassette zur Kontrolle Ihrer Aussprache.

1   2

8

2B I'm very well, thank you

1 Setzen Sie ein: *am, 'm not, are(n't), 's* oder *isn't.*

1. Hello. How _are_ you?
2. How _is_ your daughter today?
3. 'Are you English?' 'Yes, I _am_.'
4. 'Judith _is_ a doctor.' 'No, she _isn't_. She's a dentist.'
5. 'Are you an artist?' 'No, I _'m not_.'

2 *Morning, afternoon, evening* oder *night?*

  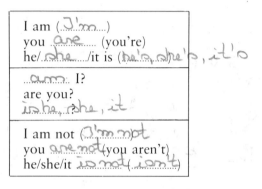

1 _morning or evening_   2 _afternoon_   3 _morning_

4 _night_   5 _morning afternoon_   6 _morning_

3 Vervollständigen Sie die Gespräche.

Dialogue 1
A: _Hey John. How are you_
B: Not bad. And you?
A: _Good, thank you_.

Dialogue 2
A: _Good afternoon, Dr Watson. How are you_
B: Good afternoon, Mr Kowalski. I'm fine, thank you. And you?
A: _I'm well, thanks._

Dialogue 3
A: Hello. I'm Polly. What's your name?
B: _I'm Steve._
   Are you from Spanish?
A: No, I'm Australian. And you?
B: _I'm from Britain_
   Are you a teacher?
A: Yes, I am. Oh, dear! It's 10.45! I must go. Bye!
B: _Bye_.

4 Tragen Sie die Wörter im Kasten in die entsprechende Liste ein.

~~artist~~ ~~Chinese~~ ~~doctor~~ ~~electrician~~ ~~engineer~~ ~~he~~ ~~her~~ ~~his~~ ~~housewife~~ ~~Italian~~ ~~John~~ ~~Mary~~ ~~photographer~~ ~~secretary~~ ~~she~~ ~~shop assistant~~ ~~Spanish~~ ~~student~~ ~~Susan~~ ~~Tom~~

WOMAN	MAN	WOMAN OR MAN
Mary	John	artist

5 Kopieren und vervollständigen Sie die Tabelle.

I am (_I'm_)   you _are_ (you're)   he/_she_/it is (he's, _she's, it's_
_am_ I?   are you?   _is he, she, it_
I am not (_I'm not_   you _are not_ (you aren't)   he/she/it _is not (isn't_

6 Übersetzen Sie ins Deutsche.

1. Good morning. _Guten Morgen_
2. Hello. _Hallo_
3. Good afternoon. _Guten Tag_
4. Good evening. _Guten Abend_
5. I'm very well, thank you. _Mir geht's sehr gut,_
6. Fine, thanks. _Fein, danke._ _danke schön._
7. I'm not well today. _Mir geht's heute nicht gut_
8. Oh, I'm sorry to hear that. _Oh, Ich entschuldige mich das höre ich._

7 Wenn Sie *Student's Cassette A* haben, suchen Sie *Unit 2, Lesson B, Exercise 2.* Üben Sie die Gespräche aus *Student's Book, Exercise 2.* Benutzen Sie die Cassette zur Kontrolle Ihrer Aussprache.

Good morning, Mr Roberts.

Good morning, Mr Roberts.

1   2

2C I'm an actress. And you?

1 Setzen Sie ein: *I, you, he, she, am, 'm, are, 're, is* oder *'s*.

1. George is Swiss. _He_ is from Geneva.
2. 'Mrs Alexander isn't English.' 'No? Where's _She_ from?'
3. 'Are you American?' 'Yes, I _am_.'
4. 'What do _you_ do?' '_I_'m a doctor.'
5. '_Are_ you married?' 'Yes, I _am_.'
6. 'What'_s_ your name?' 'Charles.'
7. '_Is_ your name Alice?' 'No, it _is_n't.'
8. 'What does Mary do?' '_She is_ a shop assistant.'

2 Schreiben Sie die Fragen.

1. '_Are you married_?' 'No, I'm single.'
2. '_What do you do_?' 'I'm a doctor.'
3. '_Where are you from_?' 'Australia.'
4. '_What's your name_?' 'John Cagney.'
5. '_Is your name Michelle_?' 'No, it's Mary.'

3 Setzen Sie die fehlenden Wörter ein.

1. 'Are you Italian?' 'No, I'm _from_ France.'
2. I _speak_ a little Portuguese.
3. 'What's your _first name_?' 'Michael.' 'And your _surname_?' 'Smith.'
4. Excuse _me_.
5. '_How_ are you?' 'Fine, _thanks_.'

4 *First name* oder *surname*?

Alice	Anne	Barker	Bill	Catherine
Dan	Jackson	James	Jane	Jennings
John	Manning	Mary	Miriam	Perkins
Peter	Philip	Sarah	Steve	Susan	Tom
Wagner	Watson	Webber	Wharton

First name	Surname
Alice	Barker

5 Übersetzen Sie ins Deutsche.

1. eleven _elf_
2. twelve _zwölf_
3. thirteen _dreizehn_
4. nineteen _neunzehn_
5. She's married. _Sie ist verheiratet._
6. He's single. _Her ist single_
7. That's interesting. _Das ist interessant_

6 Wenn Sie *Student's Cassette A* haben, suchen Sie *Unit 2, Lesson C, Exercise 1*. Hören Sie zu und üben Sie. Achten Sie auf die Betonung.

| thir**teen** | four**teen** | fif**teen** | six**teen** |
| seven**teen** | eigh**teen** | nine**teen** | |

1   2

7 Trennen Sie die beiden Geschichten voneinander.

Alice is sixteen.
Steve is twenty.
His surname is Berczuk; it's a Ukrainian name.
She is a student from Aberdeen, in Scotland.
Her surname is MacAllen.
He's an artist, so his job is interesting.
He is from Australia, but now he is both British and Australian.
MacAllen is a Scottish name, not an English name.
Alice lives at 6 Menzies Way.
He is from Sydney.
His address in London is 113 Beech Road, NW2.
She is not very well today.

Alice	Steve
Alice is sixteen.	Steve is twenty. H

"Me?"

10

2D How old are you?

1 Korrigieren Sie die Sätze.

1. whats your name
   What's your name ?
2. how old are you
3. im an engineer
4. suzanne is french
5. are you an architect
6. john isnt in england
7. shes twenty seven

2 Ordnen Sie die Zahlen den entsprechenden Wörtern zu.

55	five	6	sixty-six	99	ninety
15	fifty-five	16	six	90	nineteen
50	fifty	60	sixteen	19	nine
5	fifteen	66	sixty	9	ninety-nine

3 Schreiben Sie die Zahlen aus. Beispiel:

76 *seventy-six*

82	23	14	30	61
47	88	17	54	12

4 Welches Wort paßt nicht?

1. morning   evening   night   (name)
2. (Hi)   How   Where   What
3. Italian   British   (Japan)   American
4. Hi.   (Thanks.)   Hello.   Good morning.
5. fine   very well   not bad   (good)
6. two   twenty-eight   (seven)   sixteen   six
7. (eighty-two)   five   thirty   ninety-five   ten

5 Vervollständigen Sie das Gespräch.

'Good morning. I'm Ms Wharton. Do sit down.
   Now, what's your name, please?'
'*Bill Perkins*'
'And your address?'
'*113 Beech Road.*'
'Is that a London address?'
'*Yes it is*'
'I see. Now, how old are you, please?'
'*42*'
'And what's your job?'
'*I'm an engineer*'
'Fine. Now, how are you today?'
'*Not bad, thanks.*'
'OK. Please read this . . .'

6 Übersetzen Sie ins Deutsche.

1. How old are you? *Wie alt bist du?*
2. How are you? *Wie bist du?*
3. He's separated. *Er ist getrennt.*
4. She's divorced. *Sie ist geschieden.*
5. She's a widow. *Sie ist Witwe.*
6. a hundred *ein hundert*
7. Mr Jackson *Mister Jackson*
8. Mrs Jackson *Misses Jackson*
9. Miss Jackson *Miss Jackson*
10. Dr Jackson *Doktor Jackson*

7 Wenn Sie *Student's Cassette A* haben, suchen Sie *Unit 2, Lesson D, Exercise 1.* Üben Sie die Aussprache der Zahlen aus *Student's Book, Exercise 1.* Benutzen Sie die Cassette zur Kontrolle Ihrer Aussprache.

twenty-one   twenty-one

1   2

8 🔊 Lesen Sie mit Hilfe Ihres Wörterbuchs.

IT'S A LONG STORY
1

Judy Parker is twenty-two. She is a medical student. Judy is intelligent and very pretty, with a good sense of humour. She is a nice woman. Her boyfriend's name is Sam Watson. Sam is twenty-seven. He works in a bank as assistant manager. He is good-looking, but he is not a very nice man. Judy loves Sam very much. Sam loves money, cars, good food, whisky, travel and beautiful women.

🔊   Dieses Symbol bedeutet, daß Sie diese Episode von *It's a Long Story* auf einer der *Student's Cassettes* hören können.

Unit 3 People

3A Andrew's bag's under the table

1 Formulieren Sie die Sätze wie in den Beispielen.

1. Where is Ann's hat? *Where is her hat?*
2. Dan's an architect. *Dan is an architect.*
3. Ann's married.
4. John's bag is under the table.
5. Is Susan's book French?
6. Tom's pen isn't on the table.
7. Harry's coat's on the chair.
8. Mary's single.
9. Where's Alice's pen?
10. Dan's Italian.

2 Schreiben Sie Fragen.

1. Fine, thanks. *How are you?*
2. It's under the table. *Where's John's pen?*
3. How do you do?
4. I'm an engineer.
5. It's on the chair.
6. No, he isn't. He's a teacher.
7. No, it isn't. It's under my coat.
8. I'm very well, thank you.
9. No, I'm divorced.
10. She's not well today.
11. 17 Church Lane.
12. Q, U, I, N, T, O, N.
13. The United States.

3 Welcher Begriff paßt zu welchem Bild?

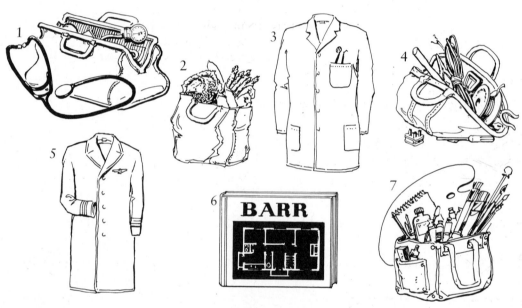

| 6 an architect's book | 7 an artist's bag | 3 a dentist's coat | 5 a pilot's coat |
| 1 a doctor's bag | 4 an electrician's bag | 2 a housewife's bag |

4 Schreiben Sie die Antworten.

1. What's your surname?
2. What's your first name?
3. What's your nationality?
4. How old are you?
5. Are you an architect?
6. Are you married?
7. How are you today?
8. Where's your bag?
9. Where's your Practice Book?

5 Übersetzen Sie ins Deutsche.

1. John's coat is on the table.
2. Where's Polly's bag?
3. Is Ann's coat on the chair?
4. Ann's pen is on John's book.

6 Wenn Sie *Student's Cassette A* haben, suchen Sie *Unit 2, Lesson B, Exercise 2*. Hören Sie sich die Gespräche an und versuchen Sie sie aufzuschreiben. Benutzen Sie *Student's Book, Unit 2, Lesson B, Exercise 2* zur Kontrolle.

Good morning, Mr Roberts.

3B This is Judy

1 Kopieren und vervollständigen Sie die Tabelle.

I	am
you	are
he/she/it	is
we	are
you	are
they	are

2 Ändern Sie die Sätze. Nehmen Sie Ihr Wörterbuch zu Hilfe.

1. My friend Alice and I are tall.
   We are tall.
2. Eric and George are very good-looking.
   They
3. Susan is a doctor.
4. My father and I are fair.
5. My children are quite intelligent.
6. Eric is very slim.
7. Andrew is not very tall.
8. Joan and Philip are tall and dark.
9. Mr and Mrs Carter are American.
10. John and I are quite good-looking.
11. You and your brother are engineers, aren't you?

3 Bilden Sie Fragen. Nehmen Sie Ihr Wörterbuch zu Hilfe.

1. your friend | a policeman
   Is your friend a policeman?
2. they | American
   Are
3. his father | English
4. Alice | married
5. you and your wife | British
6. John and Polly | doctors
7. Susan | pretty
8. Eric's girlfriend | tall
9. your secretary | good-looking
10. Ingrid and Christiane | German
11. your name | Sam Lewis
12. your boyfriend's name | Peter

4 Übersetzen Sie ins Deutsche.

1. She is very pretty.
2. He is quite good-looking.
3. This is Sam's friend, Eric.
4. This is Sam's girlfriend, Judy.
5. 'She's English.' 'No, she's not. She's French.'

5 Schneiden Sie Bilder aus Illustrierten aus und beschreiben Sie die Personen.

3C I've got three children

1 Setzen Sie ein: *his, her, their, is* oder *are*.

1. Monica and **her** mother **are** both doctors.
2. Philippe **is** French, and **his** wife .... German.
3. Joyce Price .... a photographer, and .... brother .... an accountant.
4. My sister and I .... American, but our grandparents .... Greek.
5. Sonia .... a doctor, and .... mother is a doctor too.
6. Henry's mother .... a shop assistant. .... name is Lucy.
7. George and Karen .... British; .... daughter .... married to an American.
8. Alice and Bill .... doctors, and .... son is a medical student.
9. What .... your brother's name?
10. 'John and Matthew .... brothers.' 'What .... surname?'

2 Üben Sie die Aussprache.

John's   Mark's   Joyce's   Ann's   Alan's   Ronald's
Greece's   an artist's   Alice's   Mr Nash's   my parents'

3 Ändern Sie die Sätze dem Beispiel entsprechend.

Joyce has got a son. He is fourteen.

Joyce's son is fourteen.

1. Peter has got a sister. She is very pretty.
2. My mother has got a brother. He is a doctor.
3. Anne has got a boyfriend. He is tall and good-looking.
4. Robert has got a girlfriend. She is not very pretty.
5. Mrs Lewis has got children. They are students.

4 Schreiben Sie fünf Sätze über Ihre Familie.

5 Schreiben Sie die Mehrzahlformen.

1. engineer *engineers*
2. boyfriend
3. artist
4. secretary
5. woman
6. doctor
7. child
8. country
9. daughter
10. man

6 Übersetzen Sie ins Deutsche.

1. Joe and Ann have got three children.
2. I've got two daughters and a son.
3. What are their names?
4. My son's name is Fred.
5. My daughters' names are Alice and Lucy.
6. Who is John's daughter?

3D   An interview

1 Vervollständigen Sie die Sätze.

1. I have .... three children.
2. How many children .... you got?
3. My father .... got two sisters.
4. I haven't .... any sisters.
5. .... any brothers or sisters?

2 Vervollständigen Sie das Gespräch.

A: Good morning, Mrs Martin.
B: ....
A: Please sit down.
B: ....
A: .... ?
B Thirty-three.
A .... ?
B: Yes, I ....
A: What is .... 's name?
B: Alex.
A: And .... ?
B: Thirty-two.
A: Have you got any .... ?
B: Yes, ... A boy and a ....

(Phone rings)

A: .... me, Mrs Martin. Hello? Yes. Yes.
I'm .... , I .... know. No. Goodbye.
I'm .... , Mrs Martin. Now, you want to
borrow some money.
B: Yes.

3 Übersetzen Sie ins Deutsche.

1. Sit down, please.
2. You're Canadian, aren't you?
3. Excuse me a moment.
4. How many children have you got?
5. Pardon?

4 Wenn Sie *Student's Cassette A* haben, suchen Sie *Unit 3, Lesson D, Exercise 1.* Hören Sie zu und sprechen Sie nach.

1   2

"Here's to you and me and your husband and my wife."

5 📼 Lesen Sie mit Hilfe Ihres Wörterbuchs.

IT'S A LONG STORY 2

Judy is worried. She doesn't know where Sam is. The bank manager doesn't know where Sam is, either. He is very worried.

Sam is in Brazil, in a small town on the coast near Rio de Janeiro, with £50,000 of the bank's money. He is sitting in a bar near the beach, drinking a large martini and writing a letter to Judy.

Rio, Tuesday.

Darling Judy,
Well, here I am in Brazil. It's very warm here, and the sea is nice for swimming. The women here are very beautiful, and very, very friendly. But I miss you, Judy. Please come and stay with me in Brazil. Can you take the 13.25 flight from London to Rio on April 14th? I'll meet you at the airport.
All my love
Sam

6 Ein Kreuzworträtsel.

ACROSS

C. 4 + 2.
E. Leonardo da Vinci was a poet, ... artist and an engineer.
G. 3 × 2 − 1.
I. 6 − 5 + 4 − 3 − 2 + 1.
J. C across × 3 + 2.
N. 'Is Karsten Danish?' 'Yes, ... is.'
O. 'Are your grandparents Italian?' 'No, ... not.'
Q. 1, 2, 3, 4, etc.
T. 'Is your name Mary?' 'Yes, ... is.'
U. Three threes.
V. I've got .... children: two girls and a boy.
Y. My mother's American. ....'s from California.
Z. I speak a little ....
BB. G across × 2.
CC. .... you married?
EE. Mother's brother.
FF. No, I'm ....
GG. .... she Japanese?
HH. Good morning, ... Harris.

DOWN

A. 'Where are you from?' '................?' 'Where are you from?'
B. I'm sorry, I .... know.

C. 10 − 3.
D. 'Is your name Bernard?' 'No, ... isn't.'
F. 'Are you married?' '................, I'm not.'
G. C down − 3.
H. G down × 2.
J. Sonia is Alan and Peter's mother; Philip is .... father.
K. 'Are you Mr and Mrs Harris?' 'Yes, ... are.'
L. The same as F down.
M. Thank ....
P. 6 + 5.
R. Good morning. .... name is Henry Martin.
S. Alice is English. She's from ....
V. 'Sit down, please.' '................ you.'
W. She's tall, but .... husband is very short.
X. We are.
AA. .... down, please.
BB. ...., 4, 6, 8, 10.
DD. Mary and .... sister are very pretty.
EE. United States.

Unit 4 Consolidation

4A Things to remember: Units 1, 2 and 3

1 Vervollständigen Sie Catherines Familienstammbaum.

GEORGE — ANN .... JOE — MARY
my father

ERIC — CATHERINE LUCY TOM — ALICE
me! .... my .... brother's ....

SUSAN .... PHILIP .... DAN ....

4 Schreiben Sie die Mehrzahlformen.

1. student students
2. age   9. parent
3. widow   10. sister
4. man   11. wife
5. woman   12. address
6. boyfriend   13. housewife
7. child   14. secretary
8. family

5 Schreiben Sie die Zahlen aus.

100	12	58	95
83	32	10	76
17	14	2	29
70	40	61	11

2 Setzen Sie ein: *Where, Who, What* oder *How*.

1. '................ are you?' 'Fine, thanks.'
2. ....'s your name?
3. .... is your mother from?
4. .... old is John?
5. '................'s your dentist?' 'Mr Phillips.'
6. '................ do you do?' '................ do you do?'
7. .... do you spell your surname?
8. '................ do you do?' 'I'm a shop assistant.'
9. '................'s my bag?' 'I'm sorry, I don't know.'
10. .... does *slim* mean?

3 *Excuse me, Pardon* oder *I'm sorry?*

6 Ein Kreuzworträtsel.

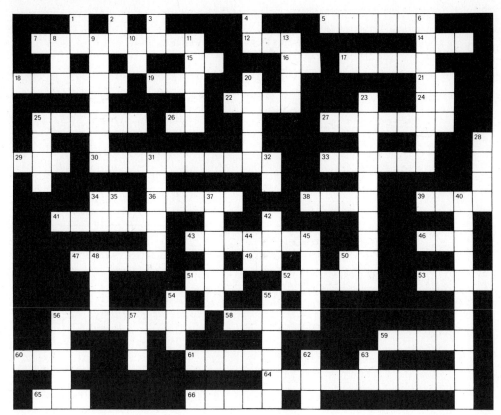

ACROSS

5. .... sit down.
7. Morning, ..., evening, night.
12. .... down.
14. *isn't = is* ....
15. My hat is .... my bag.
16. '................' 'Hello.'
17. Not old.
18. Parent; man.
19.
21. Not on, not under, not near.
22.
24. ...., I'm not.
25. Mother, father, sisters, brothers = ...
26. 'Is your name Harry?' 'No, ... isn't.'
27. Your mother's son = your ....
29. Child; boy.
30. Tom is Jane's boyfriend; Jane is Tom's ....
33. Your father's daughter = your ....
34. ...., here's my bus.
36.
38. 'What's his name?' 'I don't ....'
39. Not dark.
41. Mother or father.
43. I'm a medical ....

46.
47. Not on, not in, not near.
49. Not under, not in, not near.
50. You + I; or he + I; or she + I; or they + I.
51. Not young.
52. Plural of *wife*.
53. Not fair.
56. I've got a ....: what does *strong* mean?
58. I .... a little German.
59. 'Are you Italian?' 'Yes, that's ....'
60. Not fat.
61. 'How old is Alice?' '................ forty, I think.'
64. Job; it has got two Es, two Is, and two Cs in it.
65. 'Are you married?' '................, I am.'
66.

DOWN

1. I, you, he, she, ..., we, you, they
2. Is 'Jennings' a first name .... a surname?
3. What .... you ....?
4. *What's = What* ....
6. A job.
8. Not slim.
9. Good ....
10. Not 'yes'.
11.

13. 'I'm an actress.' '................'s interesting.'
20. Girl, boy, ..., man.
23. Plural of *housewife*.
25. Where are you ....?
28. One + one + two
31. A or B or C or D or E or F . . .
32. How .... you ....?
34. Is your child a girl .... a boy?
35. 'Is your brother a student?' 'No, ...'s a shop assistant.'
37. I speak a .... Spanish.
40. 'I'm a photographer.' 'That's ....'
42.
44. How .... you spell it?
45. 'How old is Dan?' 'About twenty-two, I ....'
48. First name + surname
50. *50 across*
54. Man, woman, ..., girl.
55. G or H or I or J or K or L . . .
56. Miriam is .... tall.
57. Alice is strong, and her daughter is very strong ....
62. My, your, his, ...
63. Is he fair .... dark?

17

4B Please write

1 Schreiben Sie die Fragen.

1. Spain. _Where are you from?_
2. It's near the table.
3. Not bad, thanks. And you?
4. I'm a housewife.
5. L, O, P, E, Z.
6. Lopez.
7. Teresa.
8. She's seven.
9. No, I'm sorry, it's not. It's Jake Barker.
10. How do you do?
11. Good night.
12. Yes, a girl and two boys.
13. No, they're dentists.

2 Setzen Sie passende Wörter in die Lücken ein.

1. 'How old are you?' '.............. fifteen.'
2. 'Are you Japanese?' 'Yes, ...'
3. 'Is John an electrician?' 'Yes, ...'
4. .... surname is Brown.
5. .... student.
6. My sons are very ....
7. 'How old is Mickey Mouse?' 'He's .... fifty.'
8. Is Robin a man's name .... a woman's name?
9. 'I'm from Texas.' 'Oh! I'm from Texas, ...'
10. 'How do you spell your name, Polly?' 'P, O, ..., Y.'

3 Ordnen Sie die Wörter im Kasten gemäß ihrer Betonung den entsprechenden Listen zu. Können Sie die Listen erweitern?

```
address    afternoon    brother    divorced
doctor    double    engineer    evening
excuse    family    goodbye    hello
housewife    husband    interesting    letter
little    married    morning    number
question    secretary    single    sister
sorry    student    surname    table
teacher    widow    woman
```

☐☐ ☐☐ ☐☐☐
brother   address   family
doctor   divorced   interesting

☐☐☐
afternoon

Achten Sie auf die Betonung beim Aussprechen folgender Wörter:

separated   intelligent   electrician   university

4 Welches Wort paßt zu welchem Bild?

tall
quite tall
very tall

intelligent
quite intelligent
very intelligent

Good evening.
Hi.
Good night.

It's Italy.
It's Italian.

in
near
on
under

fair
dark
slim
fat

5 Kennen Sie diese Wörter? Nehmen Sie Ihr Wörterbuch zu Hilfe, falls nötig.

ex-   good   holiday   home   international   newspaper
page   player   swimmer   tennis court

Erstellen Sie einen zusammenhängenden Text.

She's a journalist for the international page of a daily newspaper.
She's a dark, slim, pretty woman, and very intelligent.
My friend Solange is from Paris.
She speaks English, German, Spanish and a little Italian.

Her holiday home has got a swimming pool,
He is quite tall and fair, and a good swimmer.
she and her ex-husband have got one son, Julien.
and a good tennis player.
Solange is divorced;
and it is near a tennis court.
Solange is a good swimmer, too,
He is fifteen.

6 Lesen Sie noch einmal den Text über *Solange*. Schreiben Sie dann über *Ihre/n*
Mutter, Vater, Ehefrau, Ehemann, Schwester, Bruder, Freund/in, Lehrer/in, Chef/in ...

4C I've got a new girlfriend

1 Kopieren und vervollständigen Sie die Tabelle.

I	....	....	I'm	....	....	am I?
....	your	....	....	you are not	....	....
....	....	he is	....	....	he isn't	....
she	....	....	she's	....	....	is she?
....	(its)	....	....	it is not	....	....
....	our	we are	....	....	we aren't	....
....	....	you are	....	....	you aren't	....
they	....	....	they're	they are not	....	are they?

2 Schreiben Sie die unverkürzten Formen.

1. *Susan's* an engineer. Susan is
2. *They're* Italian.
3. *I've* got five brothers.
4. Dan and Catherine *aren't* in England.
5. They *haven't* got any children.
6. *He's* a photographer.
7. *How's* your daughter?
8. *John's* not very tall.
9. *What's* your name, please?
10. *I'm* quite tall.

3 *'s: is, his* oder *her?*

1. John's pen is under your book. his pen
2. John's an electrician. John is
3. Susan's secretary isn't well. her secretary
4. Where's Ann's bag?
5. Are Dan's books in your bag?
6. I think Ann's about fifty.
7. Tom's English.
8. Is Tom's mother English?
9. I haven't got my daughter's coat.
10. My daughter's very pretty, and very intelligent.

4 's oder s'?

1. Lucy has got a daughter. Her daughter is fair.
   Lucy's daughter is fair
2. My sons have got pens. The pens are in their bags.
   My sons' pens are in their bags
3. Eric has got a son. He is fourteen.
4. My daughters have got a teacher. She is Canadian.
5. My father has got a sister. She is an artist.
6. Alice has got a doctor. He is not very intelligent.
7. My students have got books. Their books are on the table.
8. Dr Wagner has got two brothers. They are doctors too.

5 Setzen Sie passende Wörter in die Lücken ein.

1. 'How .... your name, Philip?'
   'P, H, I, L, I, P.'
2. Are you American .... Canadian?
3. My daughters are very ....
4. .... surname is Gomez.
5. .... engineer.
6. 'How old is James Bond?' 'I think he's .... thirty-five.'
7. 'My sister is a photographer.' 'That's interesting. My sister is a photographer, ...'
8. 'Is Alice an engineer?' 'Yes, ...'
9. 'How old is your mother?' '................ forty-three.'
10. 'Are you Italian?' 'Yes, ...'

6 Lesen Sie das Rätsel und beantworten Sie die Frage.

Elizabeth, John, Harry, Mary and Tom are a family. The two doctors are fair. The father and the daughter are dark. Mary's children are an actress, an artist, and a doctor. Tom is an architect. Harry is dark. What is John's job?

7 Wenn Sie *Student's Cassette A* haben, suchen Sie *Unit 4, Lesson C, Exercise 1*. Hören Sie sich an, was *Andrew* sagt. Versuchen Sie dann, sich daran zu erinnern, was *Dan* sagt.

1   2

8 ▣ Lesen Sie mit Hilfe Ihres Wörterbuchs.

IT'S A LONG STORY
3

Judy is at home. (She lives in a small flat near the bank. It's not very nice.) She's in the living room, drinking a cup of coffee and thinking. Judy's very worried, because she doesn't know what to do. She loves Sam, and she doesn't want to tell the police where he is. But she doesn't want to go to Rio, either. She wants a quiet life.
  Judy goes to the window and looks out. There's a police car in the street. Two big policemen are walking towards her house.

ÜBUNGEN ZU *LESSON 4D* ENTFALLEN.

Unit 5 Where?

5A Home

1 Schauen Sie sich das Bild an und beantworten Sie die Fragen.

1. Is there a table in the room?
   Yes, there is.
2. Are there any children in the room?
   Yes, there are three (children).
3. Is there a hat on the table?
   No, there isn't. There's a hat on the TV.
4. Are there any women in the room?
5. Is there a television near the table?
6. Are there any windows in the room?
7. Are there any books in the room?
8. Is there a cupboard in the room?
9. Is there a woman on the sofa?
10. Is there a man on the sofa?
11. Are there any bags under the table?
12. Are there any coats in the room?

2 Schneiden Sie aus einer Illustrierten das Bild eines Zimmers aus. Schreiben Sie fünf Fragen über das Bild und geben Sie das Blatt an eine/n andere/n Kursteilnehmer/in weiter.

3 Unterstreichen Sie die betonten Silben.

1. There are two bedrooms in the house.
2. There's a table in the living room.
3. There are three armchairs in the living room.
4. There's a woman on the sofa.
5. There are two children in the room.

4 *A/an* oder *the*?

1. Look at .... picture on page 123.
2. There are five rooms in .... house.
3. There is .... armchair in .... living room.
4. There isn't .... garage.
5. There is .... fridge in .... kitchen.
6. My father is .... shop assistant.
7. He lives in .... flat in Manchester.

5 Lesen Sie die Informationen zu den Wohnungen.

Jenny lives in a small flat and Sally lives in a big flat.

Jenny's flat

two rooms:
bed-sitting room   very small kitchen

and:
small bathroom with a shower and a toilet

in the kitchen:
small fridge

in the bed-sitting room:
black and white TV

Sally's flat

four rooms:
living room   two bedrooms   big kitchen

and:
bathroom   separate toilet

in the kitchen:
big fridge   dishwasher

in the living room:
colour TV

Schreiben Sie über Sallys Wohnung, indem Sie die folgende Beschreibung vervollständigen.

There .... four .... in Sally's flat: a living room, two .... and a big .... is .... bathroom too, and a separate .... In the kitchen .... a big .... and a dishwasher. .... colour .... in the ....

Schreiben Sie jetzt über Jennys Wohnung.

6 Schreiben Sie über eins der folgenden Themen: Ihr Haus bzw. Ihre Wohnung, Ihr Traumhaus oder das Haus bzw. die Wohnung von jemandem, den Sie kennen (Ihrer Mutter/Ihres Bruders/Ihrer Freundin/Ihres Freundes . . .).

7 *Kaum zu glauben:* Lesen Sie mit Hilfe Ihres Wörterbuchs.

There are only twelve letters in the Hawaiian alphabet: A, E, H, I, K, L, M, N, O, P, U and W.
There is a street in Canada that is 1,900km long.
There are about 790,000 words in English.
There are about 5,000 languages in the world (845 in India).
There are six different languages in Great Britain and Ireland (English, Welsh, Scots Gaelic, Irish Gaelic, Manx and Cornish).

5B Where do you work?

1 Setzen Sie das richtige Verhältniswort ein (*at, in* oder *on*).

1. I live .... 14 St Andrew's Place, Dundee.
2. My father lives .... a small house .... North London.
3. My girlfriend's flat is .... the seventh floor.
4. Do you live .... a house or a flat?
5. 'Where's the toilet, please?' '................. the second floor.'
6. 'Is there a doctor near here?' 'Yes, ... 37 High Street.'
7. I lived .... America from 1976 to 1978.
8. She lives .... Pentonville Road.

2 *Live* oder *lives?*

1. My Aunt Sally .... in New Jersey.
2. Where do you ....?
3. We .... at 141 Riverside Avenue, Cardiff.
4. My brother's wife .... in Chicago.
5. The Prime Minister .... at 10 Downing Street.

3 Sprechen Sie diese Buchstaben laut aus.

A E I H Y R K W G Q
V J X Z U

Buchstabieren Sie diese Wörter.

address age John eighteen sorry
intelligent night interesting Japan
housewife evening widow married

Wie werden diese Abkürzungen ausgesprochen?

USSR TWA BBC EEC USA OK

4 Lesen Sie den Text und füllen Sie die Tabelle aus.

There are four floors in a block of flats. Two women and two men live in the flats; they are an architect, an artist, a doctor and a photographer. The architect lives on the ground floor. The photographer and the doctor are women. Philip is not an artist. Jane lives on the first floor. Susan is not a doctor; she lives under Dan.

NAME	JOB	FLOOR

5 Wenn Sie *Student's Cassette A* haben, suchen Sie *Unit 5, Lesson B, Exercise 3*. (Sie werden dort nur das erste Gespräch hören.) Hören Sie sich das Gespräch an und schreiben Sie es auf.

A hundred and sixteen Market Street.

1

2

*"What do you mean other man? He's my husband.
You live next door."*

5C Where's the nearest post office?

1 Vervollständigen Sie die Gespräche.

A: ....?
B: Over there by the stairs.
A: ....

*   *   *

A: Excuse me. Where's Room 8, please?
B: ....
A: ....

*   *   *

A: Excuse me. Where's the nearest ....?
B: ....
A: ....

2 Beantworten Sie diese Fragen mit *Yes, there is/are; No, there isn't/aren't* oder *I don't know.*

1. Is there a bank in your street?
2. Is there a swimming pool near your home?
3. Is there an armchair in your bedroom?
4. Is there a television in your living room?
5. Is there a bus stop in your street?
6. Are there tigers in Canada?
7. Are there elephants in Thailand?
8. Are there penguins in Brazil?
9. Are there camels in India?
10. Is there a cat in your home?

3 *True* oder *false?* Schreiben Sie T oder F hinter jeden Satz. Sie können Ihr Wörterbuch benutzen.

1. The USSR is 31 miles (50km) from the USA.
2. In 1710, there were 350 Europeans living in North America.
3. Mont Blanc is 6,000 metres high.
4. There are twenty pence (20p) in a pound sterling (£1).
5. There are a hundred cents (100¢) in a US dollar ($1).
6. There are three kilometres in a mile.
7. The President of the United States lives in the White House.
8. There are penguins in the Arctic.

4 Bilden Sie Fragen mit *Is/Are there . . .?*

1. lions | Uganda? _Are there lions in Uganda ?_
2. an armchair | your bathroom?
3. a hotel | your street?
4. a bank | the station?
5. camels | Argentina?
6. a bus stop | this street?
7. a fridge | your kitchen?
8. crocodiles | Texas?

5 Wenn Sie *Student's Cassette A* haben, suchen Sie *Unit 5, Lesson C, Exercise 3.* Hören Sie sich das Gespräch Satz für Satz an und versuchen Sie, sich an den jeweils nächsten Satz zu erinnern. Benutzen Sie *Student's Book, Exercise 3* zur Kontrolle.

6 Lesen Sie mit Hilfe Ihres Wörterbuchs.

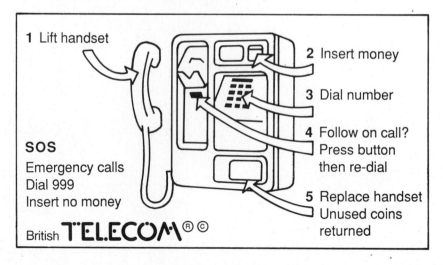

5D First on the right, second on the left

1 Sie sind in der Straße, in der Sie wohnen *oder* im Zentrum Ihres Wohnorts. Beantworten Sie die Fragen.

1. Excuse me. Where's the nearest bus stop, please?
2. Excuse me. Is there a car park near here?
3. Excuse me. Is there a swimming pool in the town?
4. Excuse me. I'm looking for the post office.
5. Excuse me. Where's the police station, please?

2 Setzen Sie die richtigen Verhältniswörter ein *(at, in, on, from, for, under).*

1. 'Where are you ....?' 'San Francisco.'
2. She lives .... 37 Paradise Street.
3. Go straight on .... 600 yards.
4. I work .... the fifth floor.
5. Is there a fridge .... your kitchen?
6. I think your book is .... my coat.
7. 'Thank you very much.' 'Not .... all.'
8. Have you got a pen .... your bag?
9. 'Please sit down. Now, a few questions.' 'Yes, ... course.'
10. Tom's hat is .... the table.

3 Achten Sie auf die richtige Betonung beim Aussprechen folgender Wörter:

bathroom · **car** park · living room · **phone** box
police **second station supermarket**
swimming pool TV **toilet win**dow

4 Tragen Sie weitere Wörter in die Listen ein.

1. armchair, chair, . . .
2. artist, doctor, . . .
3. bank, post office, . . .
4. bedroom, living room, . . .

5 Übersetzen Sie ins Deutsche.

1. There are two bedrooms in the house.
2. There's a sofa in the living room.
3. My sister works in Edinburgh.
4. I live at 37 Valley Road.
5. My sister lives on the ground floor, and my brother lives in a small flat on the third floor.
6. Excuse me. Where's the nearest post office?
7. It's over there on the right.
8. 'Thank you very much.' 'Not at all.'
9. I'm sorry, I don't know.
10. Thank you anyway.
11. Go straight on for about three hundred metres.
12. First on the right, then second on the left.
13. How far is it?

6 Wenn Sie *Student's Cassette A* haben, suchen Sie *Unit 5, Lesson D, Exercise 3.* (Sie werden dort nur die ersten drei Wegbeschreibungen hören.) Hören Sie sich die Beschreibungen an und versuchen Sie, sie aufzuschreiben.

1   2

7 🔊 Lesen Sie mit Hilfe Ihres Wörterbuchs.

IT'S A LONG STORY 4

Hello – is that Croxton 43122? Dr Wagner? Listen, Dr Wagner, this is Judy . . . Yes, Judy Parker. Listen, I'm in very bad trouble. Can you help? . . . Trouble with Sam and the bank and the police. I haven't got time to explain . . . Yes, OK. Please come to my house *at once* with your car. As fast as you can – it's really urgent . . . 23 Carlton Road. Turn right at the station and it's the second street on your left. *Please* hurry! Oh, and come to the *back* door.

Unit 6 Habits

6A What do you like?

1 Vervollständigen Sie die Sätze.

1. '.................. Mozart?' 'No, I ....'
2. 'I .... orange juice, but I .... apple juice at all.' 'Don't you?'
3. 'I like Picasso very much.' '.................. you?' 'Yes, I ....'
4. What sort of books .... you ....?
5. Everybody .... Sally. Nobody .... Ann.
6. 'Do .... big dogs?' 'No, I ....'
7. Only two people in my family .... dancing.

2 Setzen Sie ein: *he, she, him, her, it, they* oder *them*.

1. 'Where are my pens?' '..................'re on the table.'
2. John's nice. I like .... a lot.
3. 'Have you got any dogs?' 'No, I don't like ....'
4. 'Is Mary at home?' 'Yes, ... is.' 'Can I speak to ...., please?' 'Yes, of course.'
5. 'Where are your books?' 'Ann's got ....'
6. Ann likes Bill, but he doesn't like .... much.
7. 'Are your children here?' 'Yes, ...'re in the garden.'
8. 'My brother's a shop assistant.' 'Where does .... work?'
9. 'Do you like shopping?' 'I hate ....'
10. 'Do you like cats?' 'No, I don't like .... at all.'
11. 'Is the car in the garage?' 'No, ...'s in the street.'
12. 'What do you think of Peter?' 'I quite like ....'

3 Achten Sie auf die richtige Betonung beim Aussprechen folgender Sätze:

1. I like the **Greek** statue very **much**.
2. I **quite** like the **mask**.
3. The **mask** is **OK**.
4. I **don't** like the **Vermeer** picture **much**.
5. I **don't** like it at **all**.
6. I like the **Greek** statue **best**.
7. **Yes**, I **do**.
8. **No**, I **don't**.
9. I **love** it.
10. I **hate** them.
11. It de**pends**.

4 Lesen Sie den Text und beantworten Sie die Frage.

Four people work in an office: two women and two men.
Anne likes Catherine, but she dislikes the two men.
Peter doesn't like the person that Anne likes, but he likes Anne.
Only one person likes Catherine.
John likes two people.
One person doesn't like Anne. Who is it?

5 Schreiben Sie ein Gedicht über das, was Sie mögen und was Sie nicht mögen. Sie können Ihr Wörterbuch benutzen. Beispiel:

I quite like the sea.
I like my friends and my family.
I love the sun, strawberries, dancing and cats.
I don't like fast cars or snails.
I hate violence.

"You don't like my mother, do you?"

6B Where are you at seven o'clock?

1 Beantworten Sie die Fragen.

1. Where are you at six o'clock in the morning?
2. Where are you at eight o'clock in the morning?
3. Where are you at ten o'clock in the morning?
4. Where are you at ten to one in the afternoon?
5. Where are you at a quarter past seven in the evening?

2 Schreiben Sie die Uhrzeiten.

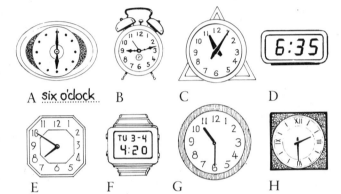

A six o'clock   B   C   D

E   F   G   H

3 Verbinden Sie die Buchstaben in *Box 2* mit den Wörtern, auf die sie sich reimen.

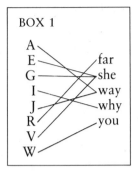

BOX 1

A	
E	far
G	she
I	way
J	why
R	you
V	
W	

BOX 2

A	
E	are
G	day
I	my
J	we
R	who
V	
W	

4 Wenn Sie *Student's Cassette A* haben, suchen Sie *Unit 6, Lesson B, Exercise 3*. Hören Sie sich Nummer 1 bis 4 an und schreiben Sie die Buchstaben der Sätze, die Sie hören.

A. Thank you very much.
B. What time is your train?
C. Is that OK?
D. Oh yes, that's fine.

5 Ein Kreuzworträtsel.

ACROSS

1. 'What time is it?' 'Eight ....'
5. 10 × 8.
8. This clue is number .... *across*.
11. At five o'clock in the morning I'm still .... bed.
12. Yes, ... course.
14. 'Do you like the music?' 'It's ....'
15. 'Do you like cats?' '................, I don't.'
16. It's under the first floor.
19. Half of two.
20. I live in a small .... on the third floor.
21. 3 × 2.
22. .... name's Michael.
23. .... is Judy. She is tall and fair.
25. 3.15 = a .... past three.
27. Is .... a table in the living room?
28. I like dogs, but I don't like ....
30. Half of 26.
34. 1.30 = half past ....
36. Good .... How are you?
37. Are you .... or single?

DOWN

1. The same as *12 across*.
2. I .... cats, but I don't .... dogs.
3. It's over there .... the left.
4. 'What time is it?' 'I'm sorry, I don't ....'
5. 'Do you speak ....?' 'Yes, a little.'
6. .... afternoon. How are you?
7. 5 × 2.
9. Judy is Sam's ....
10. 'Is your name Anne?' 'Yes, ...'s right.'
12. The same as *1 down*.
13. We live on the fourth ....
14. .... one person in the class likes maths.
17. .... you speak English?
18. The same as *12 down*.
21. 'Please .... down.' 'Thank you.'
22. I like music very ....
23. At a quarter to eight I am on my way .... work.
24. Are you married .... single?
26. Three threes.
29. Half of four.
31. She's a teacher. .... name's Alice.
32. My brother's .... engineer.
33. There are two chairs .... the bathroom.
35. 'Do you like dancing?' '................, I don't.'

6C Work

1 Setzen Sie *do* oder *does* ein.

1. .... your father work in a garage?
2. What time .... you finish work in the evening?
3. What .... your husband do?
4. .... both your children go to the same school?
5. Where .... they have lunch?
6. .... your grandmother work?
7. When .... Andrew's sister have lunch?

2 Setzen Sie die richtigen Formen der Zeitwörter ein.

1. Mechanics usually .... work at eight o'clock.
2. In Spain, people .... dinner at ten o'clock in the evening.
3. My cousin Tom .... in Germany.
4. The village shop .... at nine o'clock in the morning.
5. Anita .... children's clothes and shoes.
6. I .... cereal and milk for breakfast.
7. Brian .... old clocks.

VERBS	
have/has	repair/repairs
live/lives	sell/sells
open/opens	start/starts

3 Schreiben Sie acht Sätze.

Where What time	do does	Mr Carter you your sister your mother her children Jane Dr Wagner	work? live? have lunch? start work?
	Do Does		work? start work early? work in a garage? live in London? have lunch?

Beispiel: Where does Jane have lunch?

4 Üben Sie die Aussprache folgender Wörter und Sätze:

if it is six British
English kitchen live listen
It is in the kitchen.
It isn't in the living room.

5 Lesen Sie die Texte ohne Wörterbuch. Können Sie die Berufe der sechs Personen erraten? Mögliche Antworten: *electrician, secretary, doctor, dentist, air hostess, photographer, bank manager, bus driver, artist, lorry driver, singer.*

A. She speaks four languages. She works very long hours, but she does not work every day. She likes people and travel, and she travels a lot in her work.

Antwort: She is an ...

B. She doesn't work in an office. She works very long hours, and she often gets up at night – it's a tiring job. She likes people. She does not speak any foreign languages. She loves her job.

Antwort: ....

C. He gets up at half past seven every day, has breakfast at eight o'clock, and starts work at half past nine. He works in an office; he has two secretaries and two telephones. He does not work on Saturdays. He likes people and mathematics.

Antwort: ....

D. He usually gets up at eleven o'clock, and has breakfast at lunchtime. He works at home. He works in the afternoons, but not every day. Sometimes he works very long hours; sometimes he does not work at all. He loves his job.

Antwort: ....

E. She lives in a big city. She gets up at two o'clock in the afternoon, and has breakfast at three o'clock. She works from 9 p.m. until 2 a.m. She goes to and from work by taxi. She does not like her job much, and she does not like the people where she works.

Antwort: ....

F. He gets up at two o'clock in the morning. He has breakfast and lunch in motorway restaurants. He works sitting down, and he travels a lot in his work. He likes his job.

Antwort: ....

6D What newspaper do you read?

1 Wählen Sie die richtige Form des Zeitworts.

1. Stan *have/has* breakfast at half past seven.
2. Karen does not *have/has* breakfast.
3. How does Karen *go/goes* to work?
4. Stan *go/goes* to work by bus.
5. My father *work/works* in Cardiff.
6. He does not *like/likes* travelling.
7. He *get up / gets up* at six o'clock every day.
8. He does not *work/works* on Saturdays.
9. My parents *live/lives* in a big flat.
10. What does your father *do/does*?

2 *It, them, him* oder *her*? Ändern Sie die Sätze. Sie können Ihr Wörterbuch benutzen.

1. I like bananas.
   I like them.
2. I hate whisky.
3. Alice loves children.
4. Children love Alice.
5. I don't like rock music.
6. Can I speak to Bill, please?
7. Do you like your work?
8. She loves fast cars.
9. I don't like Mrs Harris very much.
10. I hate rain.
11. You can't speak to John. He isn't here.
12. Do you like big dogs?

3 Setzen Sie ein: *never, sometimes, often, usually* oder *always*. (Seien Sie ehrlich!) Sie können Ihr Wörterbuch benutzen.

1. I eat bananas.
2. I go to the cinema.
3. I drink coffee.
4. I speak French.
5. I work at home.
6. I get up before six o'clock.
7. I eat fish.
8. I go dancing.
9. I drink tea.
10. I read poetry.
11. I watch TV on Sundays.
12. I play tennis.

4 Übersetzen Sie ins Deutsche.

1. I don't like cats, but my brother likes them very much.
2. 'Do you like dogs?'   'Yes, I do.' / 'No, I don't.'
3. It depends.
4. What time is it?
5. ten past three; half past three; a quarter to four; five to four
6. She's at home.
7. He's at school.
8. Stan gets up at seven o'clock.
9. After breakfast, he goes to work by bus.
10. What time does Karen get up?
11. What newspaper do you read?
12. What sort of music do you like?

5 Wenn Sie *Student's Cassette A* haben, suchen Sie *Unit 6, Lesson D, Exercise 2*. (Sie werden dort nur die ersten 16 Fragen finden.) Hören Sie zu und schreiben Sie mindestens fünf der Fragen auf.

6 Wie, glauben Sie, sieht ein typischer Tag einer dieser Personen aus? Schreiben Sie darüber.

7 🔊 Lesen Sie mit Hilfe Ihres Wörterbuchs.

IT'S A LONG STORY
5

Dr Wagner and Judy are on their way to the airport in Dr Wagner's car. There is another car behind them, with a pretty blue lamp on top. Dr Wagner accelerates, and the police car disappears.

'But what's the problem, Judy?' asks Dr Wagner.

'I can't explain,' says Judy. 'It's too complicated.'

'I know what it is,' says Dr Wagner. 'It's that Sam. I don't like him at all. He's a very dishonest young man.'

'Sam is my boyfriend,' says Judy, 'and I love him. He has sensitive eyes and beautiful hands.'

Dr Wagner does not answer.

Unit 7 Counting and measuring

7A How many calories?

1 Schreiben Sie die unverkürzten Formen.

aren't _are not_
haven't   we're
doesn't   you're
don't   they're
I'm

2 Setzen Sie ein: *I, you, he, she, we, they, my, your, his, her, our* oder *their.*

1. We live in London. .... address is 17 Fox Terrace, Hampstead.
2. 'Where does your sister work?' '............... works in Sheffield.'
3. Susie and Ingrid are German – .... are from Dortmund. .... father is a bank manager.
4. My mother lives with .... second husband in Edinburgh.
5. My wife and I are architects. .... work in an office in the centre of Cambridge.
6. 'There's Mr Parslow.' 'What's .... first name?' 'Sam.'

3 Antworten Sie mit *Yes, I do; No, I don't; Yes, I am* oder *No, I'm not.*

1. Are you tall?
2. Do you like cats?
3. Are you married?
4. Are you American?
5. Do you speak French?
6. Do you work on Saturdays?
7. Are you a student?
8. Do you like your work?
9. Do you like children?

4 Schreiben Sie für folgende Zeitwörter die Formen der dritten Person Einzahl *(he/she/it).*

work _works_

like   watch   get   go   finish   have   sell
study

5 *Do* oder *does?*

1. Where .... your parents live?
2. What time .... you start work?
3. .... your mother like cooking?
4. .... you like your job?
5. How .... you travel to work?
6. What sort of books .... Mary read?
7. What languages .... Mr Andrews speak?
8. What newspaper .... you read?

6 Schauen Sie sich das Bild an und vervollständigen Sie die Sätze.

1   2   3   4   5   6   7   8   9   10

1. The _sixth_ person is a tall, dark woman.
2. The .... person is a fair, slim man.
3. The .... person is a fair, slim woman.
4. The .... person is a dark, slim girl.
5. The .... person is a good-looking, dark man.
6. The .... person is an artist.
7. The .... person is a photographer.
8. The .... person is a doctor.
9. The .... person has got a hat.
10. The .... person has got a book.

For dinner, you have:
prawns (112g)
two pork chops and a baked potato
fresh raspberries (226g)
How many calories?

Antwort: ....

Food	Portion	Calories	Fibre g
Plaice, fillets, fried in crumbs	6oz (170g) raw weight	435	1.0
Plums Victoria, dessert cooking, stewed without sugar, weighed with stones	2½oz (70g), average-sized fruit	15	1.5
Pork chop, grilled	6oz (170g)	40	3.5
leg, roast	7oz (220g) raw weight, fat cut off after grilling		
Pork sausages, grilled	3oz (85g), lean only	315	0
	2oz (56g), large sausage, raw weight	155	0
	1oz (28g), 1 chipolata, raw weight	135	0
Porridge	1oz (28g) oatmeal or porridge oats made up with water	65	0
Potato baked	7oz (200g), eaten with skin	110	2.0
roast	2oz (56g)		
instant, mashed	1oz (28g) dry weight	170	5.0
old, boiled and mashed	4oz (113g)	90	1.0
new boiled		90	4.5
canned	4oz (113g)	90	1.0
Prawns, shelled	4oz (113g) drained weight	85	2.5
Prunes, dried with stones	2oz (56g)	60	3.0
stewed without sugar		60	0
Puffed wheat	1oz (28g), four to five prunes		
Rabbit, stewed	4oz (113g) cooked weight	20	2.0
Radishes, raw	¾oz (21g), average breakfast bowl	85	8.5
Raisins	6oz (170g), weighed on the bone	70	3.5
Raspberries raw	1oz (28g), salad serving	150	0
canned in syrup	½oz (14g), serving with cereal etc.	5	0.5
Redcurrants, stewed without sugar	4oz (113g)	35	1.0
	4oz (113g), fruit and syrup	30	8.5
	4oz (113g)	95	5.5
		20	8.0

(from *The F-Plan Calorie and Fibre Chart* by Audrey Eyton)

7B   It's terrible

1 Setzen Sie *the* ein, falls nötig.

1. 'There's a small piece of cheese and a small orange in the fridge.' 'I'll have .... cheese.'
2. .... rump steak is very expensive.
3. There are no calories in .... tea.
4. 'Where's .... milk?' 'In the fridge.'
5. .... boys and .... girls like imagining they're adults.
6. She's got two boys and two girls. .... girls are both fair, and .... boys are both dark.
7. I like .... oranges, but I don't like .... orange juice.
8. There are 50 calories in 5ml of .... sugar.

2 Setzen Sie ein: *am, is, are, was* oder *were.*

1. I .... an accountant – what do you do?
2. I .... in Patterson's yesterday.
3. Milk .... not so expensive when I .... a child.
4. Where in China .... Shanghai?
5. .... both your sisters in Britain?
6. My grandchildren .... here yesterday.
7. .... you tall as a child?
8. .... your son tall?

3 Schreiben Sie einige Preise auf. Beispiel:

Oranges are 75 cents a kilo.

4 Suchen Sie die richtigen Antworten in dem Kasten.

1. 'Are you Spanish?'
2. 'Do you know what time it is?'
3. 'Is he married?'
4. 'Does Mary live with her parents?'
5. 'Are we in London?'
6. 'Am I speaking to Mrs Collins?'
7. 'Do they drink beer?'
8. 'Does he speak Chinese?'
9. 'Are they married?'

'No, I'm not.'	'No, I don't.'
'No, you aren't.'	'No, you don't.'
'No, he/she isn't.'	'No, he/she doesn't.'
'No, we aren't.'	'No, we don't.'
'No, they aren't.'	'No, they don't.'

5 Wenn Sie *Student's Cassette A* haben, suchen Sie *Unit 7, Lesson B, Exercise 1*. (Sie werden dort nur den letzten Teil des Gesprächs finden.) Hören Sie zu und schreiben Sie mindestens fünf Sätze. Benutzen Sie *Student's Book, Exercise 1* zur Kontrolle.

6 Informationssuche. Lesen Sie die Anzeigen und lösen Sie die Aufgabe.

How much will it cost to buy all of these: a girl's bicycle, a winter coat, 12lbs (pounds) of apples, two Alsatian puppies (baby dogs), a Renault 12TL, a violin and three ducks?

Total cost: ....

7C Have you got a good memory?

1 Zählbar oder nichtzählbar? Sie können Ihr Wörterbuch benutzen.

butter [U]   wool ☐   sheep ☐   beer ☐   rain ☐   bread ☐   banana ☐

£5 note [C]   tomato ☐   bank ☐   music ☐   wine ☐   money ☐

2 Welches Wort paßt zu welchem Bild? Sie können Ihr Wörterbuch benutzen.

a chicken   a glass   a melon   a paper   a potato
some chicken   some glass   some melon   some paper   some potato

3 *Some* oder *any*?

1. There is .... apple juice in the fridge.
2. Are there .... tomatoes in the kitchen?
3. I've got .... nice friends.
4. Alice hasn't got .... children.
5. Have you got .... American friends?
6. There isn't .... coffee in my cup.
7. There aren't .... flats in our street.
8. Has your father got .... brothers or sisters?
9. I know .... nice people in Canada.
10. We had .... rain this evening.

4 Welche Speisen oder Getränke haben Sie in Ihrem Kühlschrank/Ihrer Küche/ Ihrer Wohnung/Ihrem Haus? Benutzen Sie *some* und *any*. Beispiel:

There's some beer in my fridge, but there aren't any tomatoes.

5 Setzen Sie die richtige Form des Zeitworts ein.

1. What languages do you speak? (*speak*)
2. They do not know my address. (*not know*)
3. Where .... your mother ....? (*live*)
4. What time .... you .... work? (*start*)
5. Lucy .... on Friday afternoons. (*not work*)
6. .... Cathy .... reading? (*like*)
7. .... they .... German in Switzerland? (*speak*)
8. I watch football, but I .... it. (*not play*)
9. Robert .... dancing and tennis. (*like*)
10. Alexandra .... the violin very well. (*play*)

6 Wenn Sie *Student's Cassette A* haben, suchen Sie *Unit 7, Lesson C, Exercise 4*. Hören Sie zu und schreiben Sie mindestens fünf Fragen auf.

7D Not enough money

1 Setzen Sie *How much* oder *How many* ein.

1. .... brothers and sisters have you got?
2. '................ English do you speak?' 'Not much.'
3. .... people are there in your family?
4. .... calories are there in a pint of beer?
5. '................ money have you got on you?'
   'About £5.'
6. .... cheese is there in the fridge?
7. .... languages do you speak?
8. .... children have you got?

2 Bilden Sie Sätze.

I haven't got
I've got

enough   a lot of
too many   too much

money.   work.   free time.
friends.   clothes.   . . .

3 Achten Sie auf die richtige Betonung beim Aussprechen folgender Wörter:

to**ma**to	**or**ange	week**end**
water	**mem**ory	**news**paper
ba**na**na	**tra**velling	**in**terested
in**tel**ligent	de**pends**	**lan**guage
terrible	**eve**rybody	**ho**liday
supermarket	**break**fast	

4 Übersetzen Sie ins Deutsche.

1. Do you know potatoes are eighty pence a kilo?
2. Everything's so expensive.
3. It's terrible.
4. There aren't any books on the table.
5. There isn't any snow in the garden.
6. 'Are there any fair people in your family?' 'Yes, there are.' / 'No, there aren't.'
7. I don't understand.
8. How many states are there in the USA?
9. There aren't many people here.
10. There isn't enough light in this room.
11. I've got too much work.

5 Lesen Sie die Postkarte mit Hilfe Ihres Wörterbuchs. Schreiben Sie sie mit der richtigen Großschreibung und Zeichensetzung ab. Beginnen Sie mit *Dear Mary, . . .*

dear mary
well here we are at last our hotel is very nice we're on the 14th floor with a good view of the sea the room's small but it's clean and quiet the food's good and there's always enough sometimes there's too much there aren't many english people here but there's a nice couple from manchester in the next room
love carol and jim

6 Schreiben Sie einen ähnlichen Urlaubsgruß an eine/n Freund/in.

7 ⌾ Lesen Sie mit Hilfe Ihres Wörterbuchs.

IT'S A LONG STORY
6

'Single to Rio de Janeiro, please,' says Judy.
   'First class or tourist?'
   'Oh, tourist, please.'
   Judy checks in and goes through passport control to the departure gate. On the plane, she finds a seat by the window. A young man comes and sits down by her. Judy looks at him. He is tall and dark, about 25, and very well dressed. Judy is not interested in him.
   He has dark brown eyes, a straight nose, a wide humorous mouth, and strong brown hands with long sensitive fingers. He is incredibly handsome. Judy looks out of the window.

Unit 8 Consolidation

8A Things to remember: Units 5, 6 and 7

1 Setzen Sie die Verhältniswörter ein.

at	by	from	in	near	next to	of	on	opposite	outside	to	until

Michael is an accountant in a language school. He lives ....1.... a small flat ....2.... the fourth floor of a building ....3.... a small street ....4.... Tokyo. The school is not very ....5.... his home; he goes ....6.... work ....7.... bus, and leaves home at eight o'clock to arrive ....8.... work at nine. He usually does some work in the bus ....9.... his way ....10.... work.

Michael's school is ....11.... a railway station. It is very big, and it has got a lot ....12.... students. Michael likes his office; it is ....13.... the reception desk, but it is big and quiet; there are some pretty trees ....14.... his window. He works ....15.... nine o'clock ....16.... a quarter to one, and then goes to lunch. Then he starts work again ....17.... two and stops ....18.... five. On his way back ....19.... work he buys some food, and has supper ....20.... home. He likes living ....21.... Japan; he doesn't go home to England ....22.... holiday, but visits pretty places ....23.... Japan.

It is Saturday morning now, and Michael is ....24.... home ....25.... bed. ....26.... Saturdays he gets up at ten o'clock, and then sits ....27.... the living room to have breakfast. ....28.... Saturday afternoons he plays tennis or goes swimming. ....29.... Saturday evenings he usually goes out.

2 Schreiben Sie Fragen zu diesen Antworten.

1. No, she doesn't. She lives in Paris.
   Does your mother live in London?
2. No, there isn't, but there's some in the cupboard.
3. At seven o'clock.
4. No, I don't; I go by bus.
5. Yes, there are two.
6. At 23 Banbury Road.
7. Yes, I was.
8. It's over there by the police station.
9. About a hundred metres.
10. In a post office in Bradley Street.
11. Eight three two, four five four seven.
12. By car.
13. Science fiction.
14. No, but I'm interested in rock music.

3 Vervollständigen Sie die Sätze.

1. There .... apples in the cupboard.
2. .... there .... ice cream in the fridge?
3. How .... students .... there in your class?
4. .... my friends play tennis, but not many of them play badminton.
5. How .... milk have we got?
6. There are too .... chairs in here.
7. .... too .... coffee in this cup.
8. There ....n't .... cheese in the fridge, but there .... eggs.
9. There .... seven people, but only five books – that's not ....
10. Are there .... fair people in your family?

4 Schauen Sie sich die Tabelle an und schreiben Sie Sätze mit *never, sometimes, quite often, often, very often* oder *always*. Beispiele:

Ann often goes to the theatre. She never goes to the cinema.

ACTIVITY	TIMES PER YEAR	
	Ann	Joe
goes to the theatre	50	0
goes to the cinema	0	60
watches TV	100	50
plays tennis	20	100
plays football	0	60
goes dancing	50	0
goes to work by bus	0	276
goes to work by taxi	130	0
goes to work by train	100	0
travels by air	3	2
works on Saturdays	0	46
works at night	230	0
falls in love	1	10

5 *Kaum zu glauben*: Lesen Sie mit Hilfe Ihres Wörterbuchs.

There are 6,700 museums in North America.
52% of Australians, 39% of British people, and 11% of French people say that they are 'very happy'.
Your brain is 80% water.
More than one third of Britain's Prime Ministers went to the same school – Eton College.
The Wrigley's factory makes 1,360,000 kilometres of chewing gum every year.
There are 150 million bicycles in the world.
Americans use 300 litres of water per day per person.
Elephants sleep for only two hours per day.

6 Ein Kreuzworträtsel.

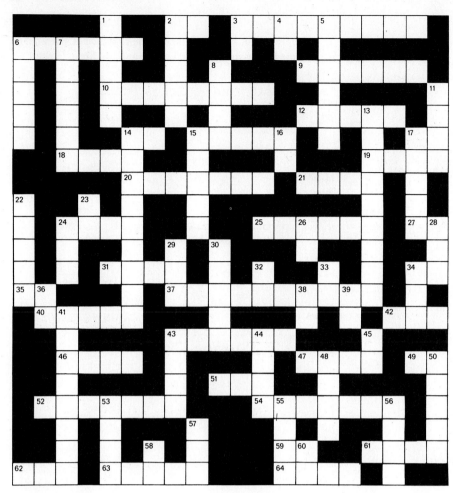

DOWN

1. This has got rooms in it.
2. There are 1,000 of these in a kilo.
3. Not 'yes'.
4. 'Do you and Alice like ice cream?' 'Yes, ... do.'
5. Five people – four people = one ....
6. I .... TV in the evenings.
7. 'Who was at home?' '...............'
8. 'A .... of rump steak, please.'
11. 'Do you know Alec and Jim?' 'Of course I do. .... live very near me.'
13. Tomatoes are £2.50 a pound. That's very ....
14. I have this in the morning.
15. There are a lot of these in a pound.
16. .... you like coffee?
17. Does your sister .... television very much?
22. You have this at about twelve o'clock.
23. The same as *39 down*.
24. This is in the bedroom.
26. A tomato, ... orange.

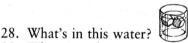

28. What's in this water?
29. What time do you .... up?
30. My sister .... work at 4.30.
32. .... dear.
33. 'Is your sister fair?' 'Yes, she ....'
34. boy → boys; man → ....
36. What time .... it?
38. Jerome has breakfast .... half past twelve.
39. It's twenty-five .... eight.
41. Food costs so much! It's ....
43. Do you .... big dogs?
44.
45. I, you, he, she, ..., we, you, they.
48. Like very, very, much.
50. John and his family live in a large flat on the fifth ....
53.
55. There's some of this under my hat.
56. My brother .... to tennis lessons every Saturday.
57. Thirteen – twelve = ...
58. Miriam is .... her way to work.
60. The hat shop is next .... the post office.

ACROSS

2. I .... to school by bus.
3. What .... do you read?
6. There's a man outside the ....!
9. How do you .... to work?
10. Is there a .... pool near your house?
12. Pounds, pence, dollars, pesetas, francs, yen, lire, and marks are ....
14. Susan is over there .... the reception desk.
15. There are a hundred pence in this.
17. I + you, or I + she, or I + he, or I + they.
18. My, ..., his, her, its, our, ..., their.
19. I don't .... tennis.
20. Morning, afternoon, ..., night.
21. What time do you .... lunch?
24. You read this.
25.

27. Hello.
31. I .... rock music; I don't like any of it at all.
34. she → her; he → him; I → ....
35. 'Hi.' '...............'
37.
40. We .... work at nine o'clock.
42. A hundred – ninety-nine = ...
43. I .... to classical music when I work.
46. You do this to books and newspapers.
47. A home, but not a house.
49. Half a litre .... milk.
51. Not small at all.
52. Don't like.
54. Where's my .... cream?
59. 'Where's the milk?' '...............'s on the table.'
61. It's terrible. Oh ....
62. A sort of water.
63. There are a hundred of these in a pound.
64. A sort of street.

8B What sort of house do you live in?

1 Schreiben Sie die richtige Form des Zeitworts.

1. Where ....? (*you, live*)
2. How .... to work? (*Miriam and Stephen, travel*)
3. My sister .... in a large flat in London. (*live*)
4. .... in London? (*she, work*)
5. Everybody in my class .... Japanese. (*speak*)
6. My brother .... in Britain. (*not live*)
7. I .... some Spanish, but I .... much. (*speak; not understand*)
8. What sort of food ....? (*they, like*)
9. .... near their parents? (*Teresa and Patricio, live*)
10. '............ Shelagh Anderson?' 'No, I don't.' (*you, know*)
11. '............ a newspaper on Sundays?' 'Yes, ... *The Observer*.' (*you, read; I, read*)
12. What time .... to bed? (*your children, go*)
13. My sister and her husband haven't got a car; .... to work by bus. (*they, go*)
14. My sister and I .... shopping, but my brother .... it. (*dislike; love*)
15. '............ tennis?' 'No, but my sister .... very well.' (*your brother, play; play*)

2 Achten Sie auf die richtige Betonung beim Aussprechen folgender Sätze:

1. I live in Curzon Street.
2. Do you like coffee?
3. Yes, I do.
4. No, I don't.
5. What time does Karen get up?
6. Does she have breakfast?
7. Yes, she does.
8. No, she doesn't.
9. Sam and Virginia live in Leeds.

3 Üben Sie die Schreibweise der Formen der dritten Person (*he/she/it*).

cost   costs

dislike   get   go   hate   like   listen to
live   love   play   read   start   stop   travel
try   watch   work

4 Wenn Sie *Student's Cassette A* haben, suchen Sie **Unit 8, Lesson B, Exercise 3.** (Sie werden dort nur den ersten Teil des Gesprächs finden.) Vergleichen Sie die Fragen im Gespräch mit den untenstehenden Fragen. Wenn Sie dieselbe Frage hören, kennzeichnen Sie sie mit einem Häkchen in Ihrem Arbeitsheft. Ansonsten schreiben Sie die Frage auf.

1. Is it a flat?
2. How many rooms has it got?
3. And your living room?
4. Do you play some sport?
5. Do you listen to classical music?

5 *Nathalie* wohnt in einer französischen Kleinstadt. Schauen Sie sich die Bilder an und schreiben Sie auf, was Sie am Abend macht. Beispiel:

On Sundays she watches football or reads.

6 Hätten Sie gerne eine/n englischsprachige/n Brieffreund/in? Wenn ja, kopieren Sie das Formular, füllen Sie es in Großbuchstaben aus und schicken Sie es an eine der folgenden Adressen. Legen Sie unbedingt VIER Internationale Antwortscheine und einen an Sie selbst adressierten Briefumschlag bei.

ADDRESS

IFL Penfriend Service
Dept FO
Saltash
Cornwall
England

Application form (please write in BLOCK LETTERS)

Personal Information

First name	Surname	Married/single	Age
....	....	....	....

Address in full (including your country)   Male/female   Occupation

....

....

....   Hobbies/interests   Languages

....

....

....

Pen friend information

Age   Male/female

....

Number of *International Reply Paid Coupons* enclosed: ....
Envelope addressed to yourself enclosed? Yes/No

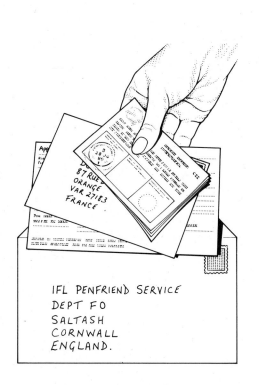

8C Choose

1 Achten Sie auf die richtige Betonung beim Aussprechen folgender Sätze:

1. Are there any **fair people** in your **family**?
2. There are some **books** under your **chair**.
3. There **aren't** any **apples** in the **kitchen**.

4. Is there any **ice cream** in your **fridge**?
5. There's some **ice** in the **fridge**.
6. There **isn't** any **money** in the **cupboard**.

2 Schreiben Sie Sätze mit *some, any, a lot of, too many, too much* und *(not) enough.*

1 2 3 4 5

6 7 8 9 10

3 Setzen Sie ein: *a/an, some, the* oder – (= kein Artikel).

1. There's .... orange in my bag.
2. .... potatoes are very expensive now.
3. Is Joanna in .... bed?
4. I think John's on his way to .... school.
5. There's .... milk over here.
6. Does she go to work by .... car?
7. Do you like .... apple juice?
8. Have you got .... pen?
9. I live in .... small flat in .... Park Street.
10. 'Where's Jack?' 'In .... living room.'
11. I have .... lunch from 12.30 to 1.15.
12. John isn't here; I think he's at .... lunch.
13. Excuse me. Is there .... post office near here, please?
14. Excuse me. Where's .... nearest post office, please?
15. First on .... right, then second on .... left.
16. About .... hundred metres.
17. I've got .... interesting books about classical music.
18. Are you interested in .... politics?
19. How do you travel to .... work?
20. Barry's wife is .... engineer.

I LOVE Y

!Ou

4 Wie heißen die Orte?

1 phone box   2   3   4   5

6   7   8   9

5 Beschreiben Sie anhand des Stadtplans auf Seite 41 im *Student's Book* den Weg zu:

1. Lenthall Road
2. The Siger Road
3. Fairfield Place

6 Wenn Sie *Student's Cassette A* haben, suchen Sie *Unit 8, Lesson C, Speaking and Listening Exercise 3.* (Sie werden dort nur die Nummern 1 und 3 finden.) Hören Sie zu und schreiben Sie die Wegbeschreibungen auf.

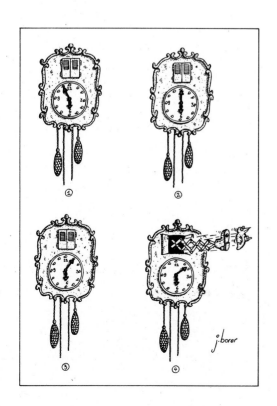

7 Lesen Sie mit Hilfe Ihres Wörterbuchs.

IT'S A LONG STORY
7

'Excuse me. Would you like a drink?'
 'Oh, er, yes. Thank you very much. A whisky, please.'
 The young man gave[1] Judy her drink and smiled at her. He had[2] an incredibly attractive smile. He really looked very nice: calm, friendly and kind. 'Perhaps he's a doctor,' she thought[3] – 'a surgeon, with those strong sensitive hands. Or perhaps an artist, or a musician.' Yes, he looked like an artist. She looked at him again and smiled.
 'What time is it, please?' he asked.
 Judy looked at her watch. 'Two thirty-five.'
 'Thank you,' he said, and smiled at her. She smiled back at him. He smiled again. He took[4] a gun out of his pocket, stood[5] up, and walked to the front of the plane.

[1]gave: past of *give*   [4]took: past of *take*
[2]had: past of *have*   [5]stood: past of *stand*
[3]thought: past of *think*

ÜBUNGEN ZU *LESSON 8D* ENTFALLEN.

Unit 9 Appearances

9A Sheila has got long dark hair

1 Bilden Sie Sätze mit *have got ('ve got)* oder *has got ('s got)*.
Beispiel:

A man in Philadelphia has got 26 names.

Mrs Calloway's flat	pretty eyes, Mary
You	a very good dentist
A man in Philadelphia	no word for 'snow'
We	four bedrooms in our house
Some Eskimo languages	three boyfriends
I	a big kitchen
My sister	26 names
My father	double nationality
Sam	TV in his bathroom
The President	enough money

2 Setzen Sie *and* ein, falls nötig.

1. Her hair is long ....*and*.... dark.
2. She has got long ......–...... dark hair.
3. My boyfriend is tall .... intelligent.
4. John has got a nice .... good-looking girlfriend.
5. I live in a big .... old house.
6. Peter's eyes are small .... green.
7. My flat is small .... dark.
8. Alex has got big .... brown eyes.
9. Bill is a tall .... good-looking man.
10. Burford is a small .... pretty .... English town.

3 Setzen Sie ein: *what, where, who* oder *how.*

1. .... is your name?
2. .... is the station?
3. '................ is the woman with dark hair?' 'She's my sister.'
4. .... time is it, please?
5. '................ do you do?' 'I'm an artist.'
6. .... are you from?
7. '................ are you?' 'Fine, thanks.'
8. '................ are you?' 'My name's Colin Watson.'
9. .... old are your children?

4 Geben Sie ehrliche Kurzantworten zu den folgenden Fragen:

1. Have you got blue eyes?
   Yes, I have. / No, I haven't.
2. Do you like classical music?
   Yes, I do. / No, I don't.
3. Have you got long hair?
4. Do you like coffee?
5. Are you hungry now?
6. Do you often travel by train?
7. Have you got pretty ears?
8. Is your home near a railway station?
9. Do you know any American people?
10. Has your teacher got brown eyes?

5 Lesen Sie die Wörter laut. Achten Sie dabei besonders auf die Aussprache von *-(e)s.*

-/z/	-/s/	-/ɪz/
doors	parents	glasses
names	nights	horses
plays	likes	buses
goes	stops	watches
potatoes	baths	oranges
Italians	works	noses
girls		houses
mornings		
lives		
eyes		

I JUST DISCOVERED WHY I'M SO CLUMSY. ...I'VE GOT 10 TOES.

EVERYBODY HAS TEN TOES!

SEVEN ON ONE FOOT AND 3 ON THE OTHER?

Jessica

My Mum

Jane is my
mummy

she is
nice is
my
mummy

May 12th
My mum is called Joy
and she is happy most of
the time as well and
she is very kind and she
looks a bit like me not much
like me at all.

my mum.

Elaine

Dad
By Philip

My Dad

My dad goes to work at 8.30 and he
comes home at 5.15 and me and my dad
play football after tea. We play with
my cars. In the morning me and my dad
play on the computer and my dad has
grey hair. My dad wears glasses. When
the breakfast goes wrong he shouts.

Philip Slater

9B A red sweater and blue jeans

1 Welche Farben?

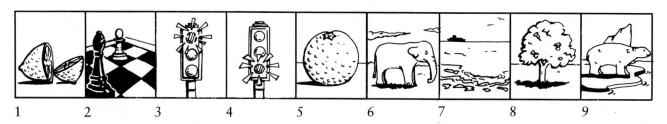

1   2   3   4   5   6   7   8   9

2 Schneiden Sie Bilder aus einer Illustrierten aus. Schreiben Sie die Namen und Farben der Kleidungsstücke auf.

blue jeans

a red coat

3 Setzen Sie ein: *am, are, is, have got* oder *has got.*

1. I .... a small flat in London.
2. A Renault 4 .... a small car, but it .... four doors.
3. Where .... my trousers?
4. Her hair .... long and black and beautiful.
5. A spider .... eight legs.
6. Jane and Isaac .... four small children.
7. My father .... a big black dog.
8. There .... some beer in the fridge, I think.
9. Los Angeles .... in the United States.
10. .... there any people from Germany in the class?
11. Lucy .... two boyfriends. They .... called Sam and Alec, and they .... both very nice.
12. An elephant .... big ears and a long nose (called a *trunk*).

4 Setzen Sie die Wörter in die richtige Reihenfolge.

1. blue have small a car we got
2. green yellow and I a dress am wearing
3. dark has long Jane hair got
4. ears have grey big got elephants
5. TV colour a and chairs green dark two are there living room my in
6. green ears , Sally long eyes has small hair and got

5 Vervollständigen Sie die Tabelle.

SUBJECT	OBJECT	POSSESSIVE
....	me	my
you	you	....
he	him	....
....	her	her
we	us	....
....	them	their

6
Wenn Sie *Student's Cassette A* haben, suchen Sie *Unit 9, Lesson B, Exercise 4.* (Sie werden dort nur die ersten sieben Fragen finden.) Hören Sie zu und versuchen Sie, die Fragen aufzuschreiben.

7
Lesen Sie einige der Kleinanzeigen mit Hilfe Ihres Wörterbuchs. Wen möchten Sie am liebsten kennenlernen? Wen möchten Sie gar nicht kennenlernen? Schreiben Sie eine Anzeige, wenn Sie möchten.

LATE IN LIFE, old but needs companion for travel. Sense of humour essential. Box G58.

YOUNG MAN, lonely, wishes to meet warm, attractive woman, for friendship etc. Box G427.

EDINBURGH (m.) research worker, 25, not tall, shy, half Jew, half Arab, sincere, seeks interesting young lady. Box G382.

MAN, 23, Edinburgh, tall, intelligent, seeks female companion for genuine friendship. Enjoys theatre, music and travelling. Box G276.

MALE, 28, sks warm relationship slim, kind, gentle understanding woman, 30–50. Box G448.

FAT, FEMALE LECTURER, dyed hair, young fifties, once married, seeks humorous, tolerant, sincere man, for living-it-up. Arts, gardening, home-life. Box G30.

AFRICAN JOURNALIST, 35, 5'5", handsome and slim-built, seeks attractive London-based, warm, intellectual fun-loving prof female, 22–30, for lasting friendship. Will appreciate photos & phone number. Box G398.

TALL, GOOD-LOOKING DIVORCEE, forties, works in London, lives in country, interested in home life, walking, books and music, would like to meet unattached, caring, warm-natured man up to 60. Box G55.

ARTISTIC good-looking man, 28, wants soul-mate for lasting relationship. Please send phr

female friend to enjoy life with. Ordinary, non-smoker. Box G84.

DAD, 30, widower; and baby seek female friend, wkends & holidays. N. Yorkshire. Box G732.

WOMAN, mid-sixties, seeks male companion, similar age. East Devon area. Box G512.

ATTRACTIVE, intelligent lady, mid-forties, seeks single, compassionate man, similar age, to talk, laugh with. Box G735.

UNATTACHED LADY, 45, not particularly attractive seeks ordinary man, 53/58, Surrey/Sussex, for happy relationship. Box G795.

SMALL, FRIENDLY, intelligent, red-headed designer, nearer 40 than 30, would like to meet man, over 28, black or white, warm-hearted, cheerful, hopefully non-smoking. Box G908.

ELEGANT, black divorcee, slim, 48, no children, wishes to meet tall, refined gentleman, 55–70, friendship/marriage. Midlands. Box G835.

TALL, SLIM, dark eyed Jewish widow, youthful, 49. Private Secretary. Sensitive, non-smoker, atheist, socialist, vegetarian, feminist, affectionate. Enjoys the arts, life, Woody Allen. Otherwise quite normal. Wish to meet male counterpart but who, unlike me, is solvent. Greater London. Box G31.

VIVACIOUS lady, mid-fifties, recently widowed, wishes to meet ...ing ... ... for friendship.

9C   I look like my father

1   Schreiben Sie die verkürzten Formen.

she is _she's_

he has got _he's got_

I have not got _I haven't got_

we are	John has got
you have got	John has not got
we have not got	they have
it is not	you are
John is	it is

2   Bilden Sie Fragen mit *have/has got*.

1. your mother | a car?

   Has your mother got a car?

2. she | a sister?
3. your parents | a nice house?
4. you | any coffee?
5. Mrs Hawkins | any children?
6. your house | a dining room?
7. you | a TV?

3   Bilden Sie negative Sätze.

1. She's got blue eyes.

   She hasn't got blue eyes.

2. I've got some Italian friends.

   I haven't got any Italian friends.

3. We've got a garage.

   We haven't got a garage.

4. My parents have got a very nice house.
5. I've got some bread in my bag.
6. Peter and Ellen have got a Rolls-Royce.
7. Sally has got long hair.
8. Robert has got his father's nose.
9. I've got my mother's personality.

4   Bilden Sie Sätze mit *looks like* und *does not look like*. Benutzen Sie *very, quite, a bit, (not) much* und *(not) at all*. Beispiele:

A camel looks very like a dromedary.
South America looks quite like Africa.
A cat looks a bit like a dog.
A radio does not look much like a TV.
The Taj Mahal does not look at all like a bird.

a modern train / Buckingham Palace / Africa / a camel / a dog / Stephenson's 'Rocket' / Chinese 你好嗎 / an aeroplane / a radio / a box / India / the Taj Mahal / Japanese 日本語 / a TV / a bird / a dromedary / a cat / a wolf / South America

5   Wenn Sie *Student's Cassette A* haben, suchen Sie *Unit 9, Lesson C, Exercise 3.* (Sie werden dort nur die ersten beiden Sprecher finden.) Hören Sie zu und versuchen Sie, mindestens fünf Wörter aufzuschreiben.

6   Beschreiben Sie sich selbst oder eine/n Freund/in. Benutzen Sie einige der folgenden Strukturen:

My name's . . . / My friend's name's . . .
I've got . . . / He/She's got . . .
I'm/He's/She's quite / very / not very / not at all . . .
I/He/She look(s) a bit / quite / very like . . .
I/He/She doesn't look (much / at all) like . . .
He/She and I are/have both . . .

"You've got beautiful eyes, Veronica."

43

9D Dear Mr Bell . . .

1 Bilden Sie Fragen mit *do you.*

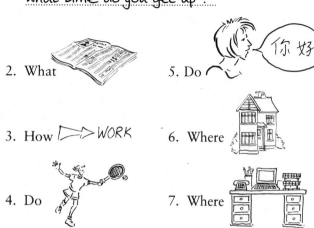

1. What time

What time do you get up ?

2. What

3. How ▷▷ WORK

4. Do

5. Do 你好

6. Where

7. Where

2 Schreiben Sie Fragen zu diesen Antworten. Benutzen Sie *does she.*

1. At seven o'clock.

What time does she get up ?

2. *The Times.*
3. By car.
4. Yes, she does.
5. No, she doesn't.
6. In Scotland.
7. In a hospital.

3 Versuchen Sie, das Gespräch zu vervollständigen. Schauen Sie im *Student's Book, Exercise 2* nach, falls Sie Hilfe brauchen.

A: Mr .... ?
B: ....
A: I'm .... journey?
B: ....
A: .... car ....
   Let's ....

4 Achten Sie auf die richtige Betonung beim Aussprechen folgender Wörter:

arrive   Tuesday   photograph   description
sincerely   conversation   station

5 Erinnern Sie sich an die folgenden Wörter? Kennen Sie ihre Aussprache? Nehmen Sie Ihr Wörterbuch zu Hilfe, falls nötig.

hair; glasses; colour; face; eyes; sweater; trousers; letter; holiday; station; person; people; family; wear; read; dark; fair; grey; blue; black; small; pretty; slim; fat; tall; good-looking; left; right; who; sorry.

6 Übersetzen Sie ins Deutsche.

1. I've got long dark hair, and my brother has, too.
2. My sister has got brown eyes and grey hair.
3. Pat is wearing a white sweater, a green blouse, and a green and black skirt.
4. I can't remember the colour of her eyes.
5. What are these called?
6. How do you pronounce this word?
7. Did you have a good journey?
8. Not bad, thanks.
9. My car's outside.
10. Yours sincerely,

7 Wenn Sie *Student's Cassette A* haben, suchen Sie *Unit 9, Lesson D, Exercise 2.* (Sie werden dort nur das zweite Gespräch finden.) Sprechen Sie diese Sätze laut aus. Hören Sie dann zu und sprechen Sie noch einmal nach.

Did you have a good journey?
Not bad, thanks.
Oh, I am sorry.
Paul Sanders?
Well, my car's outside.

8 Lesen Sie mit Hilfe Ihres Wörterbuchs.

IT'S A LONG STORY
8

'Good afternoon. This is your hijacker speaking. We are now flying at 550 miles per hour at a height of 29,000 feet. In approximately one and a half hours we will be over the north of Scotland. I wish you a pleasant flight.'

Judy's head was going round and round. First Sam, then the police, and now the hijacker. Where would it all end? Life was really much too complicated. She drank her whisky. It didn't make any difference. She looked out of the window. The sky was full of big dark clouds. So was her head.

Some time later the plane started going down. The pilot's door opened, and the hijacker came out, still holding his gun. He walked up to her and smiled. 'You know,' he said, 'you really are extremely beautiful. Come and put on your parachute.' Judy fainted.

Unit 10 Wanting things

10A I'm hungry

1 Setzen Sie ein: *am, are, is, has* oder *have.*

1. We .... breakfast at nine o'clock on Sundays.
2. I .... toast and orange juice for breakfast, and my wife .... eggs and black coffee.
3. .... you hungry?
4. How old .... your daughter?
5. When I .... cold I like to .... a bath.
6. What colour .... your new car?
7. My sister .... got three children.
8. When my wife .... ill she doesn't go to the doctor; she goes to bed.

2 Bilden Sie Sätze mit *when.*

1. John | ill | doctor
   When John is ill he goes to the doctor.
2. Mary | tired | bath
3. I | bored | shopping
4. Fred | hot | shower
5. Judy | unhappy | cinema
6. Sam | hungry | restaurant
7. Ann | bored | telephones friends
8. Lucy | happy | disco

3 Achten Sie auf die richtige Betonung beim Aussprechen folgender Sätze:

1. I'm **very hun**gry.
2. I'm a **bit tired.**
3. She's **not** at **all hun**gry.
4. **When Fred's bored** he **goes** to the **cin**ema.
5. **When Lucy's** un**hap**py she **goes shop**ping.

4 Wo würden Sie diese Dinge finden?

 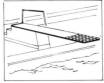  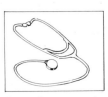

1. at a _restaurant_   2. at a ....   3. in a ....   4. at the ....'s

  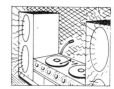

5. at the ....'s   6. at a ....   7. at ....   8. at a ....

5 Ein Kreuzworträtsel.

ACROSS ⟹

1. Are you .... in English lessons?
4. When I'm dirty I have a ....
6. Not hot.
7. A .... assistant works in a ....
11. Not happy.
12. Have you .... any brothers or sisters?
13. When I'm .... I have a 4 *across*.
15. When you're .... you go to the doctor.
16. Excuse .... What time is it?
17. I'm .... I think I'll go to bed.
18. 'Would you like some bread and cheese?' 'No, thanks, I'm not at all ....'

DOWN ⬇

1. I go to work .... car.
2. 'Where's Ann?' 'I think she's in the living ....'
3. .... you have a good journey?
4. I don't go to work by ....
5. Not *11 across.*
8. The same as *5 down.*
9. I speak a little ....
10. 'Would you like something to drink?' 'No, thanks. I'm not ....'
14. A colour.
16. More than one man.

45

10B Have you got anything in blue?

1 Setzen Sie die fehlenden Wörter ein.

A: Can I .... you?
B: I'm looking .... a blouse.
A: What ....?
B: 14.
A: Here's a lovely ....
B: Well, blue doesn't really suit ....
   Have you got anything .... yellow?
A: Yes. Here's a nice .... in yellow.
B: Can I try .... on?
A: .... course.

        *   *   *

B: How much .... it?
A: £19.95.
B: All right. I'll .... it.

2 Beantworten Sie die Fragen. Benutzen Sie *a . . . one* mit einigen der Wörter aus dem Kasten (Sie können Ihr Wörterbuch benutzen.). Beispiel:

'What colour car would you like?'   'A red one.'

large	small	modern	old	expensive
cheap	good-looking	nice	long	round
oval	red/black/brown/green		*etc.*	

1. What colour car would you like?
2. What sort of house would you like?
3. What colour shirt/blouse/tee-shirt are you wearing now?
4. What sort of watch have you got?
5. What sort of breakfast do you have on Sundays?
6. What sort of face have you got?
7. What sort of bedroom have you got?

3 Setzen Sie ein: *he, him, she, her, it, they* oder *them*.

1. .... looks like his father, and his children look like ....
2. 'What do you think of my new dress?' 'I'm afraid I don't like .... much.'
3. .... loves him, but he doesn't love ....
4. 'Here are two very nice blouses.' 'Can I try .... on?'
5. ....'s eight o'clock.
6. 'How are your parents?' '..............'re very well, thanks.' 'Say hello to .... from me.'
7. John would like us to have dinner with .... next week.

4 Setzen Sie ein: *a/an, the* oder – (= kein Artikel).

1. .... languages are difficult to learn.
2. Ann is .... secretary, but she would like to study economics.
3. 'Where's .... car?' 'In .... car park in .... Cross Street.'
4. 'Who's that?' 'It's .... my boyfriend.'
5. Do you know, ... tomatoes cost £6 .... kilo.
6. My room is on .... sixth floor.

5 Wenn Sie *Student's Cassette A* haben, suchen Sie *Unit 10, Lesson B, Exercise 2.* (Sie werden dort nur das dritte Gespräch finden.) Hören Sie zu und versuchen sie, es aufzuschreiben. Benutzen Sie *Student's Book, Exercise 1* zur Kontrolle.

10C Buying things

1 Achten Sie auf die richtige Betonung beim Aussprechen folgender Sätze:

1. **How much** are **those**?
2. There are some **books** under the **table**.
3. The **bicycle** is be**hind** the **door**.
4. The **table** is be**tween** the **window** and the **door**.
5. There is a **car** in **front** of the **house**.

2 Vervollständigen Sie die Sätze.

1. How much | those trousers?
   How much are those trousers?
2. Can | help | ?
3. Can | look | those shoes?
4. What | nice | shirt!
5. looking | French dictionary.
6. I'd like | try | on.
7. got | anything | blue?

3 Setzen Sie ein: *at, in, of, on, to, until* oder *with*.

1. The train arrives .... Bristol Parkway Station .... 7.10.
2. 'How late do you work in the evenings?' '.............. six o'clock.'
3. 'Where are Alice and Joe?' '.............. holiday in Scotland.'
4. Listen .... the recording.
5. Look .... the picture.
6. Your supper is .... the table.
7. 'Is the car .... the garage?' 'No, it's .... front .... the house.'
8. 'Are you interested .... politics?' 'Not very.'
9. I am quite short, ... dark hair and a small beard.
10. I always go to see my mother .... Sundays.

4 Setzen Sie *much* oder *many* ein.

1. how .... people?
2. too .... water
3. not .... bread
4. how .... money?

5. too .... children
6. not .... time
7. how .... rooms?

8. too .... houses
9. not .... sweaters
10. how .... milk?

5 Lesen Sie den Text, um die Antworten zu diesen Fragen zu finden, und schreiben Sie sie auf. Sie haben fünf Minuten Zeit.

1. What street is the Hilton Hotel in?
2. How many cars can be parked in the Hilton garage?
3. How far is the Hilton from Victoria Station?
4. How many restaurants are there in the Hilton?
5. How much do guests at the Hilton pay for children if they sleep in the same room as their parents?

LONDON HILTON
— ON —
PARK LANE

ROOM 3181
Hilton International

Hotel Features:
- Address: 22 Park Lane, London W1A 2HH, England
- Telephone: 01-493-8000 Telex: 24873
  Cable: HILTELS London
- Located in the heart of Mayfair, overlooking Hyde Park. Minutes from the elegant shopping and theatre districts
- 40 minutes from Heathrow Airport, 45 minutes from London–Gatwick Airport, 5 minutes from Victoria Station
- 446 comfortable guest rooms featuring:
  individual climate control
  direct-dial telephone
  electronic locks for maximum security
  radio and taped music
  self service mini-bar
  television with in-house films
- 54 one-, two- and three bedroom suites
- 2 restaurants, cocktail lounge and bar
- 24-hour room service
- Same day laundry/valet service at no extra charge (Monday–Saturday)
- Meeting facilities for up to 1000 persons
- 24-hour telex, cable, interpreter, secretarial service, typewriters, mail and postage facilities
- Pocket bleepers available for individual guest paging
- Worldwide courier service for documents guaranteeing one to three day delivery
- Teleplan – guarantees reasonable surcharges on international telephone calls
- Currency exchange at daily bank rates plus a modest handling charge of approximately 1% to cover only direct expenses
- Guest shops including beauty and barber, fashion, florist, drugstore, newsstand, speciality shops and transportation desk
- Indoor parking for 350 cars
- Hilton International Family Plan: there is no room charge for one or more children, up to the age of 16, when sharing the same room(s) with their parent(s) Maximum occupancy per room 3 persons

For reservations call your travel agent, any Hilton hotel or Hilton Reservation Service

10D Travelling

1 Vervollständigen Sie die Sätze mit den Begriffen aus dem Kasten. Nehmen Sie Ihr Wörterbuch zu Hilfe, falls nötig.

how much	how many	too much
too many	not much	not many

1. We've got .... apples this year
   – we don't know where to put them all.
2. .... people were there at seven o'clock, but at ten o'clock the restaurant was full.
3. We can have dinner or just have a drink – .... time have you got?
4. There is .... snow in the mountains this year – not enough for good skiing.
5. I'd like to go on holiday, but I've got .... work.
6. .... people were at the meeting on Thursday?
7. There's .... bread – could you buy some?
8. It was difficult to see the Queen; there were .... people.
9. .... lessons do you have at school every day?
10. There were .... buses from my village to the city when I was a child.

2 Achten Sie auf die richtige Betonung beim Aussprechen folgender Wörter und Sätze:

arrive **break**fast A**mer**ican Ex**press**

1. **What time** is the **next train?**
2. I'd **like** a **room, please.**
3. **How much** is the **room?**
4. Can I **pay** by **credit card?**
5. Could you **speak more slowly, please?**

3 Erinnern Sie sich an die folgenden Wörter und Ausdrücke? Kennen Sie ihre Aussprache? Nehmen Sie Ihr Wörterbuch zu Hilfe, falls nötig.

bread; friend; car park; dictionary; shoes; bath; shower; breakfast; money; night; number; room; speak; understand; arrive; next; under; outside.

4 Übersetzen Sie ins Deutsche.

1. I'm hungry, and I'm quite tired.
2. The children are cold.
3. She's not at all thirsty.
4. When I'm bored I go to the cinema.
5. Can I help you?
6. I'm just looking.
7. I'm looking for a sweater.
8. Yellow doesn't suit me.
9. What size?
10. Can I try it on?
11. How much is that?
12. I'd like a room, please.
13. Could you speak more slowly, please?

5 Wenn Sie *Student's Cassette A* haben, suchen Sie *Unit 10, Lesson D, Exercise 2*. (Sie werden dort nur das dritte Gespräch finden.) Hören Sie zu und versuchen Sie, es aufzuschreiben. Benutzen Sie *Student's Book, Exercise 1* zur Kontrolle.

6 Vervollständigen Sie mindestens eins dieser Gespräche. Schauen Sie im *Student's Book* nach, falls Sie Hilfe brauchen.

A: time | train | York?
B: one | 4.45 | change | Birmingham
A: there | direct | one?
B: direct | 5.52 | arriving | 8.28
A: platform | 5.52?
B: 6

A: help?
B: room
A: ?
B: double
A: one?
B: nights
A: shower?
B: bath
   ?
A: £75
B: card?
A: form

7 Lesen Sie mit Hilfe Ihres Wörterbuchs.

IT'S A LONG STORY
9

Judy opened her eyes. The sun was shining, and a cool wind was blowing on her face. She felt very light and happy. 'Where am I?' she said. Behind her, a man's voice said '100 feet above Loch Ness. Can you swim?' Judy fainted again.

When she opened her eyes, she was lying on the bank of the loch, with her head on her parachute. 'Allow me to introduce myself,' said the handsome young man. 'My name is Jasper MacDonald.' 'Why did you hijack the plane?' asked Judy. 'It's my birthday,' said Jasper. 'Now let's go to my castle and find some dry clothes.'

Unit 11 People's pasts

11A She never studied . . .

1 Schreiben Sie die Vergangenheitsformen. Beispiele:

listen ~~listened~~

hate ~~hated~~

play ~~played~~

study ~~studied~~

arrive   change   help   live
look   love   marry
pronounce   remember   start
stay   try   watch   work

2 Schauen Sie sich noch einmal *Exercise 1* im *Student's Book, Unit 11, Lesson A* an. (Die Aufnahme finden Sie auf *Student's Cassette A.*) Schreiben Sie einige Sätze über Ihre eigene Vergangenheit.

3 Drücken Sie die Uhrzeiten anders aus. Beispiel:

3.15 ~~a quarter past three~~

9.20   5.15   7.40   11.55
9.25   3.35   5.30   7.05
10.45   6.10   1.50

4 Verbinden Sie die Buchstaben in *Box 2* mit den Wörtern, auf die sie sich reimen.

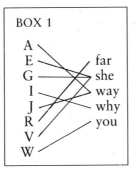

BOX 1		BOX 2	
A	far	A	car
E	she	E	play
G	way	G	see
I	why	I	try
J	you	J	who
R		R	
V		V	
W		W	

"I did say something, but that was yesterday."

11B When I was a small child . . .

1 Bilden Sie Fragen. Beginnen Sie mit *When you were a child . . .*

1. happy?
   ~~When you were a child, were you happy?~~
2. life | hard?
   ~~When you were a child, was life hard?~~
3. sometimes hungry?
4. at home a lot?
5. your parents | happy?
6. your family | rich?
7. your house | big enough?
8. your father | out all day?
9. your grandmother | pretty?
10. your mother | very young?

2 Welches Wort paßt nicht? Nehmen Sie Ihr Wörterbuch zu Hilfe, falls nötig.

1. mother   father   friend   sister
   ~~friend~~
2. chair   table   milk   fridge
3. hair   eye   moustache   beard
4. nose   ear   eye   hand
5. white   green   long   blue
6. shirt   trousers   shoes   jeans
7. small   pretty   long   mouth
8. bra   blouse   tie   skirt
9. hungry   restaurant   thirsty   tired
10. breakfast   restaurant   car park
    swimming pool

3 Achten Sie auf die richtige Betonung beim Aussprechen folgender Wörter:

be**hind** be**tween** **diff**erent en**joy** ho**tel**
interesting **mill**ion **rest**aurant **thou**sand

4 Wenn Sie *Student's Cassette A* haben, suchen Sie *Unit 11, Lesson B, Exercise 2.* (Sie werden dort nur den ersten Sprecher finden.) Schließen Sie Ihr Buch. Hören Sie zu und schreiben Sie so viel wie möglich auf. Benutzen Sie dann den folgenden Text zur Kontrolle.

My name is Adrian Webber. My age is 42 years, and I was born in Delhi, India. This was due to the fact that my father had spent most of his adult life in India in the Indian police up to that time. I have a sister who's eight years older than myself. She was also born in India, and my childhood was very varied and quite happy as I remember.

5 Schauen Sie sich die drei Texte in *Student's Book, Exercise 1* an. Schreiben Sie dann einen neuen Text anhand folgender Notizen:

– born small flat Berlin
– parents poor
– father shop assistant
– mother housewife
– sometimes hungry
– parents very good to me
– nearly always happy

11C   They didn't drink tea

1   Wie viele Jahre her?

1. 1492
   About 500 years ago
2. 1970
3. the year when you were born
4. the year when your mother was born
5. the year when you started school
6. your tenth birthday

2   Bilden Sie negative Sätze.

1. She liked cheese. (*fish*)
   She did not like fish.
2. She lived in a small village. (*London*)
3. She played tennis. (*basketball*)
4. She studied maths. (*languages*)
5. She married a dentist. (*doctor*)
6. She worked in a university. (*office*)
7. She often travelled to America. (*Africa*)

3   Bilden Sie Fragen zu den Sätzen aus *Exercise 2.*
Beispiel:

1. *What did she like?*

4   Schreiben Sie den Text mit der richtigen Großschreibung und Zeichensetzung ab. Beginnen Sie mit *Philip Hallow was . . .*

philip hallow was born in london in 1967 his father was a bus driver and his mother was a librarian they didnt have much money but philip and his two sisters jane and sarah were very happy children in 1984 philips father died so philip didnt go to university he started working in a bank but didnt like it so he changed to an import-export firm now hes the assistant manager and hes very happy

5   Achten Sie auf die richtige Betonung beim Aussprechen folgender Sätze:

1. I was **born** in America.
2. My **father** was an engi**neer**.
3. My **mother** was a **teacher**.
4. We were **all** **very** **hap**py.
5. I **liked** school, but I **didn't** **study** very **hard**.

"My son? Good heavens, no – that's me a year ago!"

50

11D Danced till half past one

1 Wie heißen die Vergangenheitsformen dieser Zeitwörter?

marry *married*

want   study   have   know   come   stop   hate   help
get   tell   shop

2 Wie heißen die Grundformen dieser Zeitwörter?

heard *hear*

woke   worked   called   died   said   could   finished   did
liked   went

3 Schreiben Sie über *Jake*.

When Jake was 20 he was very poor, and life was difficult. He had to work very hard. But he had a good time. Now he's 40. He has plenty of money and a very good job. Life is easy. And he still has a good time!

THEN	NOW
Jake worked very hard.	*He doesn't work very hard.*
He lived in one small room.	He lives in a very big house.
He started work at 7.30.	....
....	He works five hours a day.
He ate cheap food.	....
....	He often goes to restaurants.
He did not travel much.	....
He played football on Saturday afternoons.	....
....	He still has a lot of girlfriends. He doesn't want to be an artist.
....	....
His mother worked in a shop.	He's got three cars.
....	

4 Schreiben Sie einige Sätze darüber, was Sie gestern oder letztes Wochenende gemacht haben.

5 Erinnern Sie sich an die folgenden Wörter und Ausdrücke? Kennen Sie ihre Aussprache? Nehmen Sie Ihr Wörterbuch zu Hilfe, falls nötig.

age; friend; music; school; parents; teacher; question; window; travel; young; hungry; unhappy; tired; sometimes; never; quite; really; a bit; a lot; at home; except; between.

6 Übersetzen Sie ins Deutsche.

1. When I was younger I hated school.
2. I changed schools five times.
3. I was born in a village in South Africa.
4. My parents were very poor.
5. My father was a farmer.
6. We were not very happy.
7. I got home at 3 a.m. again.
8. I couldn't find my key, so I climbed in through a window.

7 Wenn Sie *Student's Cassette A* haben, suchen Sie *Unit 11, Lesson D, Exercise 2.* Hören Sie sich das Gespräch an. Sie werden die folgenden Sätze hören, aber mit kleinen Unterschieden. Können Sie sie erkennen? Benutzen Sie *Student's Book, Exercise 2* zur Kontrolle.

1. What time did you come back home last night, then, June?
2. About half past one, I think.
3. I didn't want to wake Mother up.
4. You know I hate loud music.
5. Why did you come home so late?
6. No, but we went to Alice's place and had some coffee.

8 Lesen Sie mit Hilfe Ihres Wörterbuchs.

IT'S A LONG STORY
10

It didn't take long to get to Jasper's castle. It was an enormous building, about half a mile from Loch Ness, with tall towers, battlements and a moat, and at least 200 rooms. 'What a place!' said Judy. 'Well, it's not much, but it's home,' said Jasper. 'Let me show you to your room. And I'll see if I can find you some of my sister's clothes.'

Judy's room was about ten minutes' walk from the main entrance, up a lot of stairs and along a lot of corridors. It was beautiful, decorated in light blue and lilac, with some wonderful pieces of antique furniture. There was a splendid view of the loch and the mountains. 'This is lovely!' said Judy. 'How many of you live here?' 'Just my sister and I,' said Jasper. 'And the ghost, of course. See you later.'

Unit 12 Consolidation

12A Things to remember: Units 9, 10 and 11

1 Schauen Sie sich auf Seite 56 des *Student's Book* die Liste der unregelmäßigen Zeitwörter und die Regeln für die Bildung regelmäßiger Vergangenheitsformen an. Lesen Sie dann die Geschichte und schreiben Sie die richtigen Vergangenheitsformen für die Zeitwörter in Schrägschrift auf.

I (*1. be*) very poor when I first (*2. live*) in Paris. When I (*3. go*) shopping for food, I always (*4. buy*) the cheapest things. I never (*5. travel*) by taxi; I usually (*6. walk*). But I (*7. be*) not unhappy. I (*8. love*) Paris, and people (*9. be*) very kind to me. I (*10. meet*) some people then who are still good friends today.

I only (*11. speak*) a little French, and I (*12. want*) to learn to speak and understand French well. Every day I (*13. get*) up early. Before my French lesson I (*14. read*) a newspaper and (*15. try*) to understand it; then I (*16. look*) up the difficult words in the dictionary and (*17. try*) to learn them. I (*18. go*) to lessons every day, and I (*19. talk*) to everybody I (*20. meet*).

After a few months I (*21. have got*) very little money, so I (*22. start*) a job as a part-time secretary for an American lawyer. The job (*23. not be*) interesting, but my life outside my job (*24. be*) very interesting. I (*25. have got*) friends who (*26. be*) artists, musicians and writers. I (*27. see*) and (*28. hear*) things that were new and interesting every day.

My family (*29. think*) I was coming home at the end of a year. Actually I stayed for five years, and I (*30. love*) every day of those five years. I (*31. come*) home in 1990, and I'm happy I did, but I think of Paris every day.

2 Bilden Sie Fragen in der Vergangenheit zu diesen Antworten.

1. She told me she was at home.

   <u>What did she tell you? OR</u>

   <u>Where was she?</u>
2. No, I didn't; I hated it.
3. I came by car.
4. I was quite happy.
5. No, but I liked rock music.
6. 6.30 a.m.
7. My mother was born in Ireland and my father was born in England.
8. We lived in Birmingham.

3 *Be, have* oder *have got*?

1. I .... not usually hungry in the morning, so I just .... a cup of coffee for breakfast.
2. My sister .... a very pretty cat.
3. How tall .... you?
4. That was a dirty job – I think I'll .... a shower before supper.
5. I don't know if they .... any children.
6. 'I'............... cold!' 'Would you like my sweater?'
7. What colour .... your car?
8. There .... too many people in this room.
9. 'I .... very hungry.' 'I .... some bread and cheese. Would you like some?'
10. You .... beautiful eyes, Mark.
11. The children .... thirsty – have we got anything to drink in the car?
12. I think they .... artists. They look like artists.
13. I never .... lunch on Tuesdays – there's not enough time.
14. You .... your father's nose and mouth.
15. 'Would you like a cold drink?' 'Yes, please. I'............... hot.'

4 Was sagen die Personen?

1. .... English? / It's a compact disc player.
2. .... ? / I look a bit like my mother.
3. Can I help you? / ....
4. .... red? / I'll just see.
5. .... ? / £ ....
6. .... ? / It was terrible.

5 Stellen Sie sich vor, Sie fahren mit dem Zug nach London, um Ms Hancock (eine alte Freundin Ihrer Mutter) zu besuchen. Schreiben Sie ihr einen Brief, in dem Sie ihr mitteilen, wann Sie in Victoria Station ankommen und wie Sie aussehen.

6 Finden Sie die Antworten zu den Fragen im untenstehenden Text. Sie brauchen nicht den ganzen Text zu lesen. (Im Englischen bedeutet *Continent* ganz Europa ohne Großbritannien und Irland.)

1. I was late for the 12.10 to Cardiff from London.
   When is the next train to Cardiff?
2. If a standard-class ticket to Birmingham costs £5,
   how much does a first-class ticket cost?
3. Is it possible to buy a Britrail Pass in Bristol?
4. Is it possible to buy a Britrail Seapass in the USA?

TRAVELLING BY TRAIN

British Rail operates a service of 16,000 trains a day serving over 2,000 stations; there's hardly a part of Britain that can't be reached by train. A fast InterCity network links London with all major cities, such as Bristol, Cardiff, York and Edinburgh, with trains leaving the capital every hour during the main part of the day. Also, at no extra cost, you can travel up to 125 mph (200 kph) on the High Speed InterCity Trains to many major destinations.

On most trains you have the choice between First or Standard (Economy) Class. First Class seats are more spacious and cost 50% more than the Standard Class fare. Many InterCity trains have a full meals service, and grills, snacks and drinks are also available on other trains.

Buying your rail ticket

Overseas visitors are entitled to one of the best rail travel bargains anywhere – the Britrail Pass. It gives unlimited travel throughout Britain for 8, 15, 22 days or 1 month (7, 14, 21 days or 1 month in North America). Get one from Britrail Travel International Offices in North America or from local travel agents or major railway stations in Europe. Visitors from the Continent can also buy a Britrail Seapass. This covers all the facilities offered above, plus the return sea journey across the Channel. **Remember, these passes are not sold in Britain and must be bought before you leave your own country.**

Otherwise, in addition to the normal single return fares, certain tickets can be bought at reduced rates – see this page under heading "Lots of Travel Bargains". For general rail enquiries, go to your nearest British Rail Travel Centre or any railway station.

LOTS OF TRAVEL BARGAINS

How much you pay depends on where and when you want to

7 Ein Kreuzworträtsel.

ACROSS

3. I've got four sisters, and we all look like our mother .... Ann; she looks like our father.
6. Were you .... when you were a child?
9. 'Are you ....?' 'Yes, I am; I didn't have any breakfast.'
10. Past tense of *come*.
11. I've got lots .... books about cats.
12. My brother looks very .... me.
13. I'm .... looking.
14. Not now.
15. Past of *hear*.
17. I .... some potatoes at Anderson's yesterday, and they were all bad.
18. *I see, you see, she* ....
19. You hear with this.
22. I'm looking .... some brown shoes.
24. You can have lunch here.
25. ...., you, her, him, it, us, them.
26. Where .... your sister born?
28. Can you .... me a newspaper when you're out?
29. One of the things you walk with.
30. 'We've only got two of these, a blue one and a red one. Which one would you like?' '................ red one, please.'
31. ☞
33. What's your .... colour?
34. I .... up very late yesterday.
36. Have you got these in .... 7?
38. I was .... always happy when I was a small child.
39. The opposite of *live*.
40. Football, tennis, swimming.
43. Past tense of *meet*.
44. Infinitive of *went*.
46. I look a .... like my uncle.
48. Cheese is sometimes this colour.
50. Some people have got eyes this colour.
52. Who .... you look like?
53. I am .... wearing a jacket today.

54. Would you like tea .... coffee?
55. What a .... sweater!
56. Do .... shoes cost the same as these?
59. Are you English?
63. Six and four.
64. How do you .... e-i-g-h-t?
66. Not hot.
68. The opposite of *white*.
69. Can I .... it on?
72. There is a lot of this in England.
74. A teacher's is usually small; a rock star's can be very big.
76. I told my son I was at work, but .... I was at lunch with a friend.
77. Where .... you have lunch yesterday?
79. Is *go* a regular verb?
81. Did you .... your journey?

DOWN

1. 'Here's a .... of my brother.' 'What a good-looking man!'
2. I don't earn much, but my job is very ....
3. You see with this.
4. These things work with numbers.
5. The opposite of *different* is *the* ....
6. You do this with your ears.
7. .... sincerely
8. Not cold.
16. When I'm .... I have a shower.
20. Were you .... school on Friday?
21. The same as *72 across*.
23. The same as *33 across*.
25. 'When did you meet them?' 'I .... Alice in 1988, and I .... Joan in 1989.'
27. Can I give you .... to drink?
28. Think .... you speak.
32. Where .... you live?
35. Past tense of *take*.
37. The same as *81 across*.
40. Not tall.
41. She .... she was an actress, but actually she's a secretary.
42. A colour, but no colour.
45. Look! That's Susan .... there!
47. I'd like .... see something in green.

54

49. She's tall, ... blue eyes
and dark hair.
50. Present tense of *went*.
51. *Love* is .... an irregular
verb.
53. Eyes, ears, mouth, ...
55. The same as *53 down*.
57. Yours .... ,
Emma Stockton.
58. How was your ....?

60. A thousand thousand.
61. Old people's hair is sometimes
this colour.
62. Please come and see us
.... when you are next
in England.
65. Past tense of *can*.
67. Where is ....?
70. This doesn't fit me very
....

71. A colour. Your favourite?
73. Not night.
75. .... I look round?
78. Have you got a pen ....
your bag?
80. Is that your book ....
the table?

12B On Saturday

1 Tragen Sie mindestens zwei Wörter in jede Liste ein.

1. chair, sofa, . . .
2. tomato, cheese, . . .
3. bank, post office, . . .
4. Italian, Chinese, . . .
5. I, she, . . .
6. under, in, . . .
7. hungry, cold, . . .

2 Setzen Sie jeweils eins dieser Wörter ein.

here · this · these · come/came
there · that · those · go/went

1. I .... here in 1975.
2. I go to .... hotel whenever I'm in
Washington.
3. I think .... people over there are Greek.
4. I don't understand .... sentence. Could
you come .... and help me with it?
5. .... grapes are very nice. Would you
like some?
6. Could you pass me .... newspaper?
7. 'I love walking in the Himalayas.'
'Do you .... there often?'

3 Unterstreichen Sie in jeder Liste das Wort, bei dem der Selbstlaut anders ausgesprochen wird.

1. three   eat   people   ten
2. half   all   bath   start
3. watch   want   bank   what
4. some   come   love   home
5. cost   bored   course   tall
6. her   heard   first   ear
7. where   here   there   they're
8. time   night   live   child
9. sit   feet   in   · if
10. would   look   who   foot

4 Bilden Sie Fragen.

1. Des and Jo live in Santiago. (*Bob and Liz*)
Where do Bob and Liz live ?
2. There are three rooms on the ground floor.
(*the first floor*)
How many rooms are there on the first floor ?
3. Ann has got two boys and a girl. (*Lucy*)
How many children has Lucy got ?
4. There's a bus at three o'clock. (*four o'clock*)
Is there a bus at four o'clock ?
5. My brother and his wife live in London.
(*your sister and her husband*)
6. There's some cheese in the fridge. (*butter*)
7. I've got some English friends. (*American*)
8. My uncle Edward works in a bank.
(*your aunt Helen*)
9. The 7.25 train arrives at 9.16. (*the 9.25 train*)
10. Celia and Jake have got three children.
(*Fred and Catherine*)
11. There are two chairs in the hall. (*the kitchen*)
12. King Henry VIII had six wives. (*Henry VII*)

5 Wer hat was gemacht? Schreiben Sie Sätze.

Indira Gandhi   made many famous films.
Van Gogh   wrote *Hamlet*.
Agatha Christie   was the first woman Prime
Shakespeare   Minister of India.
Karl Marx   discovered America in 1492.
Hitchcock   wrote detective stories.
Columbus   painted pictures.
wrote *Das Kapital*.

6 Lesen Sie die Notizen und schreiben Sie einige Sätze über Hemingways Leben.

Ernest Hemingway b. Illinois 1899, d. Idaho 1961.
Father doctor, mother musician and painter. Ambulance
driver in Italy during First World War. Journalist in
Paris after war for several years. Many well-known
novels, including *The Sun Also Rises*, *Farewell to Arms*,
For Whom the Bell Tolls, *The Old Man and the Sea*.
Nobel Prize for literature 1954.

7 Schreiben Sie einige Sätze über Ihr eigenes Leben oder über das Leben einer berühmten Persönlichkeit.

12C Choose

1 Können Sie die Namen all dieser Kleidungsstücke aufschreiben?

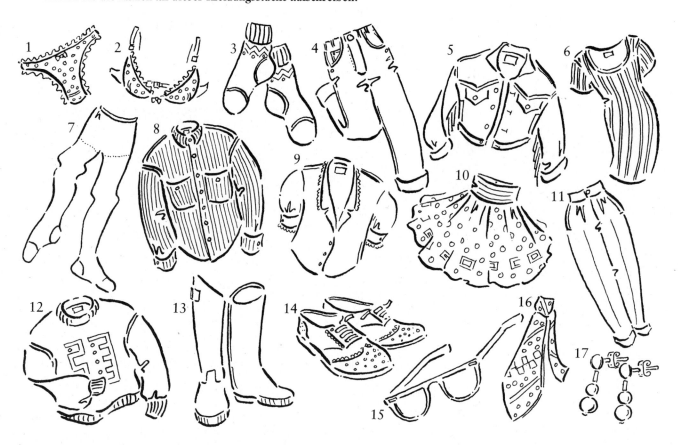

2 Kreisen Sie jeweils das Wort ein, das eine andere Betonung hat.

1. **num**ber   **hap**py   (be**hind**)   **yel**low
2. station   hotel   thousand   village
3. income   arrive   depend   police
4. Saturday   favourite   interested   eleven
5. understand   afternoon   good-looking   engineer
6. British   Chinese   German   Russian
7. again   sometimes   toothpaste   breakfast

3 Bilden Sie „Folgefragen".

1. 'Look at my new coat!' ('Where | buy?')
   <u>Where did you buy it ?</u>
2. 'Mary's here.' ('When | arrive?')
3. 'I'm tired.' ('What time | get up?')
4. 'There were some French people at the party.' ('How many . . . ?')
5. 'Karl Marx died in London.' ('When | die?')
6. 'It's my birthday today.' ('How old . . . ?')
7. 'I don't like pop music.' ('What sort . . . ?')

4 Fügen Sie *-s* hinzu, falls nötig.

1. I don't know where she work...S....
2. Does your brother live....–.... at home?
3. He arrived........... at six o'clock.
4. My father hate........... rock and roll.
5. And he doesn't like........... jazz.
6. Do you know her........... children...........?
7. My brother........... are both very tall...........
8. Most people........... like........... music.
9. She's got........... beautiful long........... hair...........

5 Setzen Sie *some* oder *any* ein.

1. I'd like .... milk, please.
2. We haven't got .... bread.
3. Is there .... cheese in the fridge?
4. I'm looking for .... cheap shoes.
5. Have you got .... American friends?
6. There aren't .... chairs in the room.
7. When I was a child, I had .... nice holidays in the mountains.
8. Did you do .... thing interesting at the weekend?

6 Wenn Sie *Student's Cassette A* haben, suchen Sie *Unit 12, Lesson C, Listening Exercise 1.* (Sie werden dort nur das dritte Gespräch finden.) Finden Sie die Bedeutung folgender Wörter: *scar; I've no idea.* Hören Sie sich dann das Gespräch an und versuchen Sie, alles aufzuschreiben.

7 Welche Sätze handeln von *Queen Elizabeth I* und welche von *Princess Grace?* Sie können Ihr Wörterbuch benutzen. Schreiben Sie beide Texte auf.

1. Grace Kelly was born on the east coast of the United States in 1929.
2. Queen Elizabeth I was the daughter of Henry VIII and his second wife, Anne Boleyn.
3. When she was three months old she went to live at Hatfield, far from the King and Queen.
4. Her mother was executed by her father when the little girl was two and a half years old.
5. When she was 21, she went to Hollywood and began acting in films.
6. The young princess learnt Italian, French, Latin and Greek from royal tutors.
7. She appeared in the film *High Noon*, and won an Academy Award ('Oscar') for her acting in *A Country Girl*.
8. In 1956 she married Prince Rainier of Monaco.
9. She followed her half-brother Edward and her half-sister Mary to the throne.
10. She then retired from her career in America and devoted herself to her royal duties.
11. She never married, and ruled for 45 years as a strong and independent queen.
12. She was much loved by the people of England, and her reign was one of power and glory for her country.
13. She died in 1982 after a car accident.

8 Lesen Sie mit Hilfe Ihres Wörterbuchs.

IT'S A LONG STORY
11

Judy had a bath, and then put on some of Jasper's sister's clothes. They fitted her perfectly. She looked at herself in the mirror, smiled, frowned, and went downstairs.

'Hello,' said Jasper. 'Did I tell you how beautiful you are?'

'Yes, you did,' said Judy.

'Fine,' said Jasper. 'Let me show you round the castle before tea.'

'But I don't want to stay for tea,' said Judy.

'This part of the castle was built in 1480,' said Jasper.

'I want to go to Rio,' said Judy.

'This is a portrait of my ancestor Donald MacDonald,' said Jasper.

'I want to see my boyfriend Sam,' said Judy.

'He was a friend of King James VI,' said Jasper.

'I love him,' said Judy.

'James VI?' said Jasper, interested.

'No, you fool,' said Judy. 'My boyfriend Sam.'

'Oh, Sam Watson,' said Jasper. 'You don't want to see him.'

'Yes, I do,' said Judy.

'No, you don't,' said Jasper. 'This is a portrait of my ancestor MacDonald MacDonald.'

'How do you know Sam?' said Judy.

'He was a friend of King Robert the Bruce,' said Jasper.

'Sam?' said Judy.

'No, you fool,' said Jasper. 'MacDonald. You don't want to see Sam. You want to stay here with me. I love you.'

Out of a door came an old man with white hair and very strange clothes. He was carrying his head under his arm. He looked very like the portrait.

'Who's that?' asked Judy.

'The ghost,' said Jasper.

'You don't want to go and see Sam,' said the ghost. 'You want to stay here with Jasper.'

ÜBUNGEN ZU *LESSON 12D* ENTFALLEN.

Unit 13 Differences

13A I can sing, but I can't draw

1 Achten Sie auf die richtige Betonung beim Aussprechen folgender Sätze:

1. Children **can't** smile when they're **born**.
2. **Most children** can smile when they're **six weeks old**.
3. How **many languages** can you **speak**?
4. Can any of you under**stand** Portuguese?
5. We can **drive** you **home** if you **like**.
6. I **can't** understand where **Jane** is.
7. 'Can you **hear** me?' 'Of **course** I **can**!'
8. 'Could I **have** some coffee?' 'I'm afraid you **can't**; there isn't any.'

2 Schreiben Sie fünf Sätze über das, was Sie können (und wie gut sie es können) und fünf Sätze über das, was Sie nicht können. Beispiele:

I can sing very well.

I can swim a little.

I can't cook.

3 Erinnern Sie sich an die folgenden Wörter und Ausdrücke? Wie viele Wörter bzw. Ausdrücke können Sie jeweils hinzufügen? Nehmen Sie *Student's Book, Lessons 4A und 8A* zu Hilfe, falls nötig.

1. dark, intelligent, . . .
2. mother, sister, . . .
3. China, India, . . .
4. Japanese, Swiss, . . .
5. engineer, shop assistant, . . .
6. never, sometimes, . . .
7. by, opposite, . . .
8. Monday, . . .
9. kitchen, bathroom, . . .
10. cooker, fridge, . . .
11. apple, bread, . . .
12. swimming pool, phone box, . . .
13. politics, music, . . .

4 Wenn Sie *Student's Cassette B* haben, suchen Sie *Unit 13, Lesson A, Exercise 2*. Hören Sie zu und sprechen Sie nach. Achten Sie auf eine möglichst gute Aussprache.

5 *Kaum zu glauben.* Sie können Ihr Wörterbuch benutzen.

Gorillas can't swim.
Mice can sing.
Horses can sleep standing up.
Elephants can't jump, and they can't remember things very well, but they can stand on their heads.
A male emperor moth can smell a female eleven kilometres away.
Leopold Stokowski could play the violin and the piano when he was five.
Thomas Young (an 18th-century scientist) could speak twelve languages when he was eight.
The Danish linguist Rasmus Rask could speak 235 languages.
The American tennis player Roscoe Tanner could serve a ball at 225 kilometres an hour.

13B Better than all the others

1 Unterstreichen Sie die betonten Silben in den folgenden Sätzen: ⌣⌣⌣.

I can drive better than my brother.

Kennzeichnen Sie dann die Selbstlaute, die /ə/ ausgesprochen werden. Beispiel: O.

I can drive better than my brother.

1. My aunt can play tennis better than Steffi Graf.
2. I can ski better now than I could when I was younger.
3. I was good at football when I was younger.

2 Üben Sie die Aussprache folgender Wörter. Nehmen Sie *Student's Book, Exercise 3* zu Hilfe, falls nötig.

wake   cat   tall   map
past   saw   came

58

3 Bilden Sie Fragen.

1. I run 5,000 metres every day. (*your sister?*)
   <u>Does your sister run 5,000 metres</u>
   <u>every day?</u>
2. I can cook quite well. (*your brother?*)
3. I can run 200 metres. (*swim?*)
4. My friend Susan came to see me on Saturday.
   (*by car?*)
5. My father was a dancer when he was younger.
   (*your mother?*)
6. My parents were very poor when they were
   young. (*unhappy?*)
7. George can type quite fast. (*How many words a
   minute?*)
8. We've got a big old piano. (*How many keys?*)

4 Lesen Sie den Text.

Fish can swim better than pigeons can fly better than
squirrels can climb trees better than kangaroos can jump
higher than horses can run faster than canaries can sing
better than fish can swim . . .

Schreiben Sie einen „Kreistext" über Ihre Familie. Beispiel:

<u>I can run faster than my father can</u>
<u>cook better than my mother can ...</u>

5 Lesen Sie den Text und versuchen Sie, die letzte Frage zu beantworten. Sie können
die Tabelle zu Hilfe nehmen.

'My four granddaughters are all very clever girls,' the bishop
said. 'Each of them can play a different musical instrument
and each can speak a different European language as well
as – if not better than – a native of the country.' 'What
instrument can Mary play?' asked someone.
   'The cello.'
   'Who can play the violin?'
   'D'you know,' said the bishop, 'I've temporarily forgotten.
But I know it's the girl who can speak French.'

The rest of the facts which I found out were of a rather
negative kind. I learned that the organist is not Valerie; that
the girl who can speak German is not Lorna; and that Mary
can speak no Italian. Anthea cannot play the violin; and she
is not the girl who can speak Spanish. Valerie knows no
French; Lorna cannot play the harp; and the organist cannot
speak Italian.
   What can Valerie do?

(from *My Best Puzzles in Logic and Reasoning* by Hubert Phillips – adapted)

	cello	violin	organ	harp		French	German	Italian	Spanish
Mary	yes	no	no	no	Mary				
Valerie					Valerie				
Lorna					Lorna				
Anthea					Anthea				

13C I'm much taller than my mother

1 Schreiben Sie die ersten und die zweiten Steigerungsformen der Eigenschaftswörter.

boring <u>more boring   most boring</u>

pretty	red	thirsty	warm
cold	talkative	large	hot
young	cheerful	tall	long
rude	terrible		

2 Schreiben Sie die Grundformen dieser Steigerungen.

slowest <u>slow</u>

funnier	oldest	cheaper	thinner
nicest	noisiest	bigger	smaller
worse	later		

3 Ändern Sie die Sätze wie in dem Beispiel.

1. I'm older than him. <u>He's younger than me.</u>
2. I'm taller than her. (Begin: *She's shorter . . .*)
3. She's bigger than me. (*I'm . . .*)
4. He's heavier than her. (*. . . lighter . . .*)
5. She's darker than me.
6. They're shorter than us.
7. Chinese is more difficult than Italian.

4 Bilden Sie wahre Sätze. Sie können Ihr Wörterbuch benutzen.

| The | highest mountain
smallest continent
largest ocean
largest sea
farthest spot from land
longest river
highest lake
largest active volcano | in the world is | Titicaca, in Peru.
the South China Sea.
in the South Pacific.
K2, not Everest.
the Nile or the Amazon.
Australia.
Mauna Loa, in Hawaii.
the Pacific. |

5 *Kaum zu glauben.* **Lesen Sie mit Hilfe Ihres Wörterbuchs.**

Fair beards grow faster than dark beards.

The most common family name in the world is Chang: there are about 75,000,000 people called Chang in China. The most common first name in the world is Mohammed.

The oldest map was made 5,000 years ago: it shows the River Euphrates.

Rats can live longer without water than camels.

Nearly three times as many people live in Mexico City as in Norway.

One of the narrowest streets in the world is St John's Lane, in Rome: it is 49cm wide. But there is a street in Cornwall, England, that is even narrower: it is 48cm wide at its narrowest point.

Loud – louder – loudest: you can hear alligators calling a mile away. You can hear the clock bell 'Big Ben' (on the Houses of Parliament, London) ten miles away. When the volcano Krakatoa erupted in 1883, it was heard 3,000 miles away.

Cold – colder – coldest: There was ice on the river Nile in 829 AD and 1010 AD. On average, New York is colder than Reykjavik (Iceland). The coldest place in the world, in Antarctica, has an average temperature of –57.8°C.

13D   The same or different?

1 Schreiben Sie sechs Sätze über sich selbst. Benutzen Sie *(not) as . . . as . . .* Beispiele:

I'm not as strong as a horse.

I'm as tall as my sister.

When I was two, I was as big as a four-year-old.

2 Schreiben Sie Sätze mit *the same as* oder *different from*.

1. your mother and your sister's mother

   My mother is the same as my sister's mother.

2. your nationality and your father's nationality
3. your nationality and your English teacher's nationality
4. your language and Italian
5. the colour of your eyes and the colour of your mother's eyes
6. your favourite TV programme and your father's favourite TV programme
7. your favourite music and your best friend's favourite music
8. where you live now and where you were born

3 Erinnern Sie sich an die folgenden Wörter und Ausdrücke? Kennen Sie die Aussprache? Nehmen Sie Ihr Wörterbuch zu Hilfe, falls nötig.

language; afternoon; cat; pen; phone number; wife; woman; long; short; tall; big; small; nice; intelligent; good-looking; old; pretty; strong; cold; cheap; expensive; late; fine; far; interesting.

4 Im Englischen haben die meisten dreisilbigen Wörter folgendes Betonungsmuster:

☐ □ □
possible

Drei Wörter in dieser Liste haben andere Betonungsmuster. Finden Sie die Wörter und schreiben Sie sie neben das entsprechende Betonungsmuster.

comfortable	good-looking	happier
anything	difficult	beautiful
expensive	understand	easiest
interesting		

1. ☐ ☐ □
2. □ ☐ □
3. □ □ ☐

5 Übersetzen Sie ins Deutsche.

1. I can sing, but I can't draw.
2. I was good at maths when I was younger, but I'm not now.
3. I'm much taller than my mother.
4. Mario's a bit older than his brother.
5. A Volkswagen is not as quiet as a Rolls-Royce.
6. She's as good-looking as a film star.

6 Vergleichen Sie zwei Personen, die Sie gut kennen. Schreiben Sie mindestens 100 Wörter.

7 Lesen Sie mit Hilfe Ihres Wörterbuchs.

IT'S A LONG STORY
12

Sam Watson was standing at the arrivals gate at Rio Airport, holding a bunch of flowers. He was worried. Judy's plane was three hours late and nobody knew why. Sam walked over to the bar and had a drink. He walked back to the arrivals gate. No news. He walked back to the bar and had another drink. Still no news . . . Back to the bar . . .

Two hours (and eight drinks) later, Judy's plane landed, and after another half hour the passengers started coming out. Sam smiled, and looked for Judy. After a time he stopped smiling. Finally, the last passenger came through. It wasn't Judy. Sam said a big bad word. What had happened? He went over to the information desk. 'My name's Sam Watson,' he said. 'Have you got any messages for me?' 'Yes,' said the stewardess. 'A telephone message from Scotland.' She handed him a paper. 'Mr Sam Watson, Rio Airport. Have a nice holiday. Don't come back. Love, Jasper MacDonald.' Sam said another big bad word, tore up the paper, and gave the flowers to the stewardess. 'What time's the next plane to London?'

Behind Sam, a tall beautiful girl was listening to his conversation. When she heard the word 'London', she smiled.

As the night plane took off, Sam closed his eyes. He loved travelling, but he was always a little afraid of flying. He couldn't really understand how the plane stayed up in the air. Also, he was worried about what would happen to him. Would there be detectives waiting for him at London Airport? It was crazy to leave Brazil. In Brazil there was sun, freedom and beautiful women. He could live happily for years with his £50,000. In Britain there was rain, trouble, policemen and a strong chance of prison. But he had to see Judy. Judy was different. Judy was special. Sam smiled and opened his eyes. Next to him there was sitting a tall, incredibly beautiful girl. 'Hello,' said Sam. 'My name's Sam.' 'I know,' said the beautiful girl. 'My name's Detective Sergeant Honeybone.' Sam closed his eyes again.

Unit 14 Personal information

14A How old are you?

1 Vervollständigen Sie das Gespräch.

DOCTOR: ...., Mr Rannoch?
PATIENT: 1 metre 76, doctor.
DOCTOR: Yes, I see. And ....?
PATIENT: About 80 kilos.
DOCTOR: Yes, right. ....?
PATIENT: 32.

2 Schreiben Sie Sätze. Beispiele:

Beryl Jones is nineteen. She
is one metre sixty-two, and
weighs sixty-four kilos.

NAME	AGE	HEIGHT	WEIGHT
Beryl Jones	19	1m 62	64 kilos
Oscar Duke	37	1m 83	86 kilos
Tony Lands	14	1m 55	47 kilos
Amelia Berry	68	1m 60	45 kilos
Oliver Ashe	33	1m 75	104 kilos

3 Schreiben Sie die Zahlen aus.

135 *a hundred and thirty-five*
    OR: one hundred and thirty-five.

| 279 | 1,500 | 4,328 | 95,767 |
| 466 | 1,799 | 17,600 | 4,000,000 |

4 Beschreiben Sie eine Person, die Sie kennen.
Wie alt ist sie? Wie groß? Wie schwer?
Wie sieht sie aus?
ODER: Beschreiben Sie Ihre/n Traumfrau/mann.

5 Schreiben Sie die Uhrzeiten aus.

1 *ten to one* 2

3 4

5 6

7 8

9 10

6 Ein Kreuzworträtsel.

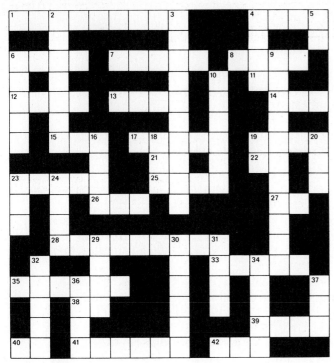

DOWN

2. In England, Spanish is a .... language.
3. You can use this to write a letter with.
4. She said .... she was at school.
5. Is *drive* a regular verb?
6. Superlative of *bad*.
9. My favourite chair is not very pretty, but it is very ....
10. The .... person in the world is over 110 years old.
16. I can't write very well, so I usually .... my letters.
18. Past tense of *run*.
19. Infinitive of *went*.
20. .... you see Mike yesterday?
23. My mother .... John Kennedy the day before he died.
24. Not difficult.
29. People do this in water.
30. A person who drives.
31. Is this .... pencil?
32. What's in your bag? It's very ....
34. Music helps you do this.
36. Past tense of *come*.
37. How many of these are irregular adjectives: *far, fast, fine, noisy*?

ACROSS

1. Not easy.
4. England is colder .... Brazil.
6. Spain is a .... country.
7. Past tense of *sleep*.
8. Your eyes are here.
11. She's on her way .... school.
12. A lot of water outside the house.
13. Past tense of *draw*.
14. Plural of *man*.
15. *Cold* is .... an irregular adjective.
17. Can you .... a bus?
19. Not bad.
21. 'Where's Yumiko?' '................. home – she's not very well today.'
22. Would you like coffee .... tea?
23. Can you .... in the daytime?
25. Take the .... right.
26. You hear with this.
27. I'm .... strong .... my sister, but she's faster than me.
28. On Friday, this is Thursday.
33. I am .... than my brother.
35. You can write with this.
38. 'Are you hungry?' 'Yes, I ....'
39. Can you make a ....?
40. My office is .... the reception desk.
41. Comparative of *easy*.
42. Infinitive of *saw*.

14B You look shy

1 Setzen Sie ein: *look(s), look(s) like* oder *like.*

1. Mrs Cowan .... a businesswoman, but actually she's a teacher.
2. You .... tired.
3. What is your new boyfriend ....?
4. I don't .... shy, but I am.
5. Alice .... her mother, but she isn't at all .... her in personality.
6. Japanese writing .... Chinese, but actually they're very different.
7. Why do you always .... so bad-tempered?
8. 'What's your job ....?' 'Boring.'

2 Setzen Sie ein: *a/an, the* oder – (= kein Artikel).

1. What's .... time?
2. My brother's .... architect.
3. I like .... steak, but I don't like .... eggs.
4. She lives in .... nice flat on .... fifth floor of .... old house.
5. Mary is .... John's sister.
6. What is .... your address?
7. What time is .... next train for Glasgow, please?
8. It's terrible – tomatoes are £5.50 .... kilo.
9. I'd like half .... litre of .... red wine.

3 Achten Sie auf die richtige Betonung beim Aussprechen folgender Wörter:

intelligent   personality   extremely
bad-tempered   talkative   optimistic   agree
information

4 Setzen Sie *as* oder *than* ein.

1. I can sing better .... you.
2. Elizabeth's much taller .... her brother.
3. I'm nearly .... old .... my teacher.
4. Your eyes are the same colour .... mine.
5. Germany is bigger .... Switzerland.
6. Your problems are not .... important .... mine.
7. English is more difficult .... Spanish.
8. She likes the same music .... I do.

5 Lesen Sie Ihr Horoskop mit Hilfe Ihres Wörterbuchs. Trifft die Beschreibung auf Sie zu? Schreiben Sie einige Sätze über sich selbst. Beispiel:

It is true that I am energetic, but I do not think that I am bossy, and I do not agree that I am often bad-tempered. I look calm, but actually I am rather nervy. I think I look like a businessman...

Aries (21/3 – 20/4): energetic, bossy, often bad-tempered, warm, generous, sensitive, artistic.
Taurus (21/4 – 21/5): hardworking, calm, friendly. Interested in business, money, friends and family.
Gemini (22/5 – 21/6): clever, witty, very talkative, changeable. Interested in books, people and ideas.
Cancer (22/6 – 23/7): humorous, conservative, often happy, anxious, shy. Interested in history.
Leo (24/7 – 23/8): proud, bossy, independent; either very tidy or very untidy; passionate and generous.

Virgo (24/8 – 23/9): practical, punctual, critical, hardworking, perfectionist. Interested in nature.
Libra (24/9 – 23/10): friendly, energetic (but also lazy), pleasant, argumentative. Interested in sport, animals.
Scorpio (24/10 – 22/11): brave, sometimes violent, extremist, possessive, passionate. Often very religious.
Sagittarius (23/11 – 21/12): talkative, self-confident, cheerful. Interested in sport, travel, living dangerously.

Capricorn (22/12 – 20/1): conservative, polite, serious, sociable but shy. Interested in home, politics, people.
Aquarius (21/1 – 19/2): tolerant, sociable but unstable. Interested in sport and politics. Often brilliant or mad.
Pisces (20/2 – 20/3): sensitive, emotional, imaginative, artistic, depressive. Very interested in themselves.

It's not true! I'm not talkative! I'm not talkative! I'm not talkative! I'm n

6 Lesen Sie mit Hilfe Ihres Wörterbuchs. Welches Bild zeigt *Leamas*?

Leamas was a short man with close, iron-grey hair, and the physique of a swimmer. He was very strong. This strength was discernible in his back and shoulders, in his neck, and in the stubby formation of his hands and fingers.

He had a utilitarian approach to clothes, as he did to most other things, and even the spectacles he occasionally wore had steel rims. Most of his suits were of artificial fibre, none of them had waistcoats. He favoured shirts of the American kind with buttons on the points of the collars, and suede shoes with rubber soles.

He had an attractive face, muscular, and a stubborn line to his thin mouth. His eyes were brown and small; Irish, some said. He looked like a man who could make trouble, a man who looked after his money, a man who was not quite a gentleman.

The air hostess thought he was interesting. She guessed he was North Country, which he might have been, and rich, which he was not. She put his age at about fifty, which was about right. She guessed he was single, which was half true. Somewhere long ago there had been a divorce; somewhere there were children, now in their teens.

'If you want another whisky,' said the air hostess, 'you'd better hurry. We shall be at London Airport in twenty minutes.'

'No more.' He didn't look at her; he was looking out of the window at the grey-green fields of Kent.

(from *The Spy Who Came in From The Cold* by John Le Carré – adapted)

14C   When is your birthday?

1 Sprechen Sie die folgenden Daten laut aus:

21 June 1919
(*'June the twenty-first, nineteen nineteen'*)

8 May 1986	3 October 1844
17 July 1600	11 March 1011
12 December 1945	20 November 1907

2 Beantworten Sie die Fragen. Nehmen Sie Ihr Wörterbuch zu Hilfe.

1. What is the date today?
2. What day is it?
3. What is the time? (Answer in words, not figures.)
4. What day is tomorrow?
5. What day was yesterday?
6. What day is your birthday this year?
7. If today is 28 February 1992, what is tomorrow's date?
8. If today is Friday, what is the day after tomorrow? What was the day before yesterday?
9. If the day before yesterday was Friday, is the day after tomorrow Tuesday?
10. What is the day after the day before the day after the day before tomorrow?
11. What month comes before August?
12. What month comes after May?
13. Seven days = one ....
14. 365 days = one ....

3 Achten Sie auf die richtige Betonung beim Aussprechen folgender Wörter:

yesterday   today   tomorrow   July
September   April   birthday

4 Wenn Sie *Student's Cassette B* haben, suchen Sie *Unit 14, Lesson C, Exercise 1*. Üben Sie die Aussprache der Monatsnamen.

→

5 Lesen Sie die Beschreibung von Bild A. Vervollständigen Sie dann die Beschreibung von Bild B.

This is a picture of a small dark room. There are only three pieces of furniture: a chair, a table and a cupboard. There are two people in the room – a man and a woman. The man is standing by the window talking to the woman, who is sitting at the table.

This is a picture of a .... There are fourteen .... : .... , ... and .... There are .... in the room – a woman .... The .... talking .... , who ....

A

B

6 Beschreiben Sie das Zimmer, in dem Sie gerade sind.

7 *Kaum zu glauben.* Lesen Sie mit Hilfe Ihres Wörterbuchs.

Human fossils found in Tanzania are about 3,500,000 years old.
There is a tree in California that is 4,600 years old.
A sequoia tree in California is 272ft (83m) tall, and 79ft (24m) round. It contains enough wood to make 500,000,000 matches.
A cat in Devon lived to the age of 36.
On June 19, 1944, a dog in Pennsylvania had 23 puppies.
A blue whale can measure 110ft 2½in (33.58m) long, and weigh 187 tons.

Living bacteria dating from 1,500 years ago have been found in a Cumbrian lake.
The eye of a giant squid is 15 inches (38cm) across.
Cheetahs can run at up to 63 miles an hour (101km an hour).
The three-toed sloth (found in tropical America) travels at 8ft (2.44m) a minute when it is in a hurry.

(from the *Guinness Book of Records*)

14D Could I speak to Dan?

1 Bilden Sie Fragen zu den folgenden Antworten. Beginnen Sie mit *What sort of . . .* oder *How many . . .*

1. Jazz.
2. Three – two boys and a girl.
3. 365.
4. Four and a kitchen.
5. Detective stories.
6. A big red one.
7. Thirteen.
8. Two and a half.

2 Setzen Sie passende Ausdrücke ein.

ANN: Cambridge 342266.
BOB: Hi. .... is Bob. Is .... Ann?
ANN: Yes. Hi, Bob.
BOB: .... I speak to Jill?
ANN: I'm afraid she's not .... at the moment. Can I .... ?
BOB: Yes, could you .... her to phone me when she gets home?
ANN: OK. I'll tell her.
BOB: Thanks a lot.
ANN: You're .... Bye.
BOB: ....

3 Einzahl eines zählbaren Hauptworts, Mehrzahl eines zählbaren Hauptworts oder nichtzählbares Hauptwort? Machen Sie drei Listen mit den Wörtern aus dem Kasten. Können Sie die Listen erweitern?

SINGULAR COUNTABLE	PLURAL COUNTABLE	UNCOUNTABLE
shirt	ears	hair

shirt	eye	hair	ear-rings	ears	
jeans	glasses	water	watch	apple	
beer	snow	foot	bank	money	feet
pounds	people	trousers	news		

4 Erinnern Sie sich an die folgenden Wörter und Ausdrücke? Kennen Sie ihre Aussprache? Nehmen Sie Ihr Wörterbuch zu Hilfe, falls nötig.

birthday; job; thousand; ask; different; heavy; nice; the same; both; other; o'clock; See you.

5 Übersetzen Sie ins Deutsche.

1. The car is about 4 metres long.
2. I'm over 20 and under 30.
3. My mother's 66, but she looks older.
4. How tall are you?
5. 'What's today?' 'Tuesday.'
6. 'What's the date?' 'The seventeenth.'
7. the day after tomorrow; the day before yesterday
8. Is that Mary? This is Peter.
9. Could I speak to Ann?
10. Just a moment.
11. I'm afraid she's not in. Can I take a message?

6 Wenn Sie *Student's Cassette B* haben, suchen Sie *Unit 14, Lesson D, Exercise 2.* (Sie werden dort nur das erste Gespräch finden.) Hören Sie zu und sprechen Sie die Sätze nach.

7 Schreiben Sie über das Leben eines Familienmitglieds. Beispiel:

My grandfather was born in 1940.
His family lived ...

8 Lesen Sie mit Hilfe Ihres Wörterbuchs.

IT'S A LONG STORY
13

When Judy woke up the next morning the sun was shining, the birds were singing, and everything was beautiful. Her room was lovely, and she felt fine. There was a knock on the door, and in walked the ghost, carrying a cup of tea. 'Did you sleep well?' he asked. 'Yes, beautifully,' said Judy. 'And thank you for a wonderful dinner last night.' The ghost blushed. 'Not at all,' he said. 'It was just a simple meal. I'm glad you enjoyed it.'

The evening before, after a magnificent dinner (cooked by the ghost), Judy and Jasper had talked far into the night – about life, love, art, death, music, books, travel, philosophy, religion, politics, economics, astronomy, biochemistry, archaeology, motor-racing and many other subjects. Most of all, they had talked about themselves. And when they had said goodnight, Jasper had kissed her, very gently. She could still feel the touch of his lips. What a perfect evening! Judy smiled at the memory. She stopped smiling. She had to go to Rio to see Sam. Sam was her boyfriend. She loved him. The sun went behind a cloud. The birds stopped singing. Judy started getting dressed as fast as she could.

Unit 15 Present and future

15A What's happening?

1 Was tragen Sie gerade? Benutzen Sie die *-ing*-Form.

2 Schreiben Sie, was diese Personen wahrscheinlich gerade tun. Benutzen Sie *probably*.
Beispiel:

My mother is probably shopping.

your mother   your father
your wife/husband/boyfriend/girlfriend
your boss   your teacher

your Prime Minister / President
one of your friends
your children

3 Achten Sie auf die richtige Betonung beim Aussprechen folgender Sätze:

1. **What** are you **do**ing?
2. **Where** are you **go**ing?
3. My **mo**ther is **prob**ably **shop**ping.

4. Some **peo**ple are **dan**cing.
5. A **man** is **ly**ing on the **floor**.

4 Schreiben Sie einige Sätze über das Bild. Was geschieht gerade? Was tun die Personen gerade? Benutzen Sie die *-ing*-Form.

"And this comment from your music teacher – 'I hope your boy enjoys his holiday as much as I'm going to enjoy mine' . . ."

15B The Universal Holiday Postcard Machine

1 Schreiben Sie die *-ing*-Formen.

speak Speaking

drive   get   go   lie   live   make   play
run   shop   smoke   start   stop   think
wear   work

2 Vervollständigen Sie die Gespräche.

A: Hello. Cardiff 945 5928.
B: Hello, Jenny. .... is Owen. .... Mike, please?
A: I'm sorry, he can't come to the phone just now, Owen. He's ....ing.
B: OK. I'll ring back later.
A: I'll tell .... you called. Bye.
B: Bye.

             *   *   *

A: What ....ing?
B: Chocolate. .... like some?
A: No, thanks. .... like chocolate.

3 Schauen Sie sich um und hören Sie zu – im Zimmer, im Haus, auf der Straße. Was geschieht gerade? Schreiben Sie mindestens fünf Sätze. Beispiele:

Somebody is singing.
My boyfriend is reading the paper.

4 Schauen Sie sich die Bilder an und vervollständigen Sie die Beschreibungen.

1. It is ....ing.

2. It is ....ing.

3. The .... is shining.

4. The weather is ....

5. The .... is fine.

5 Was haben Sie gestern oder letztes Wochenende gemacht? Schreiben Sie etwa 100 Wörter.

"'Marvellous weather, wish you were here, Regards. Sam.' When we get back to the UK., Miss Marbon, remind me that this branch needs a Xerox."

15C Who's doing what when?

1 Vervollständigen Sie das Gespräch.

PAT: Hello, Waterford 31868.
MARY: ....?
PAT: This is Pat. Who's ....?
MARY: Oh, hello, Pat. It's Mary. ....?
PAT: No, I'm sorry. I'm not. My uncle's
.... to dinner with us.
MARY: Well, are you .... on Thursday?
PAT: ....
MARY: ....?
PAT: I'd love to. What time?
MARY: Let's meet at eight at ....
PAT: OK. ....
MARY: ....

2 Was haben Sie in den nächsten Tagen vor? Schreiben Sie mindestens drei Sätze. Benutzen Sie die *-ing*-Form.

3 Wählen Sie das richtige Wort und schreiben Sie die Sätze.

1. My sister's much *taller/tallest* than me.
2. She's the *taller/tallest* person in our family.
3. My mother's 45, and my father's two years *older/oldest* than her.
4. English is *easier/easiest* than German.
5. China is the country with the *larger/largest* population.
6. *More/most* people speak Chinese than any other language.
7. I think my English is getting *better/best*.
8. But I'm afraid my pronunciation is getting *worse/worst*.
9. Anne is the *more/most* intelligent person I know – and the *nicer/nicest*.
10. You are *more/most* beautiful every day.

4 Wenn Sie *Student's Cassette B* haben, suchen Sie *Unit 15, Lesson C, Exercise 1*. Hören Sie sich das Gespräch an. Versuchen Sie, einige der Sätze nachzusprechen und aufzuschreiben.

5 Zwei Rätsel. Versuchen Sie, eins oder beide zu lösen. Nehmen Sie Ihr Wörterbuch zu Hilfe.

A

Arsenal, Manchester, Liverpool and Tottenham are four football teams.
Each team is playing against one of the others on the next three Saturdays – a different one each time.
On Saturday the 12th, Arsenal are playing against Manchester.
Manchester are playing against Tottenham on the 19th.
Who is playing against who on the 26th?

B

Here are posters for next week's entertainments in the small Fantasian town of South Lyne. Unfortunately, extremists have painted out all foreign names (Fantasian surnames always end in *-sk*). The four missing names are: James O'Connor, Maurice Ducarme, Richard Haas and Antonio Carlotti.
– Haas isn't musical.
– O'Connor is leaving Fantasia on the morning of the 22nd.
– Ducarme is a famous actor.
Who is doing what when?

15D We're leaving on Monday

1 Setzen Sie die fehlenden Wörter ein.

1. 60 minutes = 1 ....
2. 24 .... = 1 ....
3. 7 .... = 1 ....
4. 28 or 29 or 30 or 31
   .... = 1 ....
5. 12 .... = 1 ....

2 Beantworten Sie die Fragen.

1. How soon is your birthday? In a few weeks? In three months?
2. How soon is Christmas?
3. How soon is your next English lesson?
4. How soon is the year 2000?
5. How soon is next Tuesday?
6. How soon is your next holiday?

3 Setzen Sie ein: *at, on, in, for* oder kein Verhältniswort.

1. Are you free .... Friday evening?
2. Can you come round to my place .... nine o'clock tomorrow?
3. It's my birthday .... three days.
4. 'We're going to California.' 'How long ....?' 'Three weeks.'
5. We haven't got time to go shopping – the shops close .... five minutes.
6. What are you doing .... next Tuesday?
7. Can I talk to you .... five minutes?

4 Stellen Sie sich vor, Sie gehen am nächsten Montag auf eine Weltreise. Schreiben Sie über Ihren Zeitplan. Nützliche Wörter: *fly, stay, drive, hire.* Beispiel:

On Monday I'm flying to New York. I'm staying in New York for three or four days; then I'm hiring a car and driving to Los Angeles. Then . . .

5 Erinnern Sie sich an die folgenden Wörter und Ausdrücke? Kennen Sie ihre Aussprache? Nehmen Sie Ihr Wörterbuch zu Hilfe, falls nötig.

weekend; dance; get up; work; play; watch; drive; eat; sing; sleep; smoke; stand; read; write; make; happen; beautiful; really; probably; anything; this evening; Would you like to . . . ?

6 Übersetzen Sie ins Deutsche.

1. What's happening?
2. What are you doing?
3. My mother is probably shopping just now.
4. The sun is shining.
5. We are having a good time.
6. Tomorrow we are going to London.
7. Are you doing anything this evening?
8. 'Would you like to see a film with me?' 'I'm sorry, I'm not free.'
9. She's the most intelligent person I know.
10. 'I'm going to America in April.' 'That's nice. How long for?'

7 Lesen Sie mit Hilfe Ihres Wörterbuchs.

IT'S A LONG STORY
14

When Sam woke up he felt terrible. He had a headache, and there was a horrible taste in his mouth. He looked out of the window. The sun was shining, and through a gap in the clouds he could see the sea. It was a long way down. Sam shivered and turned to look at Detective Sergeant Honeybone. She looked fresh and lovely – even more beautiful than the evening before. 'Good morning,' she said. 'Did you sleep well?' 'No,' said Sam. 'Excuse me.' He got up and walked forward to the toilets.

After a wash and a shave, Sam felt a little better. He brushed his hair, put his jacket back on, and looked at his tongue in the mirror. Not a pretty sight. Sam put his tongue back in, took out his gun, and looked at his watch. Time to move. He came out of the toilet, glanced round quickly, and then walked to the front of the plane. Opening the door of the cockpit, he stepped inside. 'This is a hijack,' he said. 'Take me to Loch Ness.' 'Oh God,' said the pilot. 'Not again. What's so special about Loch Ness?' 'Jasper MacDonald,' said Sam.

Unit 16 Consolidation

16A Things to remember: Units 13, 14 and 15

1 Schreiben Sie die ersten und zweiten Steigerungsformen folgender Eigenschaftswörter. Beispiel:

big *bigger* *biggest*

comfortable economical funny heavy high late long noisy quiet slim warm

2 Vervollständigen Sie die Sätze.

1. My boyfriend | same age | me.
2. He | much taller | me.
3. Who | best footballer | world?
4. I | speak English | a bit better | my father.
5. I think | I | as good-looking | film star.
6. England | very different | United States.
7. you think | you | stronger | me?

3 Schreiben Sie diese Daten aus.

17.10.88	18.4.1900
5.3.69	21.1.94
1.12.97	2.3.36
3.6.99	20.5.1908

4 Alex möchte mit Ihnen ausgehen. Sie wollen aber nicht. Vervollständigen Sie Alex' Sätze und schreiben Sie Ihren Teil des Gesprächs.

ALEX: you | doing anything | this evening?
YOU: ....
ALEX: Well, ... about tomorrow?
YOU: ....
ALEX: free | Thursday?
YOU: ....
ALEX: Friday?
YOU: ....
ALEX: weekend?
YOU: ....
ALEX: ....

5 Setzen Sie die richtigen Formen der Zeitwörter und die fehlenden Wörter ein.

Hello, Mary. Yes, I'm sorry. I know, I (*want*) to phone you yesterday, but I (*not have*) time. It's crazy here. We (*leave*) the day .... tomorrow, and there's too much to do. Yes, China. We (*go*) .... six weeks. Jim (*work*) with some engineers on a big housing development in Beijing, and I (*give*) six concerts. Excuse me a minute – the children are very quiet, and I don't like it when I don't know what they (*do*).

*   *   *

Sorry about that, Mary. I'm back. It's OK. Sally (*watch*) TV and Peter (*make*) a cake. Yes, I know. He's a terrible cook, but if that's what he wants to do. No, they (*not come*) with us – they're staying with Granny .... three weeks, and then Sally (*go*) to Louise for the rest of the time, and Peter (*stay*) with his friends in Durham. .... about you? What (*happen*) with you and John? Really? So he (*change*) his job to be near you? I say, Mary! Perhaps this is the real thing after all these years.

Oh, dear, Sally (*ask*) for .... to eat again. Look, I can't (*talk*) any more now, but let's meet when we're back. Middle of August, OK? Thanks for phoning. Bye, Mary.

"But you're far too young to marry – why, you're only just old enough to go off and live with someone."

6 Ein Kreuzworträtsel.

ACROSS

1. If you go to this, you can see people playing football. (*Two words*)
8. When I was at school, I was good .... maths and running.
10. Mon, Tue, Wed, Thur, Fri, ..., Sun.
11. Can you .... all the questions?
13. Yes or ....?
14. 600 minutes = ... hours.
16. What sort of food .... your children like?
17. One and the other.
19. What time .... the next train leave?
20. Mike likes eating, but .... can't cook.
21. Would you like tea .... coffee?
22. A lot .... people can speak two languages.
24. I can't hear with my left ....
25. From another country.
27. I'm taller than her, but she's stronger than ....
28. The .... is shining.
29. Jan, ..., Mar.
30. Apr.
31. A lot of water between countries.
34. Can you help me? I don't know where .... glasses are.
36. A person who talks a lot is ....
39. 'What sort of discs do you want?' '.............. doesn't matter.'

40. I don't think I'm free on Thursday – I'm .... going to a concert.
43. Your son's son's father is your ....
45. Five hundred years ago, people in Europe didn't drink ....
46. Are .... doing anything this evening?
48. Just the same as *27 across*.
49. If today is Saturday, the day after .... is Monday.
50. 'Thanks a lot.' 'You're ....'

DOWN

1. He's stronger than me, but he can't run as .... as me.
2. Oct.
3. I think she's the most .... woman in the world.
4. What time did you get home .... night?
5. Present of *met*.
6. Could I speak .... Susan?
7. .... is not the same as *pretty*.
9. I've got .... much work to do.
12. .... is my favourite colour.
15. *House* is not a verb or an adjective, but a ....
18. Past of *draw*.
20. We weren't rich, but we were ....
21. Like *21 across*.
23. The month after the month before *29 across*.
26. Are you doing anything .... Saturday night?
28. Present of *sat*.
30. Sorry – .... I late?
31. I love the mountains, but I can't ....
32. A good thing to do with food.
33. Were you good .... maths when you were at school?
36. 'To be or not ...., that is the question.' (Shakespeare) (*Two words*)
37. Tomorrow we are going to Manchester. .... it will be wonderful. (*Two words*)
38. You can sleep here when you are on a journey.
41. See you .... eight o'clock .... the cinema.
42. Why did you come home so .... last night?
44. There is usually some of this in a newspaper.
46. 'I can run faster than ....' 'No, ... can't.'
47. I can't sing .... draw.
48. Excuse ....

16B Present tenses

1 Wählen Sie die richtige Form des Zeitworts.

1. I would like to go home now. It .... late. (*is getting / gets*)
2. 'What ....?' 'Beer. Can I get you some?' (*are you drinking / do you drink*)
3. 'Where's Lucy?' 'She .... a bath.' (*'s having / has*)
4. What sort of films ....? (*are you liking / do you like*)
5. 'Do you speak Chinese?' 'No, ...' (*I'm not / I don't*)
6. What time .... to bed? (*are you usually going / do you usually go*)
7. 'Is there anything to eat?' 'I .... some fish.' (*'m just cooking / just cook*)
8. 'What are you doing?' 'I .... the guitar.' (*'m just practising / just practise*)
9. .... tomorrow? (*Are you working / Do you work*)
10. No, I .... on Saturdays. (*'m not working / don't work*)

73

2 Achten Sie auf die richtige Betonung beim Aussprechen folgender Sätze:

1. **What** are you **doing**?
2. **What's** she **eating**?
3. **Where** are they **going**?
4. **What** did she **say**?
5. **How** do you **know**?
6. **When** do you **want** to **come**?
7. **What time** are you going to **work** tomorrow?
8. **Who** did you **see yesterday**?
9. **What** are you **doing** this evening?

3 Wortschatzübung. Schauen Sie sich im Zimmer um, in dem Sie gerade arbeiten. Können Sie die englischen Wörter für zehn oder mehr Dinge, die Sie dort sehen, aufschreiben?

4 Setzen Sie die Teile der Geschichte in die richtige Reihenfolge.

1. 'Didn't I tell you
2. 'Take it to the zoo,'
3. said the man,
4. a man was walking in the park
5. 'I did,'
6. He still had the penguin.
7. 'and he liked it very much.
8. answered the policeman.
9. and asked what to do.
10. he asked.
11. Now I'm taking him to the cinema.'
12. the policeman saw the man again.
13. when he met a penguin.
14. Next day
15. to take that penguin to the zoo?'
16. So he took it to a policeman
17. One day

5 Was haben Sie gestern gemacht? (Schreiben Sie etwa 100 Wörter.)

6 Lesen Sie einen dieser Texte mit Hilfe Ihres Wörterbuchs.

A long wait
The female emperor penguin lays only one egg each year. She gives it to the male, who puts it on his feet and covers it with a special pouch. The female then goes to the sea, perhaps many kilometres from the male, and does not return for three months. The male stands in the cold, with no food. When the egg hatches, the female comes back and her thin, weak mate goes off to feed.

The robin
The robin is a plump brown bird 5½ inches (14cm) long. It has a red face and breast and a white belly. Males and females look alike, but the amount of red on the breast varies in individual birds.

Robins live all over Great Britain and Ireland, and are often found in gardens. Each male or pair has a territory which the male defends.

Robins eat fruit, worms and insects. The female lays four to six eggs in a nest made of moss and hair. The eggs are white with light red spots.

Brown

Red

White

Facts about gorillas
1. A big male gorilla can weigh 200 kilograms.
2. Gorillas build a nest to sleep in each night.
3. A big gorilla's hands are 2.65 metres from its shoulders.
4. Gorillas live in groups and only move about one third of a mile a day.
5. Gorillas are afraid of snakes.
6. Gorillas never have fleas.

16C Choose

1 Schauen Sie sich die Beispiele an und bringen Sie die Wörter in die richtige Reihenfolge.

```
        1            2        3
Is your brother working today?

         1      2      3
What are those people drinking?

      1         2     3
Does Mr Allison play the piano?

             1       2       3
Where do your parents live?
```

1. does Wagner work where Mrs ?
2. fast does George like cars ?
3. eating girl that what is ?
4. often boss how on holiday does your go ?
5. this are evening doing you what ?
6. Smith dinner to us are Mr coming with Mrs and ?
7. for does what wife breakfast have your usually ?
8. Dr working today is Harris ?

2 Schauen Sie sich die Wortliste am Ende dieser Übung an. Suchen Sie etwas, das zu diesen Beschreibungen paßt. *Something that is:*

1. younger than the world
2. older than a house
3. heavier than a typewriter
4. funnier than a politician
5. more difficult than an English exercise
6. faster than a cat
7. easier than an English exercise
8. more beautiful than a car
9. more interesting than an English exercise
10. shorter than a year

Bilden Sie weitere, möglichst ungewöhnliche Vergleiche. Beispiele:

The sea is older than cities.
Love is more expensive than food.

a car   life   a teacher   love
work   a cat   food   a pencil
a typewriter   a boss   a week
a month   a year   a head
a city   the sun   the sea
a mountain   a politician
a child

3 Achten Sie auf die richtige Betonung beim Aussprechen dieser Wörter.

interesting   **com**fortable
handsome   **prob**ably
welcome   **birth**day   ex**treme**ly
to**mor**row   with**out**   per**haps**
Sep**tem**ber

4 Setzen Sie ein: *look(s), look(s) like* oder *like(s)*.

1. She .... her mother, except that her nose is much longer.
2. You .... tired – can I help you?
3. What is your boss ....?
4. He .... more .... a businessman than a teacher.
5. Your voice is .... music to my ears.
6. 'Who does the baby ....?' 'Well, she's got her father's eyes.'
7. Mary always .... worried these days.

5 Schreiben Sie einige wahre Sätze über sich selbst. Benutzen Sie mindestens fünf dieser Wörter oder Ausdrücke.

didn't   woke   knew   came
went   lived   drank   started
stopped   yesterday
last night   a long time ago

6 Übersetzen Sie ins Deutsche.

1. You look happy.
2. She looks a bit like her mother.
3. What's your new boss like?
4. Are you like your brother?
5. Do you like your brother?

7 Wenn Sie *Student's Cassette B* haben, suchen Sie *Unit 16, Lesson C, Listening Exercise 2.* Hören Sie zu und versuchen Sie, mindestens drei Sätze aufzuschreiben.

8 📟 Lesen Sie mit Hilfe Ihres Wörterbuchs.

IT'S A LONG STORY
15

Judy ran downstairs and into the dining room. No Jasper – only the ghost. 'Can I help you?' he asked politely. 'Would you like some breakfast?' 'Where's Jasper?' asked Judy. 'He's gone out,' said the ghost. 'Oh dear,' said Judy. 'Lend me a pen and paper, could you?'
    Quickly she wrote a note to Jasper:
        'Dear Jasper,
        It was wonderful. But I have to go. I'm sorry. I wanted to say goodbye to you, but perhaps it is better like this.
        Thank you for a beautiful memory.
        Judy.'
    She said goodbye to the ghost, who looked sad, and walked out of the castle. Not far along the road there was a bus stop. If she could get to Inverness before lunch, she could catch the afternoon plane to London and buy some new clothes before catching the night flight to Rio. Tomorrow morning she could be in Sam's arms. How wonderful! Judy started crying.
    At the bus stop, Judy read the timetable. Buses for Inverness ran every three hours, but she was lucky – there was one in twenty minutes. As she stood waiting, she looked out over the lake. A few hundred yards away there was a man fishing in a boat. She could hear him singing in the clear still air. He had a wonderful voice – a voice that Judy recognised – and he was singing an old Scottish love song. It was Jasper. Tears came into Judy's eyes, and she looked away from the boat, up into the peaceful sky. High above Loch Ness, a golden eagle was flying in circles. There were pretty little clouds looking like splashes of white paint against the deep blue. And two parachutes.

ÜBUNGEN ZU *LESSON 16D* ENTFALLEN.

Unit 17 Ordering and asking

17A I'll have roast beef

1 Ändern Sie *not any* zu *no*; ändern Sie *no* zu *not any*.
Beispiele:

There isn't any beer.

There's no beer.

I've got no friends.

I haven't got any friends.

1. There are no more potatoes.
2. There isn't any tea in the pot.
3. I didn't spend any money yesterday. (I spent . . .)
4. Fifty million years ago there were no people.
5. There aren't any good films on TV this evening.
6. We haven't got any food in the house.

2 Vervollständigen Sie die Gespräche.

CUSTOMER 1: .... table .... four?
WAITER: Yes, just over here, madam.

*   *   *

c1: .... tomato salad, please, and then ....
fish.
w: ...., sir?
c2: .... soup, and .... roast beef with a
green salad.

*   *   *

w: .... drink?
c1: .... lager, please.
c2: .... give .... lager, ...?
w: .... course, sir.

*   *   *

c1: .... beef?
c2: .... fish?
c1: Very good. .... potatoes aren't very nice,
....

*   *   *

w: .... everything ....?
c1: Yes, fine, thank you.

*   *   *

w: .... a little more coffee?
c1: No, ...
c2: Yes, ...

*   *   *

c1: .... bill, please?
w: ....
c1: .... service ....?
w: Yes, madam.

3 Benutzen Sie Ihr Wörterbuch. Suchen Sie die Namen dieser Dinge und lernen Sie sie.

4 Nehmen Sie *Student's Cassette B*, falls vorhanden, und suchen Sie *Unit 17, Lesson A, Exercise 3*. Hören Sie zunächst zu und versuchen Sie, sich die Antworten zu merken. Schreiben Sie dann mindestens drei der Fragen und Antworten auf.

"Steak too tough, sir?"

5 Hier sind einige Auszüge aus Tagebüchern von Jungen (zwischen 12 und 16 Jahren alt) in London. Schlagen Sie beim ersten Lesen nur die unterstrichenen Begriffe in Ihrem Wörterbuch nach.

'I got up and had sausage, egg, bacon and tomatoes for breakfast and read the *Sunday Mirror*. Then my brother Wally knocked at the door. He asked me if I wanted to go fishing with him and June, my sister-in-law. I quickly got my boots on and went with them in their van. We got to Broxbourne about 12.30 and Wally and me started fishing and June started getting the dinner with a calor gas cooker. We had sausage, egg and bacon again, after that a cup of hot orange and a piece of swiss roll. Then it started to rain. It poured down and we all got soaked, so we made for home. When we got back they came in and Mum made us a hot cup of tea. Then Wally and June went off home.'

Today I got up at eight o'clock and went swimming with my uncle. We got to the York Hall baths at nine. There were not many people in there. We fooled around and had a couple of races; I lost both. We came out at 10.30 and I came home.'

'My cousin and I took the dog out for a walk at 10.15. We stayed out quite a long while looking for girls.'

'I had my tea, washed and left for the girl-friend's house. When I arrived her mother let me in and told me to take a seat in the living-room. We watched television for most of the evening.'

8.30 p.m. My fiancée came round. We went to see my nan*, who lives in the same flats as me. We always have a good laugh when we go to see her, and my girl loves hearing her talk about the people she meets in the market every day.'

'About half past seven I went round my fiancée's flat, and sat down with her mum and dad and had a talk with them. We watched television for a while and then all went out for a drink.'

nan: grandmother

(from *Adolescent Boys of East London* by Peter Wilmott)

"We'd like a table near a waiter . . ."

"How can you say it was very nice? You slept through most of it."

17B Could you lend me some sugar?

1 Können Sie die folgenden Sätze vervollständigen, ohne im *Student's Book* nachzusehen?

1. '................ .... trouble .... lend ....
   .... tea?'
   '............, of ....'
2. '............. me. .... got .... light, ...?'
   'Just ....'
3. 'Have .... cigarette?'
   '..............., don't ....'
4. '............... .... dictionary?'
   '............... afraid .... got ....'

2 Höflich *(polite)* oder informell *(casual)*? Was sagt man in den folgenden Situationen?

You want to: 1. Borrow your teacher's car for the weekend.
2. Borrow £1 from your best friend.
3. Borrow your father's favourite jacket.
4. Get a cigarette from somebody that you don't know.
5. Get a cigarette from your sister.

Wie sagt man „nein" in den folgenden Situationen?

6. Your teacher wants to borrow your car.
7. Your brother wants to borrow your pencil.
8. A friend wants to borrow some milk, but you haven't got any.

3 *Lend* oder *borrow*? Setzen Sie das richtige Zeitwort in der richtigen Form ein.

1. Could you possibly .... me $20 for a day or two?
2. I .... my mother's car yesterday, and I lost the keys.
3. Could I .... that pencil for a moment?
4. Ann always .... me her flat when I go to Paris.
5. I'm sorry to trouble you, but could I .... an egg, please?

4 Welches Zimmer paßt zu welcher Tätigkeit?
Beispiel: 6C

1. kitchen   a. wash
2. bedroom   b. sit and relax
3. bathroom   c. keep a car
4. living room   d. sleep
5. dining room   e. cook
6. garage   f. eat

Bilden Sie nun Sätze. Beispiel:

You can keep a car in a garage.

5 Wenn Sie *Student's Cassette B* haben, suchen Sie *Unit 17, Lesson B, Exercise 2*. (Sie werden dort nur die ersten fünf Sätze finden.) Lesen Sie die untenstehenden Sätze mit der richtigen Betonung und Satzmelodie laut vor. Benutzen Sie dann die Aufnahme zur Kontrolle.

1. Sorry to **trouble you**, but could you **lend** me some **bread**?
2. Could you **lend** me a **dictionary**?
3. Could you **show** me some **black sweaters, please**?
4. Excuse me. **Have** you got a light, **please**?
5. Could you **possibly lend** me your **car** for **half** an **hour**?

6 Ein schnelles Kreuzworträtsel. Sie können Ihr Wörterbuch benutzen.

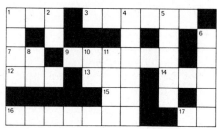

ACROSS

1. Between hip and foot.
3. .... me, have you got a light?
7. I'm sorry, there's .... more roast beef.
9. Just a ....
12. Not wet.
13. You drive it.
14. You see with it.
15. My name .... George.
16. I'm sorry to .... you.
17. United Kingdom.

DOWN

1. Could you .... me your umbrella, please?
2. I .... to work by bus.
4. 'Could I borrow your dictionary?' 'Yes, of ....'
5. You usually do this at night.
6. Do you .... English?
8. Have you got any brothers .... sisters?
10. She's a very n..e person.
11. At the end of your finger.

78

17C Somewhere different

1 Vervollständigen Sie die Gespräche.

A: Excuse me. Where can I buy a colour film near here?

B: ....

A: Thanks anyway.

* * *

A: ....?

B: At the supermarket.

A: ....?

B: First right, second left.

A: ....?

B: About two hundred yards.

A: ....

B: You're welcome.

* * *

SALLY: ....

BRUCE: Hello. Could I speak to Lorna, please?

SALLY: .... Can I take a message?

BRUCE: No, it's all right. I'll ring back later.

SALLY: OK. ....

BRUCE: ....

* * *

A: .... go to the cinema tonight.

B: No, let's .... theatre.

A: No, it's too far.

B: OK. Why .... go and see Mother?

A: No. Look, ... we stay ....
home and .... TV?

B: Good idea. OK.

2 Setzen Sie das richtige Verhältniswort ein.

1. We're leaving here .... three days.
2. I had a drink with Peter .... Tuesday.
3. I usually work .... nine o'clock .... five.
4. This is a picture of my family .... holiday.
5. We spent three weeks .... the mountains.
6. I'm getting up .... six o'clock tomorrow.
7. I'm driving .... Scotland.
8. I'm staying with friends in Edinburgh ....
four days.
9. I don't like travelling .... train.
10. 'Can you help me?' 'Yes, ... course.'

3 Wenn Sie *Student's Cassette B* haben, suchen Sie *Unit 17, Lesson C, Exercise 1.* (Sie werden dort nur den ersten Teil des Gesprächs finden.) Hören Sie zu und schreiben Sie soviel wie möglich auf.

"Artie, how would you pack if you were going to Mars?"

"Somewhere with no irregular verbs."

4 Lesen Sie mit Hilfe Ihres Wörterbuchs und beantworten Sie die Fragen.

A DREAM

Last night I had a strange dream. I was in a world where all the colours were different. The grass was orange, the trees were white; in the green sky there was a purple sun and a moon the colour of blood. I was a child again, eight years old, and I was lost. I felt very frightened and unhappy. In front of me there was a long street, stretching away as far as I could see. There were no people, but all around me I heard the noise of big insects. It was terribly hot. Suddenly a door opened on my left. I went into the house and ran up the stairs. When I got to the top, I saw a field full of blue horses. I called one of them; he came over to me and I got on his back. I don't know how far he took me – we went through forests, across rivers, past high mountains covered with black snow. At last we came to a town. The streets were full of people dressed in red. Nobody spoke. I said goodbye to my horse and walked until I came to a church. Inside I heard my mother's voice. I pushed the door, but it was too big and heavy – I couldn't move it. I called as loud as I could, but nothing happened. Then, very slowly, the door opened. In the church there were hundreds of people, all looking at me. They started to come towards me, slowly at first, then faster and faster . . . Then I woke up.

1. Do you think this was a true dream?
2. Do you like it?
3. Do you ever have dreams like this?

17D   Meet me at eight

1 Achten Sie auf die richtige Betonung beim Aussprechen folgender Sätze:

1. **What** are you **doing** this **evening**?
2. Would you **like** to **come** to the **cinema** **with** me?
3. **How** about tomorrow?
4. We're **leaving** on **Mon**day.
5. **Just** for **two days**.
6. **Back** on Friday **night**.
7. The **children** are **going** to Mother.

2 Erinnern Sie sich an die folgenden Wörter und Ausdrücke? Kennen Sie ihre Aussprache? Nehmen Sie Ihr Wörterbuch zu Hilfe, falls nötig.

window; table; minute; month; mountain; lunch; supper; give; bring; start; cost; meet; tell; different; sorry; next; tonight; tomorrow; perhaps; everything; Would you like . . . ?; of course; How about . . . ?; I'm afraid . . .

3 Übersetzen Sie ins Deutsche.

1. Have you got a table for two?
2. I'll start with soup, please.
3. Is everything all right?
4. Would you like a little more coffee?
5. Could you bring us the bill, please?
6. Is service included?
7. Sorry to trouble you, but could you lend me some bread?
8. Could you possibly lend me your car for half an hour?
9. Could I borrow your umbrella?
10. Why don't we go to California for our holiday this year?
11. Hey, wait a minute. Let's think about this.
12. I think it's a good idea.
13. Let's catch a plane to Spain.

4 Vervollständigen Sie die Geschichte mit den Wörtern aus dem Kasten.

got into	kissed	understand	when	saw
woke up	then	didn't	sing	difficult
road	drive	fast	night	couldn't

A DREAM

Last .... I dreamt that I was in a very ....
car, driving along a road in Ireland. It was raining,
and I .... see very well. Then suddenly I ....
a woman standing in the middle of the ....
.... I stopped, she .... the car and told me
to .... to Dublin. It was .... to .... her,
because she had a strange accent. She started to
..............., and .... she looked at me and smiled. I
asked her name, but she .... answer. She smiled
again, and .... me on the cheek. Then I ....

5 Beschreiben Sie einen Traum (etwa 100 Wörter). Benutzen Sie einige dieser Wörter und Ausdrücke. (In *Exercise 17C, 4* sehen Sie, wie man sie benutzt.)

I had a strange dream   I felt very frightened
in front of me   all around me   suddenly
I saw   there was   he/she came over to me
nothing happened   very slowly
faster and faster   I woke up

6 🔊 Lesen Sie mit Hilfe Ihres Wörterbuchs.

IT'S A LONG STORY
16

Sam and Detective Sergeant Honeybone hit the water together. Sam went under and came up. 'Help!' he shouted, going under again. 'I can't swim!' he shouted, as he came up again and went under for the third time. Sam's life passed in front of his eyes as he went down, down, down into the green water. His childhood in London. Visiting his mother and father in prison. His first girlfriend. His first bank robbery. Judy. Judy. He would never see her again.

'Don't worry, you lovely man,' called Detective Sergeant Honeybone. 'I'm an Olympic 400-metre gold medallist.' She swam over to him with beautiful strong strokes, caught him under the arms as he came up again, and started pulling him towards the boat.

'Hello, Isabel,' said Jasper as they pulled Sam out of the water. 'What are you doing here? And why have you got Sam with you? He's the last person I want to see.' 'It's a long story,' said Detective Sergeant Honeybone. 'I'll tell you later. Wait while I give Sam the kiss of life.' 'I don't need the kiss of life,' said Sam. 'Oh yes you do,' said Detective Sergeant Honeybone.

'All right,' said Jasper. 'I suppose we'd better go back to the castle and find you some dry clothes. Pity. I was hoping for a quiet morning's fishing.' He rowed the boat over to the bank of the loch and they got out. Detective Sergeant Honeybone picked up Sam in her beautiful strong arms and they started walking down the road towards the castle. As they passed the bus stop, Jasper walked over to Judy, who was staring up at the sky. 'Good morning, you beautiful creature,' he said. 'Going shopping? Don't forget lunch is at 12.30.' Judy turned her back, tears streaming down her face. 'Don't talk to me about lunch,' she said. 'I'm going to Rio to see Sam.' 'But Sam's here,' said Jasper. 'Don't try to talk me out of it,' said Judy. 'I've made up my mind, and I . . . what did you say?' She turned round and looked across the road. There was Detective Sergeant Honeybone, standing with a soft smile on her lips looking down at Sam, who was lying in her arms with his eyes closed. Judy's mouth fell open.

Unit 18 More about the past

18A Where was Galileo born?

1 Bilden Sie „Folgefragen".

1. Amelia Earhart took flying lessons when she was 22. (*Where . . . ?*)

   Where did she take lessons?
2. Galileo discovered sunspots. (*When . . . ?*)
3. Marie Curie was born in Warsaw. (*When . . . ?*)
4. Ho Chi Minh once went to New York. (*How . . . ?*)
5. Amelia Earhart once worked for the Red Cross. (*Where . . . ?*)
6. Galileo's lectures were very famous. (*Why . . . ?*)
7. Marie and Pierre Curie had a famous daughter. (*What . . . ?*)

2 Bilden Sie negative Sätze.

1. Shakespeare wrote plays. (*novels*)

   Shakespeare did not write novels.
2. Dickens wrote novels. (*paint pictures*)
3. Van Gogh painted pictures. (*play football*)
4. Maradona played football. (*live in London*)
5. Karl Marx lived in London. (*New York*)
6. John Lennon lived in New York. (*travel to the moon*)
7. Neil Armstrong travelled to the moon. (*write plays*)

3 Wenn Sie *Student's Cassette B* haben, suchen Sie *Unit 18, Lesson A, Exercise 3.* (Sie werden dort nur den zweiten Teil finden.) Hören Sie zu und schreiben Sie soviel wie möglich auf. Sprechen Sie dann einige Sätze nach.

4 Lesen Sie den ersten Text und die Notizen dazu. Lesen Sie dann den zweiten Text und schreiben Sie die Notizen dazu.

Margareta Gertruida Zelle was born in Leeuwarden, in the Netherlands, in 1876. She married an army officer and went with him to Indonesia, where she learnt Javanese and Hindu dances. She went back to Europe, where she became a famous dancer, calling herself 'Mata Hari'. She was accused of being a spy for the Germans and was executed in Vincennes, in France, in 1917.

Margareta Gertruida Zelle (called 'Mata Hari')
– Dutch dancer
– Leeuwarden, 1876 – Vincennes, 1917
– husband: army officer
– learnt Javanese & Hindu dances in Indonesia
– back to Europe: famous
– executed as a German spy

Marco Polo was born in Venice in 1254. With his father and his uncle, who were businessmen, he travelled to China in 1275. They were the first Europeans to do this. Marco Polo stayed at the court of the Chinese emperor for many years, and went as an ambassador for the emperor to Tonkin, Annam, India and Persia. He went back to Venice in 1295, made rich by his travels. Polo wrote a book about his experiences, but not many people believed him at first. He died in 1324.

5 Schreiben Sie über eine Persönlichkeit aus der Geschichte Ihres Landes. ODER: Schreiben Sie einen kurzen Text über die Kindheit Ihrer Mutter/Ihres Großvaters usw.

18B America invades Britain!

1 Wie lauten die Grundformen dieser Vergangenheitsformen? Beispiel:

went go

began   bought   broke
brought   fought   knew
left   saw   thought   told
took   woke

2 Setzen Sie die Vergangenheitsformen unregelmäßiger Zeitwörter ein. (In einigen Fällen gibt es mehrere Möglichkeiten.)

1. He .... to school in a very small village.
2. I .... home very late last night.
3. Charlie Chaplin .... seven children.
4. The teacher .... some photos to show us yesterday.
5. He .... he was sorry, but she .... that he wasn't.
6. I .... an aspirin half an hour ago, and my head's much better now.
7. She sat on her glasses and .... them.
8. Yehudi Menuhin .... playing the violin when he was very young.
9. He had a few minutes with nothing to do, so he .... a cake.

3 Setzen Sie Begriffe aus dem Kasten ein. (Sie können die Wörter mehrmals benutzen und in einigen Fällen gibt es mehrere Möglichkeiten.)

and	as soon as	because	but	finally	
first of all	next	so	that	then	
where	who	why			

1. I had a cup of tea and .... went straight to bed.
2. The party went on for a long time, but the last people .... went home at 5.00.
3. Could you ask her to phone me .... she comes home?
4. .... I'd like tomato salad; then I'd like steak; and after that I'll have coffee.
5. I couldn't phone her .... she hasn't got a phone.
6. I don't know .... she hasn't got a phone.
7. I was very tired, ... I went upstairs to lie down.
8. We've got a small house in the mountains .... we go in the holidays.
9. .... she studied music; .... she spent two years working in New York; .... she got married and had two children; and .... she started a computer business in San Francisco.
10. I love you .... I want to marry you.
11. I love you .... I don't want to marry you.
12. I knew .... he wasn't happy.
13. I've got some good friends .... live in Brisbane.

4 Achten Sie auf die richtige Betonung beim Aussprechen folgender Wörter:

finally   American   everything   century
university   history   because

5 Wortschatzübung. Wie viele Wörter können Sie hinzufügen?

shy, optimistic, . . .

6 Lesen Sie die Sätze. Sie können Ihr Wörterbuch benutzen. Bringen Sie dann die Sätze in den beiden Abschnitten der Geschichte in die richtige Reihenfolge.

But Florence found parties boring; she wanted to be a nurse.
Then she was in charge of a nursing-home for women in London.
Florence Nightingale came from a rich family and was very pretty.
Finally, in 1850, when she was 30, her parents accepted her decision.
In her family, young girls usually spent their time going to parties until they married rich young men.
Soon she was asked to go to the Crimea to take charge of the wounded soldiers.
So she went to study in a hospital in Germany.

＊　　＊　　＊

Forty per cent of the patients died.
By 1900 unsafe hospitals and ignorant nurses were things of the past.
The death rate dropped to two per cent.
The conditions in the Crimean hospital were terrible.
Workmen put in a proper drainage system and supplied pure drinking water.
Certain beds seemed fatal: soldiers died in them after two days.
She was an important force in the movement to reform hospitals and nursing in England.
On her return to England people greeted Florence Nightingale as a heroine.
Nightingale decided that this was because of bad drains, and insisted that the government do something about it.

18C   Who? What? Which? How? Where? When?

1 Schreiben Sie die Grundformen von zwanzig Zeitwörtern, die Sie kennen. Kennen Sie auch die Vergangenheitsformen? Wenn ja, schreiben Sie sie auf; wenn nicht, nehmen Sie Ihr Wörterbuch zu Hilfe.

INFINITIVE   PAST TENSE

go........   went........

2 Schreiben Sie den Text mit der richtigen Großschreibung und Zeichensetzung ab. (Beginnen Sie mit *On the night of April . . .*) Benutzen Sie Seite 89 im *Student's Book* zur Kontrolle.

on the night of april 24 1778 captain john paul jones quietly brought his ship ranger to whitehaven in the north-west of england as soon as he arrived he took a group of his men to one of the inns in the town broke into it and had a drink with them then they started work first of all they went to the fort and destroyed the guns next they began burning british ships the british sailors woke up and started fighting against the americans but they could not stop jones and his men

3 Setzen Sie ein: *a/an, the* oder – (= kein Artikel).

1. She was .... first woman to fly across .... Atlantic.
2. He was .... student at .... Columbia University.
3. I'm .... tallest in .... my family.
4. York is in .... north-east of .... England.
5. She looks like .... actress, but actually she's .... housewife.
6. What was .... name of .... man who discovered penicillin?
7. Who starred in .... film .... *Third Man*?
8. I play .... football every Saturday.
9. .... books are very expensive.

4 Achten Sie auf die richtige Betonung beim Aussprechen folgender Wörter:

animal   disagree   famous
across   about   member
novel   discover   football
expensive

5 Wählen Sie die richtige Form.

1. How | did Blériot travel | to England?
      | travelled Blériot |
      | did travel Blériot |

2. When | started the war?
       | did start the war?
       | did the war start?

3. Why | she left?
      | she did leave?
      | did she leave?

4. Where | did you go?
        | you went?

5. What | did want your mother?
       | did your mother want?
       | your mother wanted?

6. When | was born Shakespeare?
       | was Shakespeare born?
       | Shakespeare was born?

7. Who | did write | *Hamlet*?
      | wrote |

8. What | happened | yesterday?
        | did happen |

6 Ein Kreuzworträtsel.

ACROSS

1. The British sailors started fighting, ... they could not stop Jones and his men.
10. 'Was that television programme ....?' 'No, I fell asleep after ten minutes.'
13. How long .... did he leave?
14. I can pronounce a lot of words that I can't ...., and I can .... a lot of words that I can't pronounce.
16. I'm tired, and I'd like to go ....
17. Past tense of *get*.
18. The new telephones are smaller .... the old ones.
19. I .... cook quite well, but I don't enjoy it.
20. Present tense of *did*.
21. Past tense of *go*.
24. I'm not quite .... tall .... my boyfriend.
25. The cooker was ...., but it cooks much better than the cheaper ones.
26. I always .... with a window open.

29. Present tense of *said*.
31. My cousins .... got here at ten o'clock in the evening – their plane was four hours late.
34. His office is on the first floor, up the .... and to the right.

DOWN

2. Present tense of *told*.
3. 'When .... you leave school?' 'In 1975.'
4. When did you .... learning English?
5. Is your brother dark .... fair?
6. The same .... *24 across*.
7. She's a student at Yale ....
8. In 1778, the British .... at the American navy.
9. .... people like music.
11. My car's very fast, bit it's not very ....: it uses a lot of petrol.
12. First she phoned her boyfriend, and .... she made some coffee.
15. Judy's hair is much .... than it was the last time I saw her.
16. Past tense of *have*.
19. Oh, look! This one's much .... It's only £1.50.
22. I can .... faster than I can write.
23. Past tense of *begin*.
27. We've got a .... of bread, but we haven't got much cheese.
28. What was the name .... the man who built the Eiffel Tower?
30. What were you doing .... ten o'clock last night?
32. Nairobi is the biggest city .... Kenya.
33. 'Who's the oldest person here?' 'I ....'

18D Washed and shaved, had breakfast

1 Welche Wörter werden in diesen Sätzen besonders stark betont? Markieren Sie die Betonung und üben Sie die Aussprache der Sätze. Beispiel:

He says he's twenty-six, but he's only twenty-one.

1. I asked for orange juice, not tomato juice.
2. 'Is that Peter?' 'No, this is John.'
3. I don't like yellow. Have you got anything in red?
4. Tuesday's no good. Can we meet on Thursday?
5. French bread is much nicer than English bread.
6. French bread is nice, but French milk isn't always very good.

2 Bilden Sie mindestens zehn Sätze mit Hilfe dieser Tabelle. Benutzen Sie *neither, both* und *but.*

NAME	PLAYS FOOTBALL	LIKES BEER	READS NOVELS	IS INTERESTED IN POLITICS	GOES TO CHURCH	GOES CAMPING
Robert	No	Yes	No	Yes	No	Yes
Janet	Yes	No	Yes	No	Yes	No
Kevin	Yes	Yes	Yes	No	No	No
Philip	Yes	Yes	No	No	No	Yes
Sue	No	Yes	No	Yes	Yes	Yes

Beispiele:

Robert neither plays football nor reads novels.

Neither Robert nor Sue plays football.

Janet and Kevin both read novels.

OR: Both Janet and Kevin ...

Sue goes to church, but Philip doesn't.

3 Setzen Sie ein: *tell, tells, told, say, says* oder *said.*

1. Al .... the policeman that he got up at eight.
2. Jake .... that he met Al at 12.30.
3. Do you always .... people what you really think?
4. I saw Ann yesterday, and she .... that she didn't want to come with us.
5. Today's newspaper .... that the weather will be fine all day.
6. My brother David never .... me when he's coming to see me.
7. Kate .... me that she didn't know what to do.
8. I .... that I wanted to go back home.
9. Some people .... that Mary is very intelligent, but I don't think so.

4 Erinnern Sie sich an die folgenden Wörter und Ausdrücke? Kennen Sie ihre Aussprache? Nehmen Sie Ihr Wörterbuch zu Hilfe, falls nötig.

Europe; job; money; place; world; football match; life; size; town; help; meet; remember; study; want; show; get up; wake up; shave; have breakfast/lunch; wear; buy; free; strong; first; enough; quietly; late.

5 Übersetzen Sie ins Deutsche.

1. Galileo was born in the 16th century.
2. She was the first woman to fly a plane across the Atlantic.
3. What was the name of the man who discovered penicillin?
4. Students came from all over Europe to hear his lectures.
5. What sport was Pele famous for?
6. I got up, washed, shaved and had breakfast.
7. He told the policeman that he got up at eight o'clock, but actually he got up at ten o'clock.
8. It's not true.
9. Both Al and Jake went to bed late.
10. Neither Al nor Jake went to a football match.

6 Wenn Sie *Student's Cassette B* haben, suchen Sie *Unit 18, Lesson D, Exercise 2.* Hören Sie sich *Als* Aussage an und versuchen Sie, einiges von dem, was er sagt, aufzuschreiben.

IT'S A LONG STORY
17

JUDY:	Who is that woman?
JASPER:	May I introduce my sister Isabel? Isabel, this is Judy.
SAM:	If you're Jasper's sister, why is your name Honeybone?
ISABEL:	It's a long story. Give me a kiss, Sam.
JUDY:	Put that man down at once.
JASPER:	Ladies, . . .
ISABEL:	Who is that woman, and why is she wearing my sweater?
JUDY:	Sam, get down.
ISABEL:	He's not feeling very strong.
JUDY:	That's all right. I'm a medical student. I'll look after him.
ISABEL:	Oh, no. You're not playing doctors with my Sam.
JASPER:	Ladies, . . .
JUDY:	He's not your Sam. He's my Sam.
ISABEL:	Take my sweater off at once.
JASPER:	Ladies, please.
JUDY: }	Shut up.
ISABEL:	
JUDY:	Sam, protect me from this mad woman.
ISABEL:	It's all right, Sam. Don't pay any attention to her. I'll look after you.
JASPER:	Sam, where are you going?
JUDY: }	Sam, come back!
ISABEL:	
	(Splash!)

"Where'd you get this newspaper, boy? It's in French!"

Unit 19 Getting to know you

19A Is this seat free?

1 Vervollständigen Sie die Gespräche.

A: .... seat ....?
B: No, ... it ....

      *   *   *

A: .... car?
B: Sorry, ... need ....

      *   *   *

A: .... mind .... look at
       .... newspaper?
B: .... all.

      *   *   *

A: .... borrow .... pen?
B: .... course.

2 Einige der folgenden Wörter werden entweder mit /i:/, wie z. B. <u>ea</u>t, oder mit /ɪ/, wie z. B. <u>i</u>t, ausgesprochen; andere hingegen werden weder mit /i:/ noch mit /ɪ/ ausgesprochen. Üben Sie die Aussprache der Wörter und tragen Sie sie in die drei Listen ein.

please   live   five   give   green   pol<u>i</u>ce   d<u>i</u>nner   friend

sing   s<u>i</u>ster   ski   this   these   fine   people   him

jeans   bread   <u>E</u>ngland   pr<u>e</u>tty   steak   fridge   meat   meet

feel   speak   cheap

GROUP 1 (like *eat*)	GROUP 2 (like *it*)	GROUP 3 (other)
please	live	five
green	give	friend
police	dinner	

3 Schreiben Sie zehn Sätze.

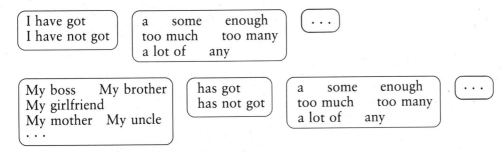

4 Wenn Sie *Student's Cassette B* haben, suchen Sie *Unit 19, Lesson A, Exercise 4*. (Sie werden dort nur die ersten sechs Bitten um Erlaubnis finden.) Hören Sie sich die Bitten an und lehnen Sie sie zunächst ab. Beim zweiten Hören erteilen Sie die Erlaubnis.

5 Lesen Sie den folgenden Text. Schlagen Sie, falls nötig, die unterstrichenen Wörter nach. (Der Autor spricht darüber, wie er sich während des Zweiten Weltkrieges in einem italienischen Krankenhaus vor den Deutschen versteckt hat.)

Then the *superiora*, the head of the <u>hospital</u>, appeared, a middle-aged woman with a gentle, <u>resolute</u> face. She was carrying a large <u>tray</u> loaded with tea things and bread and butter, ginger biscuits and raspberry jam. I tried to thank her, partly in French, partly with the few Italian words I knew, but they got mixed up with bits of school Latin, and then I ran out of words completely and looked at her in despair, and she smiled and went out of the room and came back with the girl I had met in the farmyard that morning.

She was wearing a white, open-necked shirt and a blue cotton skirt. She was brown, she was slim, she had good legs, she had ash blonde hair and blue eyes and she had a fine nose. When she <u>smiled</u> she looked <u>saucy</u>, and when she didn't she looked <u>serious</u>. She was all right.

'You have not forgotten me?' she said. I assured her that I had not done so.

'My mother has made an *apfelstrudel* for you,' she said. 'In my country we call them *struklji*. We are not Italian. We are Slovenes. You can eat it after your dinner. Tonight you have chicken. The *superiora* told me. Be kind to her and do what she says. Now I must go. I have to take food to your friends.'

I asked her when she would come again.

'I will come tomorrow, if the *superiora* allows. If you want I will teach you Italian. It will be <u>useful</u> for you, and you can teach me English. I speak badly. My name is Wanda.'

(from *Love and War in the Apennines* by Eric Newby – adapted)

19B How often do you come here?

1 Setzen Sie ein: *always, usually, very often, often, quite often, sometimes, occasionally, hardly ever* und *never*.

1. It .... rains in Britain.
2. People .... get up late on Sundays.
3. Women .... win the Nobel prize.
4. Good-looking people .... have nice personalities.
5. Policemen .... smile.
6. Politicians .... tell the truth.
7. Women .... give flowers to men.
8. Elephants .... eat meat.
9. Passport photographs .... look like the people.
10. People .... live to be 100 years old.
11. Holidays .... cost too much money.

2 Beantworten Sie die folgenden Fragen:
How often do you . . .

go to the theatre?   travel by bus?   dance?
drink wine?   play tennis?   go swimming?
go to church?   listen to the radio?
write letters?   drive a car?

Beispiele:

I travel by bus twice a day.

I play tennis every Saturday.

3 Schreiben Sie „verkürzte Fragesätze" als Reaktion auf die folgenden Aussagen (z. B. *'Are you?' 'Is it?'* usw.).

1. I work on Saturday mornings.
2. Kumiko speaks beautiful French.
3. I like swimming.
4. Andrew eats like a horse.
5. My father's got a flat in North London.
6. I've got a new car.
7. Robert came to see us yesterday.
8. Your sister looks like you.
9. You're very beautiful.

4 Vervollständigen Sie die folgenden Sätze:

1. My mother likes skiing, and so .... I.
2. All my friends can dance, but I ....
3. 'I've got a new dress.' 'That's funny. So ....'
4. 'I'm Capricorn.' 'So ....'
5. 'I'm tired.' '............... not.'
6. 'My brother can speak six languages.' 'So .... I.'
7. 'Where do you live?' 'Oxford.' 'That's funny. So .... I.'
8. 'I like smoked salmon.' 'Oh, I .... at all.'

5 Wenn Sie *Student's Cassette B* haben, suchen Sie *Unit 19, Lesson B, Exercise 3.* (Sie werden dort nur die Aussagen finden, bei denen keine Antwort vorgegeben ist.) Hören Sie sich die Sätze an und antworten Sie mit „verkürzten Fragesätzen" (z. B. *'Did you?'* usw.).

"Good morning. Now that was what I call a real party."

19C What do you think of . . . ?

1 Schreiben Sie über Ihre Vorlieben (mindestens fünf Sätze):
What (or who) is your favourite song/sport/country/town/drink/food/painter/composer/season/writer? Beispiel:

My favourite sport is cycling.

2 Beantworten Sie die folgenden Fragen:

1. Do you like horses?
2. What do you think of golf?
3. Do you like poetry?
4. Do you like Western films?
5. Do you like cats?
6. Have you ever been to the opera?
7. Have you always lived where you live now?
8. Have you ever seen the film *Casablanca*?
9. Have you always liked the same sort of music as you like now?
10. Have you ever met anyone famous?

3 Bilden Sie Fragen.

1. ever Africa to been you have ?
   Have you ever been
   to Africa ?
2. Tokyo you always lived have in ?
3. before you Rome been have to ?
4. seen Russian you films ever any have ?
5. novel have tried ever you write to a ?
6. plane have ever you a been on ?
7. driven before you bus ever have a ?

4 Achten Sie auf den Rhythmus beim Aussprechen der folgenden Sätze und ordnen Sie sie den Gruppen zu.

Where are you from?   John's a nice man.   There were two cars.
How do you do?   Buy a large steak.   Do you live here?
First on the left.   Not the green one.   English and French.
In a red car.   Do you like fish?   Thirty-five days.
What do you want?

GROUP 1	GROUP 2	GROUP 3
☐☐☐☐	☐☐☐☐	**?**
Where are you from?	John's a nice man.	....
How do you do?		

"*You know, most people's favourite number is 7, but mine is 62739901036488299100482530481038557222957100049.*"

19D   I've only known her for twenty-four hours, but . . .

1 Erinnern Sie sich an die Vergangenheitsformen? Vervollständigen Sie die Liste und lernen Sie die dritte Form (*past participle*) der unregelmäßigen Zeitwörter.

INFINITIVE	PAST TENSE	PAST PARTICIPLE
Regular verbs		
live	lived	lived
work	worked	worked
start	....	....
stop	....	....
play	....	....
change	....	....
Irregular verbs		
be		been
know	....	known
have	....	had
see	....	seen
read (/riːd/)	....	read (/red/)
write	....	written
hear (/hɪə(r)/)	....	heard (/hɜːd/)

2 Setzen Sie die dritte Form eines passenden Zeitworts ein.

1. Have you ever .... *Carmen?*
2. How long have you .... married?
3. How long have you .... my friend Andrew?
4. How long have you .... that car?
5. Have you ever .... to Scotland?
6. Have you ever .... any of Agatha Christie's detective stories?
7. Have you ever .... Beethoven's First Symphony?
8. Have you ever .... a poem? (*write*)

3 Setzen Sie die richtige Form des Zeitworts ein.

1. Where .... you ....? (*live*)
2. How long .... you .... there? (*live*)
3. .... you .... my friend Alison Haynes? (*know*)
4. How long .... you .... her? (*know*)
5. How long .... you .... that watch? (*have*)
6. .... you .... today's newspaper? (*read*)
7. .... you .... Mary today? (*see*)
8. What .... you .... of your new boss? (*think*)
9. How long .... you .... learning English? (*be*)
10. Why .... you learning English? (*be*)

4 Übersetzen Sie ins Deutsche.

1. Is this seat free?
2. 'Do you mind if I sit here?' 'Not at all. Please do.'
3. I'd rather you didn't.
4. I always come here on Sunday mornings.
5. Oh, do you? So do I.
6. I go to the theatre about every six weeks.
7. She goes skiing twice a year.
8. What do you think of the government?
9. Have you always lived in London?
10. Have you ever been to Africa?
11. for 24 hours; since yesterday
12. How long have you lived here?
13. How long have you been learning English?

5 Erinnern Sie sich an die folgenden Wörter und Ausdrücke? Kennen Sie ihre Aussprache? Nehmen Sie Ihr Wörterbuch zu Hilfe, falls nötig.

paper; window; day; week; month; year; TV; holiday; letter; place; music; look at; sit; smoke; watch; ski; come; think; cold; free; terrible; beautiful; sure; interested in; actually; every; often; sometimes; always; really; only; please; not bad.

6 Lesen Sie mit Hilfe Ihres Wörterbuchs.

IT'S A LONG STORY
18

'North-east Highlands Police Control, calling all cars. Calling all cars. The hijackers of the Boeing 707 from Rio are believed to be in the Loch Ness area after leaving the plane by parachute about twenty minutes ago. Proceed at once to the vicinity of Castle Clandonald and begin searching.

Description as follows:
Man, British, medium height, dark hair, small moustache, small brown eyes, wearing a blue suit and black shoes. He is believed to be Sam Watson, who is wanted in connection with a series of bank robberies. He is carrying a gun, and may be dangerous. Woman, nationality unknown, tall, blonde, blue eyes, attractive, athletic build, wearing dark clothes and shoes. Nothing is known about her identity.

Approach these people with caution. Repeat, approach with caution.'

"Have you been waiting long, Sir?"

20A Things to remember: Units 17, 18 and 19

1 Bilden Sie die Sätze mit *neither . . . nor* wie in den Beispielen.

I am not tall and I am not short.
I am neither tall nor short.
Alex does not speak French and Rose does not speak French.
Neither Alex nor Rose speaks French.

1. I am not fair and I am not dark.
2. She is not at home and she is not in her office.
3. John is not fat, but he is not slim.
4. It is not true and it is not false.
5. I do not speak German and I do not speak French.
6. Our village has not got a bank or a post office.
7. John is not married and Peter is not married.
8. My mother does not smoke and my father does not smoke.

2 Schreiben Sie mindestens fünf Sätze mit *neither . . . nor* über sich selbst und andere.

3 Setzen Sie die richtigen Zeitwörter ein.

1. 'I'm tired.' 'So .... I.'
2. 'Alice was very bad-tempered yesterday.' 'So .... Bill.'
3. 'We've never been to Australia.' 'Oh, we .... – three times.'
4. 'Lucy can speak five languages.' 'So .... Joe.'
5. 'Eric wants to be a doctor.' 'Oh, ... he?'
6. 'I think it's terrible.' 'So .... I.'
7. 'We went to Wales last weekend.' '................ you really? Was it nice?'
8. 'I like all her films.' 'Oh, I .... I think they're very bad.'

4 Wortschatzübung. Können Sie die fehlenden Haupt- und Eigenschaftswörter einsetzen? Können Sie die Listen erweitern?

NOUN	ADJECTIVE
Europe	European
America	American
Asia	....
....	African
Australia	....
....	English
Ireland	....
....	Scottish
Wales	....
France	....
Germany	....
....	Spanish
....	Italian
Poland	....
Turkey	....
....	Greek
....	Brazilian
....	Mexican
Egypt	....
....	Israeli
Nigeria	....
Japan	....
....	Chinese

5 Schreiben Sie passende Reaktionen auf diese Sätze.

1. I'm hungry.
   Would you like a sandwich?
2. I'm thirsty.
3. I'm bored.
4. I'm tired.
5. I'm unhappy.
6. How often do you go to the cinema?
7. I slept badly last night.
8. I can speak three languages.
9. Could you possibly lend me your car?
10. Let's have a drink.
11. Why don't we go and see a film?
12. Do you mind if I look at your paper?
13. What do you think of the government?
14. Do you like pop music?

6 Was haben Sie gestern abend gemacht?

7 Lesen Sie den Text zunächst ohne Wörterbuch. Lesen Sie ihn dann, wenn Sie wollen, noch einmal mit Hilfe Ihres Wörterbuchs.

If you are invited to an English home, at five o'clock in the morning you get a cup of tea. You must not say 'Go away'. On the contrary, you have to say, with your best five o'clock smile: 'Thank you so much. I love a cup of early morning tea, especially early in the morning.'

Then you have tea for breakfast; then you have tea at eleven o'clock in the morning; then after lunch; then you have tea for tea; then after supper; and again at eleven o'clock at night.

You must not refuse tea under the following circumstances: if it is hot; if it is cold; if you are tired; if anybody thinks that you might be tired; if you are nervous; if you are happy; before you go out; if you are out; if you have just returned home; if you have had no tea for some time; if you have just had a cup.

You definitely must not follow my example. I sleep at five o'clock in the morning; I have coffee for breakfast; I drink innumerable cups of black coffee during the day.

The other day, for instance, I wanted a cup of coffee and a piece of cheese for tea. It was a very hot day, and my wife made some cold coffee and put it in the refrigerator, where it froze* solid. On the other hand, she left the cheese on the kitchen table, where it melted. So I had a piece of coffee and a glass of cheese.

*past of *freeze*

(from *How to be an Alien* by George Mikes – adapted)

"I've spent 25 years making a name for myself and now you want me to CHANGE it?!"

20B Past, Perfect and Present

1 Suchen Sie mindestens ein passendes Zeitwort zu jedem Hauptwort. Beispiel:

letter write read

tea   tennis   steak   music   TV   a car
a door   a train   money   dirty clothes
a book   a song   a piano   a house

2 Achten Sie auf die richtige Betonung beim Aussprechen folgender Wörter:

century   animal   radio   famous
wonderful   favourite   certainly   somewhere
finally   everything   cinema

idea   policeman   believe   important
together   already   tonight   occasionally

cigarette   disagree   university

"Haven't you seen anyone posting letters before?"

3 Wählen Sie die richtigen Formen der Zeitwörter und schreiben Sie den Brief.

10 Bound Road
Wood Park
London SW17 6OJ
16.6.90

Dear Susan,

Thanks so much for your letter. It was lovely to hear from you again and to get all your news.

Things (*are starting / start*) to go very well. I (*have come / came*) to London in the first week of June, and (*have found / found*) a room the first day I was here. That was really lucky – some people (*are spending / spend*) ages looking for somewhere to live. It's a nice place in a big house. The landlady's really friendly, and there are a lot of other students. They (*came / come*) from all over the world, but most of them (*are speaking / speak*) good English, so it's easy to talk to them.

College is OK, but I think I (*change / 'm going to change*) from Design to Engineering – I (*'m / 've been*) interested in Engineering for a long time, and I really think it's the right thing for me. I (*'ve talked / talked*) to two or three of the teachers about it, and I (*'ve seen / saw*) the Principal yesterday, and they all say it's OK to change.

Social life is great! I (*'ve been / went*) out every night this week, and tomorrow I (*have / 'm having*) a party in my room for my new friends. Next weekend some of us (*go / are going*) to Wales – let's hope the weather's OK. I (*play / 'm playing*) tennis two or three times a week, too. The only problem is finding time to work!

When (*do you come / are you going to come*) over? It would be lovely to see you, and I'd really like you to meet some of my friends.

Tell Joe I (*haven't forgotten / didn't forget*) him, and I (*write / 'll write*) as soon as I can. And give my love to Alice and Ted and the others. And a big kiss to you. Write again soon.

Love,

Karen

4 Schreiben Sie einen Brief an eine/n alte/n Freund/in. Benutzen Sie einige Wörter und Ausdrücke aus *Exercise 3*.

5 Ein Kreuzworträtsel.

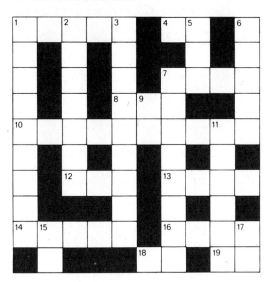

ACROSS

1. It's .... I've only known him for 24 hours, but I feel we've known each other all our lives.
4. 'Do you like music?' '............... depends what sort of music.'
7. The opposite of *rich*.
8. *So do I = I do* ....
10. A place where people study.
12. My favourite colour.
13. 'You can't do it.' 'Yes, ...' (*Two words*)
14. The opposite of *late*.
16. Could you possibly .... me some sugar?
18. Not *your*, *his*, *her*, *our* or *their*.
19. *I do too =* .... *do I*.

DOWN

1. What's your .... colour?
2. More noisy.
3. The day before the day before tomorrow.
5. Pronounced the same as *8 across*, but spelt differently.
6. Take from one place to another in your hands.
7. Could I .... borrow your car?
9. Would you like something to eat .... drink?
11. You travel on these.
15. She studied .... London University.
17. 'I think she's nice.' 'Oh, ... you?'

93

20C Choose

1 Kopieren und vervollständigen Sie die Tabelle der unregelmäßigen Zeitwörter.

INFINITIVE	PAST TENSE	PAST PARTICIPLE
fly	flew	flown
spend	....	....
show	....	....
find	....	....
catch	....	....
learn	....	....
pay	....	....
build	....	....
lead	....	....
feel	....	....

2 Setzen Sie ein: *some more, any more, a little more* oder *no more.*

1. 'Have you got .... chocolate?' 'I'm sorry, I haven't.'
2. Let me give you .... coffee.
3. 'Is there .... fish?' 'Yes, here you are.'
4. 'Here's your book back. Thanks very much.' 'I've got .... books by the same writer. Would you like to borrow them?'
5. There are .... mushrooms, but we've got some potatoes.
6. 'Can you lend me £5?' 'I haven't got .... money – I gave it all to you yesterday.'
7. 'Would you like anything more to eat or drink?' 'Just .... tea, please.'
8. I'm very hungry. Could I possibly have .... potatoes?

3 Wenn Sie *Student's Cassette B* haben, suchen Sie *Unit 20, Lesson C, Pronunciation Exercise 2*. Hören Sie zu und üben Sie die Aussprache.

4 Lesen Sie den Text, wählen Sie die fehlenden Wörter aus dem Kasten und schreiben Sie sie der Reihe nach auf. (Im Kasten ist ein Wort zuviel.)

'Don't move. ......1...... move.' The voice was calm, slow and deadly. 'Now throw your guns into the middle of the room. ......2....... That's right. Put your hands up and ......3...... back against the wall, nice and slow. Keep your hands up, lady. That's very good. Now turn round slowly and face the wall. And if you ......4...... to stay alive, just keep looking at that wall. You too, Mr Galvin.'
......5...... him, Galvin ......6...... a key turn in the door of the safe. He moved his head a little, looking at the reflection in his glasses. The big man was ......7...... with his back to them by the safe, ...8...... inside. With one smooth movement, Galvin turned and dived ......9...... the table; a moment later, the big man was ......10...... on the floor gasping for breath. Galvin picked up his gun and put it in his pocket. '......11...... them to ......12...... a younger man next time,' he said.

(From *A Gun for Your Money* by Neil MacShaw)

everybody	nobody	lying	standing
across	behind	get	heard	looking
say	send	tell	want

5 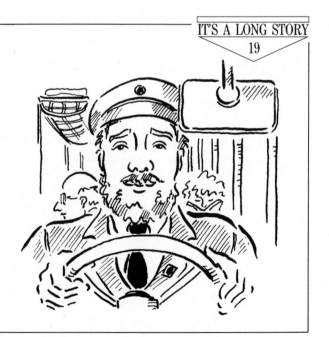 Lesen Sie mit Hilfe Ihres Wörterbuchs.

When Jock McHaverty was a little boy, he always wanted to be a bus driver. His father hoped he would go into the family business, and his mother would have liked him to be a doctor. But Jock just wasn't interested. He loved buses – all kinds of buses. He loved the way they looked, the smell of the diesel fuel, and most of all, the wonderful noise they made. When he was fourteen, he went on his first real holiday – a bus trip to the south of England and back. And when he left school two years later, he went straight into the Highland Bus Company.

Now Jock was one of the Company's most experienced drivers, working on the Fort William – Inverness route. This morning was fairly typical: he had eight passengers on board, and would probably pick up one or two more on the way. They were about twenty minutes late (Jock had stopped for a cup of tea and a chat at Strathnahuilish Post Office), but it didn't matter. 'Late' was not a word of any great importance in the Scottish Highlands. Jock leaned forward a little in his seat and smiled. It was a lovely day. The sun was shining on the loch, and the bus was running beautifully. Jock changed gear as they started up the long hill towards Clandonald Castle.

IT'S A LONG STORY
19

ÜBUNGEN ZU *LESSON 20D* ENTFALLEN.

Unit 21 Knowing about the future

21A I'm going to learn Chinese

1 Was haben Sie heute abend/morgen/nächstes Wochenende/nächstes Jahr vor? Schreiben Sie mindestens acht Sätze. Benutzen Sie *going to*.

2 Achten Sie auf die richtige Betonung beim Aussprechen folgender Sätze:

1. **What** are you going to **do**?
2. I'm **not** going to **have** a holiday **this** year.
3. I'm **never** going to **speak** to you **again**.
4. **Who's** going to **clean** the car?
5. **What film** are you going to **see**?

3 Wählen Sie die richtigen Formen der Zeitwörter.

1. I .... Lucy since Friday. (*haven't seen / didn't see*)
2. My mother .... Mrs Carpenter better than I do. (*knows / has known*)
3. She .... her for years. (*knows / has known*)
4. How long .... English? (*have you been learning / are you learning / do you learn*)
5. I .... John yesterday. (*saw / have seen*)
6. He says he .... round to see us this evening. (*'s coming / comes*)
7. What .... this evening? (*are you doing / do you do*)
8. It usually .... a lot in November. (*is raining / rains*)
9. Mark and Susan .... next month. (*are getting married / get married*)

4 Wenn Sie *Student's Cassette B* haben, suchen Sie *Unit 21, Lesson A, Exercise 3*. Hören Sie zu und versuchen Sie, das Gespräch aufzuschreiben. Schwierige Wörter: *lucky, afford, spring, summer.*

5 Persönliche Pläne.
1. Lesen Sie den ersten Text.
2. Vervollständigen Sie den zweiten Text mit Wörtern und Ausdrücken aus dem ersten Text.
3. Schreiben Sie über die Pläne eines/r Bekannten, der/die studieren will.

SATISH'S PLANS
Satish has just left school. Next year he is going to travel. He says 'I want to get some experience of life before I start studying.' He is going to spend six months in South America and six months in the Far East. First of all he is going to get a job in a factory in Brasilia – his father has got business contacts there. When he goes to the Far East he is going to try to find work teaching English.

After his year abroad Satish in going to study engineering at St Andrews University in Scotland.

RUTH'S PLANS
Ruth .... to leave school next summer. She .... to .... engineering at Brunel University, ... London, but before going there she wants to .... a year working. She says '............... .... some work experience ....' She is .... spend six months in Italy and six .... in Britain, working in car .... where her teacher has got ....

21B This is going to be the kitchen

1 Bilden Sie Sätze mit *is/are going to*.

1. What time | you | be | home tonight?
   What time are you going
   to be home tonight ?
2. When | your parents | move to London?
3. Why | your son | study engineering?
4. How | we all | travel to Scotland?
5. Where | Alice | buy her new car?
6. Who | cook supper?

2 Versuchen Sie, das Rätsel zu lösen.

Five children, still at school, are going to be a doctor, an engineer, a teacher, a lorry driver and a tennis player. Kate is not going to study after leaving school. George is going to be either the doctor or the teacher. One of the children is going to have a job which begins with the same letter as his/her name. Mark is not going to be the doctor or the engineer. Louise is not going to be the doctor. What is Phil going to be?

3 Üben Sie die Aussprache dieser drei Wortlisten.
Liste 1: Betonung auf der ersten Silbe.

breakfast   **num**ber   **dic**tionary   **bed**room
bathroom   **fin**ished   **some**where

Liste 2: Betonung auf der zweiten Silbe.

in**clud**ing   with**out**   ex**pen**sive   de**pends**
de**cide**   re**mem**ber   for**get**

Liste 3: Betonung auf der dritten Silbe.

infor**ma**tion   conver**sa**tion   under**stand**

4 Lernen Sie diese unregelmäßigen Zeitwörter.

INFINITIVE	PAST TENSE	PAST PARTICIPLE
bring	brought	brought
buy	bought	bought
begin	began	begun
take	took	taken
wear	wore	worn

5 Kennen Sie die Namen der Verkehrsmittel auf dem Bild? Benutzen Sie Ihr Wörterbuch und lernen Sie die Wörter, die Sie noch nicht kennen.

21C It's going to rain

1 Schauen Sie sich die Bilder an und sagen Sie, was gleich geschehen wird.
Benutzen Sie *going to*.

2 Was wird innerhalb der nächsten Stunde geschehen? Schreiben Sie alles auf, was Ihnen einfällt. Benutzen Sie *going to*.

3 Achten Sie auf die richtige Betonung beim Aussprechen folgender Sätze:

Where are you going to **live**?
Who are you going to **see**?
When are you going to **pay**?
Why are you going to **do** it?

My **parents** are going to **move** to **Lon**don.
The **children** are going to **leave** school.
Prices are going to **go up**.

4 Kennen Sie die Namen der verschiedenen Körperteile?

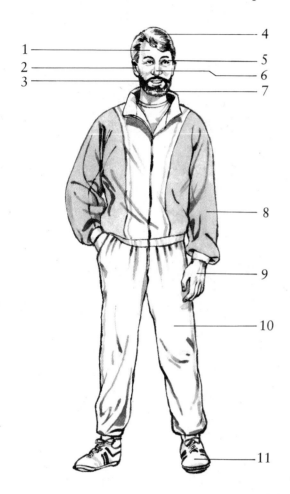

21D   Why? To . . .

1 Lesen Sie den Text und schreiben Sie dann zehn Sätze, in denen Sie sagen, weshalb Touristen nach Frankreich, Großbritannien, Indien, Japan oder in andere Länder fahren.

Tourists go to Switzerland to climb the mountains, or to ski, or to enjoy the scenery. They go to the USA to see New York, or to visit the West, or to practise speaking English.

2 Schreiben Sie mindestens fünf Sätze wie in den Beispielen.

People don't go to Nigeria to ski.
People don't go to Iceland to drink wine.

3 Schreiben Sie über einige Orte, die Sie besucht haben, und begründen Sie, weshalb Sie dort waren. Beispiel:

I went to Madrid last weekend to see my cousins.

4 Erinnern Sie sich an die folgenden Wörter? Kennen Sie ihre Aussprache? Nehmen Sie Ihr Wörterbuch zu Hilfe, falls nötig.

plane; tennis; animal; language; kiss; play; watch; listen (to); change; learn; buy; borrow; meet; understand; travel; north; south; east; west; hard; cold; tired; young; interesting; across; because.

5 Übersetzen Sie ins Deutsche.

1. Peter and Ann are going to get married.
2. This is going to be the children's room.
3. The bathroom is going to be on the ground floor.
4. She's going to have a baby.
5. I went to the library to borrow a book.
6. I went to a bookshop to buy a book.
7. People learn English all over the world.
8. I'm learning English to do business in English-speaking countries.

6 🔲 Lesen Sie mit Hilfe Ihres Wörterbuchs.

IT'S A LONG STORY
20

In her black Porsche, Dr Wagner was getting a little impatient. She was in a hurry to get to her hotel in Inverness and have a bath and a rest, after driving overnight from London. But for the last fifteen miles she had been stuck behind a bus that was driving very slowly in the middle of the road, and it seemed impossible to get past. 'Calm down, Mary,' she said to herself. 'You've got plenty of time.'

She started thinking about the holiday that was just starting. Every year, she drove up to the Scottish Highlands and spent two weeks looking for the Loch Ness Monster. Dr Wagner was a member of the West London Society for the Investigation of Strange and Unexplained Phenomena, and she was very interested in monsters, ghosts, flying saucers and things of that kind. She had never yet seen anything in Loch Ness, but she always had a wonderful holiday and went back home feeling happy and relaxed. She had a feeling about this year, though. This year was going to be special. Somehow, she just knew.

A sudden noise brought her out of her dreams. She looked in the mirror. Behind her, the road was full of police cars, with lights flashing and sirens howling. Dr Wagner frowned. She didn't like police cars. 'It's no use making all that noise,' she said. 'You'll never get past the bus.'

"This is a pretty tough library!"

Unit 22 Telling people to do things

22A I feel ill

1 Vervollständigen Sie die Gespräche.

A: I've got a cold.
B: ....?

*   *   *

A: How are you?
B: .... ill.
A: ....?

*   *   *

A: I've got ....
B: ....?

A: What's the problem?
B: ....

*   *   *

A: Why don't you go to bed?
B: ....

*   *   *

A: .... temperature?
B: I don't think so.

2 Schreiben Sie zwei oder drei Sätze darüber, wie Sie sich gerade fühlen.

3 Setzen Sie die Wörter aus dem Kasten ein.

I	you	he	she	it	we	they
me	you	him	her	it	us	them
my	your	his	her	its	our	their

1. My brothers and I all look like .... mother.
2. Tell the children to bring .... favourite toys.
3. Mum's gone to bed – .... says .... is tired.
4. Did you write to Jim or talk to .... on the phone?
5. Could you show .... that ring, please?
6. Don't worry about me and the children – .... will eat along the way somewhere.
7. I really like Don and Susan – .... are so easy to be with.
8. You can borrow .... map if you haven't got one.
9. Tell .... what the problem is and we will try to help you with it.
10. My brother lent me .... car last weekend.

4 Wenn Sie *Student's Cassette B* haben, suchen Sie *Unit 22, Lesson A, Exercise 2.* Hören Sie zu und sprechen Sie nach. Achten Sie auf eine möglichst gute Betonung und Satzmelodie.

WOMAN: **Good morning, Mr Culham. How are** you?
MAN: I **feel ill.**
WOMAN: I *am* **sorry. What's the matter?**
MAN: **My eyes hurt,** and I've **got a bad head**ache.
WOMAN: **Oh, I hope** you **aren't catching flu. Why don't** you **take an aspirin?**
MAN: **That's a good idea.**

5 Die Bilder sind in der richtigen Reihenfolge, die Textabschnitte jedoch nicht. Welcher Abschnitt gehört zu welchem Bild? Sie können Ihr Wörterbuch benutzen.

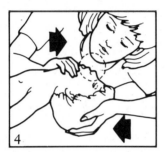
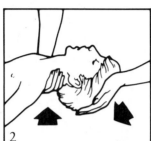

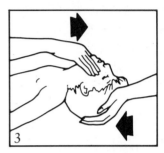
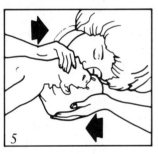

a. Breathe into the child, but not too strongly. (A small child's lungs cannot hold your entire breath.) Take your lips away and let the child's chest go down while you take your next breath. Use fairly quick, short breaths, and keep it up until the child can breathe by himself or until help comes, as long as two hours.
b. Open the air passages by pulling the neck up and putting the head down very far.
c. If the child has got water in his lungs, first get it out by putting him on his stomach for ten seconds with his hips a foot higher than his head (over your knee, on a box, etc.).
d. Keep the child's chin pushed up all the time, to keep the air passages open.
e. With a child's small face you can breathe into nose and mouth together.

(from *Baby and Child Care* by Dr Benjamin Spock – adapted)

99

22B Always warm up

1 Hier sind einige Anweisungen zum Autofahren. Setzen Sie *always*, *never* oder *don't* an den Anfang der Sätze. Nehmen Sie Ihr Wörterbuch zu Hilfe.

1. .... look in the mirror before driving off.
2. .... drive fast in fog.
3. .... drive too close to the car in front.
4. .... forget to check the oil from time to time.
5. .... wear your seat belt.
6. .... put a small child in the front seat.
7. .... drive on the right in Britain.
8. .... overtake when you can't see a long way in front.
9. .... drive at over 30 miles an hour in towns.
10. .... park on a double yellow line – it can be expensive.

2 Kopieren und vervollständigen Sie die Tabelle.

INFINITIVE	PAST TENSE	PAST PARTICIPLE
come	came	come
....	cost	....
....	....	drawn
drink	....	....
....	ate	....
....	....	forgotten
get	....	....
....	gave	....
....	....	gone/been
leave	....	....

3 Wenn Sie *Student's Cassette B* haben, suchen Sie *Unit 22, Lesson B, Exercise 2*. (Sie werden dort die Antwort des Jungen nur zum Teil finden.) Hören Sie zu und schreiben Sie möglichst viel auf.

4 Lesen Sie den Text und bringen Sie die Bilder in die richtige Reihenfolge.

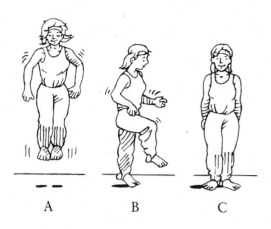

A   B   C

> **Exercise Ten   Run and hop**
>
> **Start** Stand erect, feet together, arms at sides. Starting with left leg, run in place raising feet at least four inches from floor.
> (When running in place lift knees forward, do not merely kick heels backwards.)
>
> **Count** Each time left foot touches floor counts one. After each fifty counts do ten hops.
>
> **Hops** Hopping is done so that both feet leave floor together. Try to hop at least four inches off floor each time.

(from Physical Fitness)

5 Schnelles Lesen. Lesen Sie die Anweisungen zügig aber sorgfältig und führen Sie sie genau aus. Sie haben zwei Minuten Zeit.

Write your surname on a piece of paper. Don't write your first name. If it is Tuesday, write your age, but if it is Thursday, write the date. If it is not Tuesday or Thursday, don't write anything, but draw a big O round your name. Write the name of your country, in English, under your name. If you have not already written the date, write it to the left of the name of your country. If you are over thirty, do not write the name of an animal, but if you are thirty or under, write the name of an animal and the name of a bird at the bottom of the page.

"Very good, chaps, now we'll try if from the plane."

22C   Look out!

1 Welches Spiel paßt zu welchem Bild? Nehmen Sie Ihr Wörterbuch zu Hilfe.

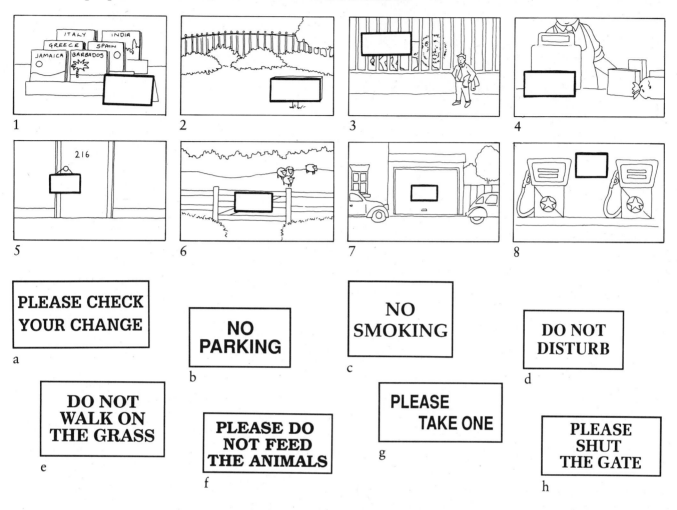

PLEASE CHECK YOUR CHANGE

a

NO PARKING

b

NO SMOKING

c

DO NOT DISTURB

d

DO NOT WALK ON THE GRASS

e

PLEASE DO NOT FEED THE ANIMALS

f

PLEASE TAKE ONE

g

PLEASE SHUT THE GATE

h

2 Schreiben Sie mindestens drei Schilder für Ihr Schulgebäude.

3 Setzen Sie die Ausdrücke aus dem Kasten ein.

| look out   come in   look   don't worry |
| wait here   follow me   be careful |
| please hurry   take your time |

1. *Be careful* — there are eggs in that box.
2. .... Everything's all right.
3. .... and sit down, Mr Pearson. What can I do for you?
4. .... My plane is at four o'clock, and it's 3.15 now.
5. ...., please. Your seats are right over here.
6. ....! There's your brother over there!
7. ....! There's a car coming!
8. Ms Wilsdon is busy at the moment. Could you ...., please?
9. 'I'm terribly sorry.'   'That's all right. I'm not in a hurry. ....'

4 Kopieren und vervollständigen Sie die Tabelle.

INFINITIVE	PAST TENSE	PAST PARTICIPLE
lend	....	....
....	lay	....
....	....	made
....	....	meant
meet	....	....
....	ran	....
....	....	said
send	....	....
....	showed	....
....	....	sung

5 Erinnern Sie sich an die folgenden Wörter? Kennen Sie ihre Aussprache? Nehmen Sie Ihr Wörterbuch zu Hilfe, falls nötig.

leg; eye; idea; water; road; run; walk; drink; right; better; comfortable; fast; rich; somebody; until; over.

6 Wenn Sie *Student's Cassette B* haben, suchen Sie *Unit 22, Lesson C, Exercise 2.* (Sie werden dort nur den ersten Teil finden.) Schlagen Sie folgende Wörter nach: *comfortably; cow; farm.* Hören Sie dann so oft Sie wollen zu und versuchen Sie, alle Wörter aufzuschreiben.

7 Ein Kreuzworträtsel.

31. Susan is the .... interesting person I know.
32. There's a lot of .... in my study; it has got four windows.
33. Alice is taller than her sister, but they both weigh the same; Alice is ....
34. 'Jane, you look ill!' 'Yes, I feel ill. I think I've got a ....'

DOWN

1. My brother .... a beautiful cake for his girlfriend's birthday.
2. You can't talk in my car – it's too ....
3. I always wear comfortable clothing .... I run.
4. How many people .... there in your English class?
5. I don't like my son to walk home .... at night.
7. Everybody .... Ann caught the early train.
9. A Volkswagen is more .... than a Rolls-Royce.
10. I don't think .... her brother can drive.
11. He's not .... tall .... his wife.
15. My daughter is fair now, but I think that she'll be .... when she's older.
16. I can't phone her .... I haven't got her number.
17. People are in this room about one third of their time.
20. When you wake up in the morning, you .... your eyes.
22. '................?' 'Because.'
26. She's .... tall, but not as tall as I am.
27. How far is it .... the nearest phone box?
29. The same as *32 across*.
30. I don't like opera; rock music is much .... interesting.
31. Yesterday at a party I .... somebody who has got the same birthday as me.

ACROSS

1. £ $ DM ¥
6. .... are you from?
8. The opposite of *cheap*.
10. My sister can run faster .... me.
12. Eyes can be this colour.
13. Why don't you go .... and lie down?
14. Opposite of *good*.
18. .... the first left.
19. I can't drink this coffee – it's .... hot.
21. The opposite of *hot*.
22. Husband and ....
23. Mountains are ....
24. He can't walk home; it's .... too far.
25. Me, ..., her, him, us, them.
26. The opposite of *2 down*.
28. Their children are still ....; the oldest is three.

22D Please speak more slowly

1 Machen Sie Umstandswörter aus diesen Eigenschaftswörtern.

tired _tiredly_

easy last sensitive possible probable certain careful different quick heavy

2 Setzen Sie das Umstandswort an die richtige Stelle.

1. She opened every book. (*carefully*)
2. I like British television. (*very much*)
3. She read the newspaper. (*quickly*)
4. He said 'No' and walked away. (*angrily*; *fast*)
5. He answered the phone. (*sleepily*)
6. Please say your name and age. (*clearly*)

3 Auffrischung. Setzen Sie die Vergangenheitsformen der Zeitwörter ein.

1. I .... your mother yesterday. She's looking fine. (*see*)
2. You .... a letter from Sylvia this morning, didn't you? (*get*)
3. Who .... St Paul's Cathedral? (*build*)
4. I .... ill yesterday, so I .... to see the doctor. (*feel*; *go*)
5. It .... very late when I .... home last night. (*be*; *come*)
6. Alex .... a new car last week. (*buy*)
7. A man once .... 6,700m without a parachute, and lived. (*fall*)
8. My boss .... to New York again last week. (*fly*)

4 Übersetzen Sie ins Deutsche.

1. What's the matter?
2. I feel ill.
3. I've got a cold.
4. I've got toothache.
5. My leg hurts.
6. Don't run if you feel tired.
7. Please hurry, darling.
8. Take your time.
9. Be careful.
10. Look out!
11. Follow me, please.
12. I'm very angry with you.
13. She spoke to me very angrily.
14. You speak English very well.

5 Wenn Sie *Student's Cassette B* haben, suchen Sie *Unit 22, Lesson D, Exercise 1*. Hören Sie zu und versuchen Sie, die Sätze aufzuschreiben.

6 Lesen Sie den Brief. Sie können Ihr Wörterbuch benutzen. Schreiben Sie dann einen ähnlichen Brief über Ihr Zuhause an eine/n Freund/in.

Dear Alice,

I'm so happy I can lend you my flat while you're here: I'm only sorry I can't be here with you.

Mrs Rogers on the first floor has got the keys for you, and she is looking forward to seeing you. She is very friendly, and she will happily tell you about shopping and so on.

Please lock the door carefully when you go out, and when you are in the flat; remember that this is a big city, not like your little village! The milkman will leave you a pint of milk every two days, but if you want to change that just leave him a note. And could you water my plants when they are dry? They will do well if you water them every three days or so, but they will die fast if you give them too much water.

I hope you have a lovely time. I will leave a note in the flat about interesting places to go and interesting things to do.

Love,

Janice

7 🔲 Lesen Sie mit Hilfe Ihres Wörterbuchs.

IT'S A LONG STORY
21

Down at the bottom of Loch Ness, things were very calm. The Monster scratched her ear with the third leg on the right and decided that it was time to do something. She didn't usually go up to the surface during the day because the light hurt her eyes, but she was getting bored out of her mind sitting down at the bottom of the loch with nothing to do except talk to the fish. She scratched her ear again, yawned, stretched, and started swimming slowly up towards the light.

Five minutes later, the Monster reached the surface, stuck her head and fifteen metres of neck out of the water, and looked around. She closed her eyes and opened them again. It was a little difficult to understand what was happening. Scotland was generally a fairly quiet place, but today a lot of things seemed to be going on.

On the bank of the loch, two women were fighting. A man was trying to stop them; another man was trying to learn to swim. The road was full of cars with pretty blue lights on top, coming from all directions. A helicopter landed on the bank of the loch and some soldiers got out and lay down. There was a bus driving along very slowly with the driver looking out of the window. The bus driver caught sight of the Monster and drove into the loch. The two women stopped fighting and stood with their mouths open. All the police cars crashed into each other. A sports car stopped and a woman got out and started taking photographs.

It was all too much. The Monster closed her eyes and went back down to the bottom of the loch.

Unit 23 Predictions

23A Are you sure you'll be all right?

1 Welche Geschenke erwarten Sie zu Weihnachten oder zum nächsten Geburtstag? Benutzen Sie *I (don't) think, I'm sure, perhaps, probably.* Beispiele:

I think my father will give me a book.
Perhaps somebody will give me perfume.
I don't think anybody will give me a car.

2 Achten Sie auf die richtige Betonung beim Aussprechen folgender Sätze:

I'm going to **hitchhike** round the world.
Where will you **sleep?**
You'll **get lost.**
What will you **do** for **money?**
Of **course** I'll be **all right.**

3 Schreiben Sie einige wahre Sätze über sich selbst. Benutzen Sie mindestens fünf dieser Wörter.

didn't   last night   woke   knew   came
went   lived   will   never   happy

4 Kopieren und vervollständigen Sie die Tabelle.

INFINITIVE	PAST TENSE	PAST PARTICIPLE
go	went	gone/been
say	....	said
....	took	....
buy	....	....
....	....	spoken
....	left	....
understand	....	....
....	....	given
....	knew	....
write	....	....
....	....	read
....	came	....

5 Wenn Sie *Student's Cassette B* haben, suchen Sie *Unit 23, Lesson A, Exercise 1.* Hören Sie sich das Gespräch an und üben Sie die Aussprache.

23B If you push lever B, . . .

1 Vervollständigen Sie die Sätze. Versuchen Sie dies zunächst, ohne die Wörter im Kasten anzuschauen. (Im Kasten sind drei Wörter zuviel.)

1. I was .... in London, ... 16 June 1942, ... three o'clock .... the morning. I was a beautiful ....
2. I had a very strange .... last night. I was in a big red Rolls-Royce. We were going .... York, and we were .... very fast in the dark, without .... Suddenly I .... a white horse in the road .... front .... us. Then I .... up.
3. 'What did she want?' 'I don't know. She .... so quietly that I couldn't .... what she said.'
4. What's that noise in the street? Look .... the window and see what's ....

again	at	baby	born	dream	driving
happening	hear	in	in	lights	long
of	on	out of	saw	shop	spoke
to	woke				

2 Sagen Sie, woher Sie einige persönliche Dinge haben. Beispiele:

I got my sweater in London.
I got my watch from my mother.
I got my shirt at the shop round the corner.

3 Achten Sie auf die richtige Betonung beim Aussprechen folgender Sätze:

What are they **doing?**
Where are you **going?**
What do you **think?**
When can I **come?**
How do you **know?**
Who did you **see?**
Why do you **ask?**
What does she **want?**
When did they **arrive?**
How can I **help?**

4 Schnelles Lesen. Lesen Sie den Text so zügig wie möglich, um die Antworten zu den Fragen zu finden. Sie haben zwei Minuten Zeit.

mph	km/h	Record	mph	km/h	Record
		SPEED IN SPORT			
622.287	1001.473	Highest land speed (four wheeled rocket powered)	43.14	69.40	Track cycling (219 yd 200 m unpaced in 10.369 s)
		(Official land speed record)	41.72	67.14	Greyhound racing (410 yd 374 m straight 26.13 s)
429.311	690.909	Highest land speed (wheel driven)	41.50	66.78	Sailing – 60 ft 18,29 m proa Crossbow II (36.04 kts)
319.627	514.39	Official water speed record	35.06	56.42	Horse racing – The Derby (1 mile 885 yd 2.41 km)
318.866	513.165	Highest speed motor cycle	27.00	43.5	Sprinting (during 100 yd 91 m)
250.958	403.878	Motor racing – closed circuit	25.78	41.48	Roller skating (400 yd 402 m in 34.9 s)
188	302.5	Pelota	21.49	34.58	Cycling – average maintained over 24 hr
170	273	Golf ball	13.46	21.67	Rowing (2187 yd 2000 m)
163.6	263	Lawn tennis – serve	12.26	19.74	Marathon run (26 miles 385 yd 42.195 km)
140.5	226.1	Cycling, motor paced	9.39	15.121	Walking – 1 hr
128.16	206.25	Water skiing	5.28	8.50	Swimming (50 yd) – short course in 19.36 s
124.412	200.222	Downhill Schuss (alpine skiing)	4.53	7.29	Swimming (100 m) – long course in 49.36 s
63.894	102.828	Downhill alpine skiing (Olympic course) (average)			
52.57	84.60	Speedway (4 laps of 430 yd 393 m)			
43.26	69.62	Horse racing (440 yd 402 m in 20.8 s)			

(from *Guinness Book of Answers* – abridged)

1. What is the record speed for a tennis serve?
2. What is the record average speed for 24-hour cycling?
3. What is the official land speed record?
4. What is the water skiing record speed?
5. What is the record speed for a one-hour walk?

23C   What do the stars say?

1 Setzen Sie die richtige Form ein. (Zukunft mit *will* oder einfache Vergangenheit.)

1. My horoscope said 'You will have a wonderful week' (*have*)
2. but actually, I .... a terrible week. (*have*)
3. My horoscope said 'You .... on a long journey' (*go*)
4. but actually, I only .... to the post office. (*go*)
5. My horoscope said 'Money .... to you' (*come*)
6. but actually, I .... the whole week paying bills. (*spend*)
7. My horoscope said 'You .... a tall dark stranger' (*meet*)
8. but actually, I .... a short fat policeman. (*meet*)
9. My horoscope said 'This .... a good time for love' (*be*)
10. but actually, my girlfriend .... very unkind to me. (*be*)
11. My horoscope said 'There .... bad news on Wednesday'. (*be*)
12. Actually, there .... bad news every day. (*be*)

2 Wählen Sie mindestens drei dieser Listen aus und fügen Sie so viele Wörter wie möglich hinzu.

1. red, blue, . . .
2. coat, sweater, . . .
3. table, chair, . . .
4. orange, fish, . . .
5. secretary, shop assistant, . . .
6. happy, tired, . . .
7. shy, bad-tempered, . . .
8. post office, station, . . .

3 Lernen Sie diese unregelmäßigen Zeitwörter.

INFINITIVE	PAST TENSE	PAST PARTICIPLE
sit	sat	sat
sleep	slept	slept
speak	spoke	spoken
spend	spent	spent
stand	stood	stood
swim	swam	swum
tell	told	told
think	thought	thought
understand	understood	understood
wake	woke	woken

4 Übersetzen Sie eins der Horoskope von Seite 114 im *Student's Book* ins Deutsche.

5 Stellen Sie sich vor, Sie machen im nächsten Jahr Ihren Traumurlaub. Was wird geschehen? Wohin werden Sie fahren? Wen werden sie treffen? Was werden Sie tun? Benutzen Sie die Zukunft mit *will*.

→

6 Lesen Sie mit Hilfe Ihres Wörterbuchs.

(*Which?* is the magazine of the Consumers' Association. It tests different things that you can buy, and says which is the 'best buy'. One month, *Which?* tested horoscopes.)

Most people will say there's nothing in horoscopes. So you would expect that most people wouldn't read them. But they do.

We thought we would try to find out how useful forecasts from stars really are, in their most accessible form – horoscopes in the press.

First of all we asked 1,000 people whether they read horoscopes, whether they found them useful, and what their reactions were.

Their reactions ranged from 'nonsense' and 'a load of rubbish' through 'they're fun' and 'amusing', to one person who always looked at them 'before making any major decision'.

To find out how good the advice and predictions really are, and see if there was any best buy, we asked some 200 people, some men, some women, some believers and some not, to read their horoscopes in the papers and magazines every day for a month, and to comment on them at the end of each day.

Rather sadly, 83 per cent reported that the advice was very little help at all. There wasn't much to choose between any of the newspapers and magazines we looked at but *Woman*, *Woman's Own* and the *Daily Mirror* were thought marginally less unhelpful than the average, while the *Sun* and the *News of the World* were thought worse.

"*Separate futures, please.*"

"*I've already met the tall, dark man. What I'd like to know is, where is he now?*"

23D What will happen next?

1 Wie wird die Mode in fünfzig Jahren aussehen? Vervollständigen Sie einige oder alle der folgenden Sätze:

I think skirts will be *longer.*
I think the fashionable colour will be . . .
I'm sure people will wear . . .
I'm sure people won't wear . . .
I don't think people will wear . . .
People certainly won't wear . . .
Perhaps men will wear . . .
Perhaps women will wear . . .
Clothes will be . . .

2 Üben Sie die Aussprache dieser Wörter. (Alle Wörter haben den gleichen Selbstlaut.)

first   heard   word   early   certain
Thursday   work   shirt   skirt   turn
third   learn   sir   dirty   girl

3 Vervollständigen Sie die Sätze mit passenden Verhältniswörtern.

1. Our house is right .... the police station.
2. I heard a strange noise .... the night.
3. Don't run until two hours .... eating.
4. We're very old friends. We met ....
   university.
5. I've been here .... six weeks, and I still can't
   understand anybody.
6. Would you like a drink .... you go to bed?
7. I'll meet you at the station, ... the clock.
8. The bus arrives .... the airport ....
   about 10.25.
9. Come and sit .... me. I want to tell you
   something.
10. Are you doing anything .... Tuesday?

4 Erinnern Sie sich an die folgenden Wörter und Ausdrücke? Kennen Sie ihre Aussprache? Nehmen Sie Ihr Wörterbuch zu Hilfe, falls nötig.

money; driver; help; party; parents; street; sleep;
need; get up; hope; open; agree; sure; hard;
interesting; strange; rich; terrible; early; late; again;
enough; round the world.

5 Übersetzen Sie ins Deutsche.

1. I'm going to be a racing driver.
2. That's very dangerous.
3. I don't mind.
4. You'll get killed.
5. No, I won't.
6. My English is getting better.
7. What time do you usually get up?
8. Get on the bus outside the station, and get off at
   the post office.

6 📼 Lesen Sie mit Hilfe Ihres Wörterbuchs.

IT'S A LONG STORY
22

'Hello, Judy,' said Dr Wagner. 'What are you doing here? I thought you were in Rio.' 'It's a long story,' said Judy. 'I'll tell you later.' 'Did you see the Monster?' said Dr Wagner. 'Wasn't she just *wonderful*? I got hundreds of photos.'

'I'm sorry to interrupt,' said Jasper, 'but I think this is a very good time to go on holiday. Isabel, go and get Sam out of the water and follow us up to the castle. Judy, come with me. I hope the ghost remembered to fill the plane up with petrol.' 'Ghost?' said Dr Wagner. 'You have a ghost in your castle? *A ghost?*' 'Come along with us and you can meet him,' said Judy. 'But hurry.'

Twenty seconds later, they drove in through the front gate of the castle in Dr Wagner's Porsche, and a minute or so after that Isabel ran up carrying Sam over her shoulder. The ghost closed the gate and led the way to the back of the castle. There, standing on the grass, shining in the sun, was a powerful-looking six-seater aeroplane. 'Get in,' said Jasper. 'We haven't got a moment to lose.' 'Can I come too?' asked Dr Wagner. 'I must talk to that beautiful ghost.' 'Of course,' said Jasper, 'but get in fast, or you'll be talking to our wonderful police. Fasten seat-belts, everybody. Take-off in fifteen seconds.' 'Where are we going?' asked Judy. 'Rio,' said Jasper. 'That's where you wanted to go, isn't it?' 'Sounds good to me,' said Sam. 'Jasper,' said Judy, 'I have been a blind, blind fool. I love you.'

Unit 24 Consolidation

24A Things to remember: Units 21, 22 and 23

1 Schreiben Sie die Umstandswörter.

angry *angrily*	economical	sure
hungry	noisy	real
beautiful	quiet	comfortable
free	warm	

2 Setzen Sie die Umstandswörter an die richtigen Stellen.

1. She speaks Chinese. (*very well*)
2. Please write your address. (*clearly*)
3. He wrote my name without looking at me. (*slowly*)
4. He closed the door. (*angrily*)
5. Please read this paper. (*carefully*)

3 Vervollständigen Sie die Sätze.

1. If you __don't eat__, you'll get thin.
2. If you . . . , you'll get tired.
3. If you . . . , you'll get thirsty.
4. If you . . . , you'll get wet.
5. If I . . . , I'll be very happy.
6. If . . . , I'll be very unhappy.
7. If . . . , it will be very bad for the country.
8. If . . . , it will be very good for the country.

4 Lesen Sie den Text, ohne Ihr Wörterbuch zu benutzen. Schauen Sie sich dann rechts unten die Wörter und Ausdrücke an und wählen Sie die jeweils beste Erklärung. Nehmen Sie danach Ihr Wörterbuch zur Kontrolle.

'The best car in the world'

The first Royce car (1904)

The Silver Ghost (1906–1925)

The Silver Cloud (1959–1966)

The Silver Spirit (1981)

Henry Royce did not like his Decauville car, which ran badly and often broke down. So he decided to make a better car himself, and in 1904 he produced his first two-cylinder model. Charles Rolls, a car manufacturer, was very impressed by Royce's car, and soon Rolls and Royce went into business together. One of their first models was the Silver Ghost. In 1907, a Silver Ghost broke the world's endurance record by driving 14,371 miles (23,120km) without breaking down once. After the drive, it cost just over £2 to put the car back into perfect condition. It is not surprising that the Silver Ghost was called 'the best car in the world'. Rolls-Royce cars are famous for running quietly: an advertisement for one model said 'the loudest noise is the ticking of the clock'. The cars are made very carefully. A lot of the work is done by hand, and they take a long time to manufacture: only twelve cars leave the factory every day.

1. *It broke down*: (a) It made a noise. (b) Pieces fell off it. (c) It stopped working.
2. *Charles Rolls was very impressed by Royce's car*: (a) He thought it was good. (b) He wanted it. (c) He did not understand it.
3. *model*: (a) picture (b) small car (c) sort of car
4. *endurance*: (a) going fast (b) going on for a long time (c) being easy to drive
5. *Rolls-Royce cars are famous*: (a) They are very good. (b) Everybody knows about them. (c) They are very quiet.
6. *ticking*: (a) a sort of clock (b) a part of a car (c) a sort of noise
7. *manufacture*: (a) make (b) sell (c) finish
8. *factory*: (a) town (b) place where cars are made (c) shop

5 Ein Kreuzworträtsel.

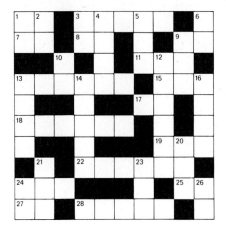

11. You'll get thin if you don't .... enough.
13. Cold time of the year.
15. You can .... a dictionary if you like.
17. Let's meet .... eight o'clock.
18. Warm time of the year.
19. Past of *meet*.
22. After *13 across* and before *18 across*.
24. If you don't eat at all, you'll ....
25. I'm tired – let's .... home.
27. Are you doing anything .... Tuesday?
28. Argentina is in .... America.

DOWN

1. I'm not .... tall as my father.
2. I'm going to the bank .... get some money out.
3. I'm sorry – there's .... more steak.

ACROSS

1. Get off the bus .... Park Street.
3. The USA is in .... America.
7. 'I like her.' '............... do I.'
8. Get .... the bus outside the station.
9. I'll phone you again .... three days.

4. I write to my mother .... a week.
5. My eyes are .... same colour as my mother's.
6. This word comes in two other places in the crossword.
9. *It is* = ...
10. My sister's .... architect.
12. After *18 across* and before *13 across*.
13. The sun is here in the evening.
14. Can you tell me the .... of trains to Exeter?
16. The sun is here in the morning.
20. Food that comes from a bird.
21. Infinitive of *won*.
23. Capitalist without capital.
24. 'How .... you ....?' 'How .... you ....?'
26. This is the end .... the crossword.

24B Choose

1 Können Sie diese Wörter aussprechen, obwohl Sie sie nicht kennen? (Schauen Sie nicht in Ihrem Wörterbuch nach.)

tope	dune	slot	cope
dram	glide	slid	pride
hack	cube	grid	grate

2 Achten Sie auf die richtige Betonung beim Aussprechen dieser Wörter.

morning   aspirin (/ˈæsprɪn/)
medicine (/ˈmedsən/)
headache   problem   terrible
understand   pronounce
remember   forget   invite
prefer   included   examine
prescription   tomorrow

3 Setzen Sie die Vergangenheitsformen dieser Zeitwörter ein.

begin	buy	can	come	go	have	hear	know
put	say	see	take	tell	wake up		

1. When I .... this morning I was still very tired.
2. I .... Janet at the disco last night.
3. John .... Michael Jackson when he was a boy.
4. I .... some grape juice for you when I went shopping.
5. We .... the children to the Science Museum last week.
6. 'Where's my jacket?' 'I think you .... it on the bed.'
7. He .... he .... a headache, but I think he just didn't want to come.
8. The postman .... very early this morning.
9. When she was younger she .... run much faster than now.
10. They .... to Bali for two weeks in September.
11. Who .... you that I was unhappy?
12. I .... studying English when I was twelve.
13. I was just going to bed when I .... a terrible noise in the street.

4 Erinnern Sie sich an die folgenden Wörter? Kennen Sie ihre Aussprache? Nehmen Sie Ihr Wörterbuch zu Hilfe, falls nötig.

buy; dog; fall; horse; next; o'clock; pull; sing; turn; word.

5 Vervollständigen Sie den Text mit den Wörtern und Ausdrücken aus dem Kasten.
Sie können einige Wörter mehrmals benutzen.

because	but	finally	first of all	how	I'm afraid	so
then	what	when	who			

Yesterday was not a good day. ....1......., I woke up late ....2....... I didn't hear my alarm clock. ....3....... I got out of bed I put my foot on a teacup that was standing by the bed. I can't think ....4....... it got there – perhaps somebody ....5....... doesn't like me put it there while I was asleep. ....6....... I cleaned the tea off the carpet and got dressed as quickly as I could. There wasn't much time, ...7....... I was going to Chester for a job interview, and my train was at seven-forty, and it was already seven twenty-five. ....8....... I couldn't find my keys to open the door. I looked everywhere. ....9....... I decided there was only one thing to do. I opened a window and started climbing out. This was not difficult, ...10....... my flat is on the ground floor, and I am still quite young and athletic – I play tennis every Saturday afternoon, and I do a lot of swimming on holiday. But just as I stood up and closed the window somebody said 'Excuse me, sir.' I turned round and saw that it was a policeman. It was now seven-thirty, ...11....... I didn't really have time for conversation. 'Good morning, officer,' I said. 'I'd like to talk to you, ...12....... I'm afraid I can't stop, ...13....... I've got a train to catch.' 'I'm sure you have, sir,' he said. 'But ....14....... I'll have to ask you a few questions first.' ....15....... I spent an hour and a half at the police station, and I missed the train, and ....16....... I finally got to Chester they said I was too late for the interview. The next train home was at six in the evening, ...17....... I had to spend the day in Chester. It rained all day. Do you want to know ....18....... there is to do in Chester on a wet Thursday afternoon? Don't ask.

6 Schreiben Sie über einen Tag, an dem für Sie alles schiefging.

24C   When you grow up

1 Vergleichen Sie sich und Ihr Leben heute und vor zehn Jahren. Schreiben Sie mindestens fünf Sätze.
Beispiele:

Ten years ago I lived in a flat; now I live in a house.
Ten years ago I weighed 55 kilos, and I still do.
I can run faster than I could ten years ago.

2 Schreiben Sie den Text mit der richtigen Groß-schreibung und Zeichensetzung ab. Schauen Sie dann auf Seite 107 zur Kontrolle nach.

hello judy said dr wagner what are you doing here i thought you were in rio its a long story said judy ill tell you later did you see the monster said dr wagner wasnt she just wonderful i got hundreds of photos

3 Wortschatzübung. Überlegen Sie sich fünf wichtige Wörter, die Sie nicht auf englisch kennen. Schlagen Sie sie in Ihrem Wörterbuch nach und lernen Sie sie.

4 Wenn Sie *Student's Cassette B* haben, suchen Sie *Unit 24, Lesson C, Exercise 3.* (Sie werden dort nur das zweite Gedicht finden.) Hören Sie zu und versuchen Sie selbst, das Gedicht aufzusagen. Der Text steht auf Seite 121 im *Student's Book.*

5 ⊙⊙ Lesen Sie mit Hilfe Ihres Wörterbuchs.

IT'S A LONG STORY
23

As the plane flew peacefully south-west across the Atlantic, Judy put her head on Jasper's shoulder and closed her eyes. 'I'm so glad I'm in love with you instead of Sam,' she said. 'It's much nicer. I'm sure we're going to be very happy together. Do you think the others will be all right?' 'I think so,' said Jasper, and kissed her.

Judy listened to the fragments of conversation that came from the seats behind. 'Isabel, you are my favourite detective. Will you teach me to swim?' 'Have some more champagne, ghost.' 'Yes, please. Call me MacDonald.' 'You've got beautiful eyes, Sam.' 'Can ghosts get married?'

'Sounds all right,' said Judy. 'Tell me, are you really terribly rich? How did you get your money? What do you do, actually? How did you get to know Sam? Why did you really hijack that plane?'

'I'll tell you later,' said Jasper. 'It's a long story.'

ÜBUNGEN *ZU LESSON 24D* ENTFALLEN.

Mini-grammar (Kurzgrammatik)

Besondere Zeitwörter: *be, have (got)* und *can*

Be (sein)

Gegenwart		
I am (I'm)	am I?	I am (I'm) not
you are (you're)	are you?	you are not (aren't)
he is (he's)	is he?	he is not (isn't)
she is (she's)	is she?	she is not (isn't)
it is (it's)	is it?	it is not (isn't)
we are (we're)	are we?	we are not (aren't)
you are (you're)	are you?	you are not (aren't)
they are (they're)	are they?	they are not (aren't)

I **'m** sixteen.
  Ich bin sechzehn Jahre alt.
'**Are** you English?' 'Yes, **I am**.' ('Yes, I'm?')
  „Sind Sie/Bist Du Engländer/in?" „Ja."
Her name's Ann.
  Sie heißt Ann.
'**Is** Susan an engineer?' 'Yes, she **is**.' ('Yes, she's')
  „Ist Susan Ingenieurin?" „Ja."
Are John and his father doctors?
  Sind John und sein Vater Ärzte?
'**You're** Canadian, **aren't** you? 'Yes, that's right.'
  „Sie sind/Du bist Kanadier/in, oder (nicht)?" „Jawohl!"

Vergangenheit		
I was	was I?	I was not (wasn't)
you were	were you?	you were not (weren't)
he/she/it was	was she *etc.*?	he *etc.* was not (wasn't)
we were	were we?	we were not (weren't)
you were	were you?	you were not (weren't)
they were	were they?	they were not (weren't)

'When you **were** a small child, **were** you happy?'
('When you a small child were …')
  „Warst Du glücklich, als Du ein kleines Kind warst?"
'Yes, I **was**.' 'No, I **wasn't**.' 'I **was** quite happy.'
  „Ja." „Nein." „Ich war ganz glücklich."
Were your parents poor?
  Waren Deine Eltern arm?
We **weren't** poor, but we **weren't** rich.
  Wir waren nicht arm, aber auch nicht reich.
Life **wasn't** hard, but white people **were not** always kind to me.
  Das Leben war nicht so schwer, aber die Weißen waren nicht immer freundlich zu mir.

Aussprache und Rhythmus

I was (/wəz/) **hun**gry.   **Yes**, I **was** (/wɒz/).
I **wasn't** (/wɒznt/) **hap**py.   **No**, I **wasn't** (/wɒznt/).
We were (/wə/) **poor**.   **Yes**, we **were** (/wɜː/).
We **weren't** (/wɜːnt/) **hap**py.   **No**, we **weren't** (/wɜːnt/).

Present Perfect und Zukunft

I **have been** a teacher for ten years.
(I am teacher for ten years.)
  Ich bin seit zehn Jahren Lehrer.
Where **has** John **been** all day? (Where is John been …)
  Wo ist John den ganzen Tag gewesen?
Tomorrow **will be** cold and wet.
  Morgen wird es kalt und naß sein.
I**'ll be** back home about six o'clock.
  Ich werde gegen sechs Uhr wieder zu Hause sein.

There is (es gibt)

there is (there's) there are (–)	is there? are there?	there is not (isn't) there are not (aren't)
there was there were	was there? were there?	there was not (wasn't) there were not (weren't)

There is/was wird für die Einzahl benutzt. *There are/were* wird für die Mehrzahl benutzt.

There is a swimming pool in the garden.
  Es gibt ein Schwimmbecken im Garten.
There isn't any tea left.
  Es gibt keinen Tee mehr.
There are three chairs in the kitchen.
  Es gibt drei Stühle in der Küche.
There aren't any glasses in the cupboard.
  Es gibt keine Gläser im Schrank.

Zu *some/any* siehe Seite 123

Rhythmus und Betonung

There's a **big** table in my **kit**chen. (/ðəz ə/)
Is there **any milk** in the **fridge**? (/ɪz ðər 'eni/)
Yes, there **is**. (/ðər 'ɪz/)
No, there **isn't**. (/ðər 'ɪznt/)
There **isn't** a **ga**rage. (/ðər 'ɪznt/)
There was some **cof**fee on the **table**. (/ðə wəz səm/)
There **wasn't** any **ice** in her **glass**. (/ðə 'wɒznt/)
There are **two chairs** in the **hall**. (/ðər ə/)
There are some **ap**ples **here**. (/ðər ə səm/)
Are there any **or**anges? (/'ɑː ðər 'eni/)
Yes, there **are**. (/ðər 'ɑː/)
No, there **aren't**. (/ðər 'ɑːnt/)
Yes, there's **one**. (/ðəz 'wʌn/)
There **aren't enough eggs**. (/ðər 'ɑːnt/)
There **weren't a**ny po**ta**toes. (/ðə 'wɜːnt/)

Have (got) (haben)

Have got (Zugehörigkeit, Beziehungen usw.)

Gegenwart		
I have (I've) got you have (you've) got he *etc.* has got (he's got) we have (we've) got you have (you've) got they have (they've) got	have I got? have you got? has she *etc.* got? have we got? have you got? have they got?	I have not (haven't) got you have not (haven't) got he *etc.* has not (hasn't) got we have not (haven't) got you have not (haven't) got they have not (haven't) got

You've **got** beautiful eyes.
   Sie haben/Du hast schöne Augen.
'**Have** you **got** any brothers or sisters?'
(Have got you …?)
   „Hast Du Geschwister?"
'Yes, I **have**. I've **got** two sisters.' 'No, I **haven't**.'
   „Ja. Ich habe zwei Schwestern." „Nein."
'**Has** your mother **got** any sisters?'
(Has got your mother …?)
   „Hat Deine Mutter Schwestern?"
'Yes, she **has**. She's **got** two.' 'No, she **hasn't**.'
   „Ja. Sie hat zwei Schwestern." „Nein."
We've **got** a new car.
   Wir haben ein neues Auto.
I **haven't got** any money.
   Ich habe kein Geld.

1. *Have got* und *have* haben die gleiche Bedeutung, wenn es um Zugehörigkeit und Beziehungen geht. Im alltäglichen britischen Englisch ist *have got* üblicher. Amerikaner benutzen häufiger *have* ohne *got*.
2. Bei *had* (Vergangenheit) wird *got* seltener benutzt. Frage und Verneinung in der Vergangenheit werden gewöhnlich mit *did* gebildet (siehe unten).
3. *Have* (**ohne** *got*) kann auch in der Bedeutung von *eat*, *take*, usw. (essen, nehmen, usw.) benutzt werden (siehe unten). Frage und Verneinung werden dann mit *do* gebildet.
4. *Have* wird auch benutzt, um die *Perfect*-Formen anderer Zeitwörter zu bilden (siehe unten). In diesem Fall werden weder *got* noch *do* verwendet.

Have (= eat, take, etc.)

Gegenwart		
I have you have he/she/it has we have you have they have	do I have? do you have? does he/she/it have? do we have? do you have? do they have?	I do not (don't) have you do not (don't) have he/she/it does not (doesn't) have we do not (don't) have you do not (don't) have they do not (don't) have

What time **do** you **have** lunch? (What time have you …)
   Wann essen Sie/ißt Du zu Mittag?
Have another sandwich!
   Nehmen Sie noch ein Sandwich!
Have a good holiday!
   Mach Dir einen schönen Urlaub./Schöne Ferien!

Die Vergangenheit von *have got* und *have*

I had you had he/she/it had we had you had they had	did I have? did you have? did he/she/it have? did we have? did you have? did they have?	I did not (didn't) have you did not (didn't) have he/she/it did not (didn't) have we did not (didn't) have you did not (didn't) have they did not (didn't) have

When she was a young girl she **had** long fair hair.
   Als sie ein junges Mädchen war, hatte sie lange, blonde Haare.
We **didn't have** a car when I was a child.
   Wir hatten kein Auto, als ich klein war.
We **had** a wonderful holiday last summer.
   Wir hatten sehr schöne Ferien im letzten Sommer.
What time **did** you **have** breakfast this morning?
   Wann hast Du heute morgen gefrühstückt?

Present Perfect und Zukunft

I **have had** a lot of problems this year.
   Ich habe dieses Jahr viele Probleme gehabt.
He **has** just **arrived**. (He is just arrived.)
   Er ist gerade angekommen.
I think I'**ll have** a bath now.
   Ich glaube, ich nehme jetzt ein Bad.
I don't know if we **will have** enough time.
   Ich weiß nicht, ob wir genügend Zeit haben werden.

Have und *be*

Es gibt Redewendungen, die im Deutschen mit *haben*, aber im Englischen mit *be* gebildet werden:

I'**m** hungry/thirsty.   (~~I have hunger/thirst.~~)
   Ich habe Hunger/Durst.
What colour **is** your car?   (~~What colour has …?~~)
   Welche Farbe hat Dein Auto?
What size **are** your shoes?
   Welche Größe haben Deine Schuhe?

Can (können)

Gegenwart
I/you/he/she/it/we/they can   (~~he/she/it cans~~)   can I/you/*etc.*?   (~~do I can?~~)   I/you/*etc.* cannot (can't)

Vergangenheit und Bedingungsform
I/you/*etc.* could   could I/you/*etc.*?   I/you/*etc.* could not (couldn't)

I **can** sing.   (~~I can to sing~~)
   Ich kann singen.
I **can't** dance.   (~~I don't can dance.~~)
   Ich kann nicht tanzen.
'**Can** you swim?' 'Yes, I **can**.' 'No, I **can't**.'
   „Kannst Du schwimmen?" „Ja." „Nein."
'Hans **can** dance, but Heidi **can't**.'   (~~… Heidi can't it.~~)
   Hans kann tanzen, aber Heidi nicht.
Sorry, I **can't** see you tomorrow.
   Leider kann ich Dich morgen nicht treffen.

I **could** swim very well when I was younger.
   Ich konnte sehr gut schwimmen, als ich jünger war.
I **couldn't** find my keys.
   Ich konnte meine Schlüssel nicht finden.
Could I speak to Alice?
   Könnte ich bitte (mit) Alice sprechen?
Could you speak more slowly, please?
   Könntest Du bitte langsamer sprechen?

Aussprache, Rhythmus und Betonung

I can (/kən/) **swim**, but I **can't** (/kɑːnt/) **dance**.
Yes, I **can** (/kæn/).

Normale Zeitwörter: Gegenwartsform

Einfache Gegenwart

I play	do I play?	I do not (don't) play
you play	do you play?	you do not (don't) play
he/she/it plays	does he *etc.* play?	she *etc.* does not (doesn't) play
we play	do we play?	we do not (don't) play
you play	do you play?	you do not (don't) play
they play	do they play?	they do not (don't) play

Do spielt hier die Rolle eines Hilfszeitworts bei der Bildung von Fragen, Verneinung und Kurzantworten. Es hat nichts mit dem normalen Zeitwort *do* (= *tun/machen*) zu tun.

What do you do when the weather is bad?
(~~What do you when …~~)
   Was tust Du bei schlechtem Wetter?
'I live in Curzon Street.' 'Oh? I do, too.'
   „Ich wohne in der Curzon Street." „Aha? Ich auch."
'Do you like orange juice?' 'Yes, I do.'
(~~'Like you orange juice?'~~) (~~'Yes, I like.'~~)
   „Mögen Sie/Magst Du Orangensaft?" „Ja."

'What time does Karen get up?' 'Half past seven.'
   „Wann steht Karen morgens auf?" „Um halb acht."
'Does she go to work by car?'
'Yes, she does.' 'No, she doesn't.'
   „Fährt sie mit dem Auto zur Arbeit?" „Ja." „Nein."
'Do Sam and Virginia live near you?' 'No, they don't.'
   „Wohnen Sam und Virginia in Deiner Nähe?" „Nein."

Die Aussprache der *he/she/it*-Formen

1. /z/ nach Selbstlauten und den meisten stimmhaften Mitlauten (/b/, /d/, /g/, /v/, /ð/, /l/, /m/, /n/, /ŋ/)

   goes /gəʊz/   sees /si:z/   stands /stændz/   lives /lɪvz/
   tells /telz/   runs /rʌnz/

2. /s/ nach den meisten stimmlosen Mitlauten (/p/, /t/, /k/,
   /f/, /θ/)

   stops /stɒps/   starts /stɑːts/   looks /lʊks/

3. /ɪz/ nach /s/, /z/, /ʃ/, /ʒ/, /tʃ/, /dʒ/

   presses /ˈpresɪz/   uses /ˈjuːzɪz/   pushes /ˈpʊʃɪz/
   watches /ˈwɒtʃɪz/

Betonung

Do you (/dju/) **like o**range **juice?**
Yes, I **do.**   **No,** I **don't.**
What time does (/dəz/) **Karen get up?**
Does (/dəz, dʌz/) she **have break**fast?
Yes, she **does** (/dʌz/).   **No,** she **doesn't** (/ˈdʌznt/).

Rechtschreibung der *he/she/it*-Formen

Die meisten Zeitwörter:	get ⟶ gets
	play ⟶ plays
	live ⟶ lives
Zeitwörter, die auf einen Mitlaut + -*y* enden:	try ⟶ tries
	marry ⟶ marries
Zeitwörter, die auf -*ch*, -*sh* oder -*s* enden:	watch ⟶ watches
	wash ⟶ washes
	pass ⟶ passes
Unregelmäßige Formen:	have ⟶ has
	do ⟶ does
	go ⟶ goes

Verlaufsform der Gegenwart

I am ('m) eating	am I eating?	I am ('m) not eating
you are ('re) eating	are you eating?	you are not (aren't) eating
he/she/it is ('s) eating	is he *etc.* eating?	she *etc.* is not (isn't) eating
we are ('re) eating	are we eating?	we are not (aren't) eating
you are ('re) eating	are you eating?	you are not (aren't) eating
they are ('re) eating	are they eating?	they are not (aren't) eating

I'm looking for a blue sweater.
   Ich suche einen blauen Pullover.
Some people **are dancing.**
   Einige Leute tanzen (gerade).
What **is** the woman in the red dress **doing?**
(~~What is doing the woman …~~)
   Was macht die Frau im roten Kleid (gerade)?
'**Are** George and Tom **wearing** their blue jackets?
('~~Are wearing George and Tom …~~)
   „Tragen George und Tom ihre blauen Jacken?"
'Yes, they **are**.'   'No, they **aren't**.'
   „Ja."   „Nein."
I'm not working today.
   Ich arbeite heute nicht.

Rechtschreibung der -*ing*-Formen

Die meisten Zeitwörter:	sing ⟶ sing**ing**
	eat ⟶ eat**ing**
Zeitwörter, die auf -*e* enden:	make ⟶ mak**ing** (~~makeing~~)
	write ⟶ writ**ing**
Kurze Zeitwörter, die auf einen Selbstlaut + einen Mitlaut enden:	stop ⟶ sto**pping**
	sit ⟶ si**tting**
	run ⟶ ru**nning**
Zeitwörter, die auf -*ie* enden:	lie ⟶ **lying**

Der Unterschied zwischen einfacher Gegenwart und der Verlaufsform

Die deutsche Gegenwartsform drückt eine Reihe von verschiedenen Bedeutungen aus,
die im Englischen streng aufgeteilt werden zwischen einfacher Gegenwart und der Verlaufsform:

1. Die einfache Gegenwart wird benutzt:
– um allgemeingültige Sachverhalte auszudrücken

The earth **goes** round the sun.
(The earth is going …)
   Die Erde dreht sich um die Sonne.
Water **boils** at 100 degrees Celsius.
(Water is boiling at …)
   Wasser kocht bei 100 Grad.
I **understand** French.
   Ich verstehe Französisch.

– um regelmäßige oder wiederholte Handlungen auszudrücken, besonders mit Umstandswörtern der Häufigkeit wie *often, usually, sometimes, etc.* (oft, normalerweise, manchmal, usw.)

I usually **study** from five to seven o'clock.
(I'm usually studying …)
   Ich lerne gewöhnlich von fünf bis sieben Uhr.
Helen often **wears** red.
(Helen is often wearing …)
   Helen trägt oft rot.

2. Die Verlaufsform der Gegenwart wird benutzt:
– um Handlungen auszudrücken, die jetzt oder nur vorübergehend stattfinden

The water**'s boiling**. I'll make coffee.
(The water boils.)
   Das Wasser kocht jetzt. Ich mache den Kaffee.
I'm studying very hard just now.
(I study very hard just now.)
   Ich lerne sehr fleißig zur Zeit.
Look. Helen**'s wearing** a lovely red dress.
(Helen wears …)
   Schau! Helen trägt ein schönes, rotes Kleid.

– um für die Zukunft fest geplante Handlungen auszudrücken (siehe Seite 119)

We**'re going** to Ann and Peter's for Christmas.
(We go …)
   Weihnachten fahren wir zu Ann und Peter.
What **are** you **doing** tomorrow?
(What do you do tomorrow?)
   Was machst Du morgen?

Die einfache Gegenwart und die Verlaufsform beim Erzählen

Geschichten können im Englischen, ebenso wie im Deutschen, in der Gegenwart erzählt werden. Auch hier muß auf den Unterschied zwischen einfacher Gegenwart und der Verlaufsform geachtet werden.

One day, Anna **is walking** in the Tuileries when a man **stops** her. It **is** Boris. He **tells** her …
   Eines Tages, als Anna in den Tuilerien spazierengeht, wird sie von einem Mann angehalten. Es ist Boris. Er erzählt ihr, …

Normale Zeitwörter: Vergangenheitsformen

Die einfache Vergangenheit

I stopped	did I stop?	I did not (didn't) stop
you stopped	did you stop?	you did not (didn't) stop
he/she/it stopped	did she *etc.* stop?	he *etc.* did not (didn't) stop
we stopped	did we stop?	we did not (didn't) stop
you stopped	did you stop?	you did not (didn't) stop
they stopped	did they stop?	they did not (didn't) stop

Did you **go** to the cinema last Friday?
   Bist Du letzten Freitag ins Kino gegangen?
I **didn't watch** television last night. (I watched not …)
   Ich habe gestern abend nicht ferngesehen.
When Angela was younger she **hated** school.
   Angela haßte die Schule als sie jünger war.
'**Did** your family **have** a television when you were a child?'
('Had your family …?')
   „Hattet Ihr zu Hause einen Fernseher als Du ein Kind warst?"
'No, we **didn't**.'
   „Nein."

'**Did** you **like** school when you were a child?'
   „Bist Du als Kind gerne zur Schule gegangen?"
'Yes, I **did**.' ('Yes, I liked.')
   „Ja."
I **didn't like** cheese when I was a small child, but I do now.
(I liked not cheese …) (I not liked cheese …)
(I didn't liked …)
   Als Kind habe ich nicht gerne Käse gegessen, aber jetzt schon.

Rechtschreibung der regelmäßigen Vergangenheitsformen

Die meisten regelmäßigen Zeitwörter:	work ⟶ work**ed**
	start ⟶ start**ed**
	wait ⟶ wait**ed**
	play ⟶ play**ed**
Zeitwörter, die auf -*e* enden:	hate ⟶ hat**ed**
	like ⟶ lik**ed**
Kurze Zeitwörter, die auf einen Selbstlaut + einen Mitlaut enden:	st**op** ⟶ st**opped**
	sh**op** ⟶ sh**opped**
	fit ⟶ fi**tted**
Zeitwörter, die auf Mitlaut + -*y* enden:	stu**dy** ⟶ stu**died**
	hurry ⟶ hur**ried**

Aussprache der regelmäßigen Vergangenheitsformen

1. /d/ nach Selbstlauten und stimmhaften Mitlauten (/b/, /g/, /v/, /ð/, /l/, /z/, /ʒ/, /dʒ/, /m/, /n/, /ŋ/)

   agreed /əˈgriːd/   played /pleɪd/   lived /lɪvd/
   pulled /pʊld/   used /juːzd/

2. /t/ nach /p/, /k/, /f/, /θ/, /s/, /ʃ/, /tʃ/

   stopped /stɒpt/   worked /wɜːkt/   watched /wɒtʃt/

3. /ɪd/ nach /t/ und /d/

   started /ˈstɑːtɪd/   decided /dɪˈsaɪdɪd/

Das *Present Perfect*

(*have* + dritte Form)		
I have ('ve) seen	have I seen?	I have not (haven't) seen
you have ('ve) seen	have you seen?	you have not (haven't) seen
he/she/it has ('s) seen	has he *etc.* seen?	she *etc.* has not (hasn't) seen
we have ('ve) seen	have we seen?	we have not (haven't) seen
you have ('ve) seen	have you seen?	you have not (haven't) seen
they have ('ve) seen	have they seen?	they have not (haven't) seen

Alle englischen Zeitwörter bilden das *Present Perfect* mit *have/has* + dritte Form: **I have** seen him.   Ich **habe** ihn gesehen.
They have arrived.   Sie **sind** angekommen.

'**Have** you ever **been** to Africa?' 'Yes, I **have**.'
   „Bist du schon einmal in Afrika gewesen?"   „Ja."
   „Warst du schon einmal in Afrika?"   „Ja."
'**Have** you **seen** Carmen before?' 'No, I **haven't**.'
   „Hast du *Carmen* schon einmal gesehen?"   „Nein."
I**'ve** never **learnt** to drive.
   Ich habe nie Auto fahren gelernt.
I**'ve changed** my job three times this year.
   Ich habe meine Arbeitsstelle in diesem Jahr dreimal gewechselt.
How long **have** you **lived** in this town?
(How long do you live in this town?)
   Wie lange wohnst du schon in dieser Stadt?

How long **have** you **known** Maria?
(How long do you know Maria?)
   Wie lange kennst du Maria schon?
I**'ve known** her since 1986.   (I know her since 1986.)
   Ich kenne sie seit 1986.
I**'ve been** in this class for three weeks.
(I am in this class for three weeks.)
(I've been in this class since three weeks.)
   Ich bin seit drei Wochen in dieser Klasse.
How long **have** you **been** learning English?
(How long are you learning English?)
   Wie lange lernst du schon English?

Since und *for*

Das Englische hat für das deutsche *seit* zwei Wörter:
– *seit* + Anfangspunkt des Zeitraums = *since*

I've had this car **since 1986**.
   Ich habe dieses Auto seit 1986.
I've been learning English **since I was nine**.
   Ich lerne seit meinem neunten Lebensjahr Englisch.
I haven't seen him **since last Friday**.
   Ich habe ihn seit letztem Freitag nicht mehr gesehen.

– *seit* + Dauer des Zeitraums = *for*

I've had this car **for five years**.
   Ich habe dieses Auto seit fünf Jahren.
I've been learning English **for two months**.
   Ich lerne seit zwei Monaten English.
I haven't seen him **for a long time**.
   Ich habe ihn seit langem nicht mehr gesehen.

Der Unterschied zwischen einfacher Vergangenheit und *Present Perfect*

Im Deutschen ist der Unterschied zwischen den zwei Vergangenheitsformen, der einfachen und der zusammengesetzten Form, meistens nur stilistisch. Im Englischen aber besteht ein strenger Bedeutungsunterschied zwischen einfacher Vergangenheit und *Present Perfect*.

1. Das *Present Perfect* wird benutzt:
   - wenn von einem noch nicht abgeschlossenen Zeitraum die Rede ist, z. B. *this week/month/year, since …* (diese Woche/diesen Monat/dieses Jahr/seit + Anfangspunkt des Zeitraums)
   - wenn von „irgendwann bis jetzt" die Rede ist, z. B. *ever, never, before* (jemals, noch nie, schon einmal)

I've changed my job three times **this year**.
   Ich habe meine Arbeitsstelle in diesem Jahr dreimal gewechselt.
Have you **ever been** to America?
   Bist du schon einmal in Amerika gewesen?
   Warst du schon einmal in Amerika?
She **has never learnt** to drive.
   Sie hat nie Auto fahren gelernt.
I've never wanted to live anywhere else.
   Ich wollte noch nie irgendwo anders wohnen.
   Ich habe noch nie irgendwo anders wohnen wollen.

2. Die einfache Vergangenheit wird benutzt:
   - wenn von einem abgeschlossenen Zeitraum die Rede ist, z. B. mit *ago, yesterday, last week/month/year,* etc. (vor …, gestern, letzte Woche/letzten Monat/letztes Jahr, usw.) *then* (damals), *when* (als)

I **changed** my job **last week**.
(I have changed my job last week.)
   Ich habe letzte Woche meine Arbeitsstelle gewechselt.
I **saw** *Carmen* **three years ago**.
(I have seen *Carmen* three years ago.)
(… for three years.)   (… before three years.)
   Ich habe *Carmen* vor drei Jahren gesehen.
Did you **go** to California **last summer**?
(Have you been/gone to California last summer?)
   Bist du im letzten Sommer nach Kalifornien gefahren?
She **learnt** to fly **when** she was eighteen.
(She has learnt to fly when she was eighteen.)
   Sie hat das Fliegen gelernt, als sie 18 Jahre alt war.

Der Unterschied zwischen *Present Perfect* und Gegenwart

Um auszudrücken, *wie lange (how long)* eine Handlung oder ein Vorgang bereits andauert, wird im Englischen das *Present Perfect* benutzt. Im Deutschen steht die Gegenwart.

Beispiele: I **have known** her **since 1980**.
   (I know her since 1980.)
      Ich kenne sie seit 1980.
   We **have lived** here **for ten years**.
   (We live here for ten years.)
      Wir wohnen seit zehn Jahren hier.
   She**'s been** in this class **for three weeks**.
   (She is in this class for three weeks.)
      Sie ist seit drei Wochen in diesem Kurs.

Grundform, Vergangenheit und dritte Form

	Grundform	Vergangenheit	dritte Form
regelmäßige Zeitwörter	work	worked	worked
	play	played	played
	live	lived	lived
	stop	stopped	stopped
	try	tried	tried
	etc.		
unregelmäßige Zeitwörter	be	was/were	been
	come	came	come
	go	went	been/gone
	know	knew	known
	learn	learnt	learnt
	see	saw	seen

(Eine vollständige Liste der unregelmäßigen Zeitwörter, die im *New Cambridge English Course 1* vorkommen, finden Sie im *Student's Book,* Seite 136.)

Wie man Zukünftiges beschreibt

Wir sprechen über die Zukunft, um Pläne, Absichten, Erwartungen, Voraussagen usw. auszudrücken.
Das Deutsche hat dafür zwei Formen zur Auswahl: Gegenwart oder Zukunft.
Im Englischen wird je nach Sprechabsicht zwischen mehreren Formen unterschieden.

Verlaufsform der Gegenwart (um Pläne/Verabredungen auszudrücken)

Are you **doing** anything this evening?
  Hast Du heute abend etwas vor?
I'm working on Thursday.   (I work on Thursday)
(I will work …)
  Ich werde am Donnerstag arbeiten.

We're **leaving** on Monday.
  Wir fahren am Montag.
Jane's Granny **is** probably **coming** on Thursday.
(Jane's Granny probably comes …)
  Janes Großmutter wird wahrscheinlich am Donnerstag
  kommen.

Be going + Grundform
(um Pläne/Absichten auszudrücken; um Voraussagen zu treffen)

Pläne

I'm **going to learn** Chinese.
  Ich habe vor, Chinesisch zu lernen.
What **are you going to do** next year?
  Was machst Du im nächsten Jahr?
This **is going to be** the kitchen.
  Dies wird die Küche sein.

Voraussagen

It's **going to rain**.
  Es wird gleich regnen.
The plane's **going to crash**.
  Das Flugzeug wird gleich abstürzen.
She's **going to have** a baby.
  Sie bekommt ein Kind.
  (Sie ist schwanger.)

Will (um Voraussagen zu treffen)

I/you/he/*etc.* will ('ll) go (I will to go   he wills go)
will I/*etc.* go? (do I will go?)
I/*etc.* will not (won't) go

I think Manchester **will beat** Liverpool 2 – 0.
  Ich glaube, Manchester wird Liverpool 2:0 schlagen.
Something very strange **will happen** next Thursday.
(… will be happen …)
  Etwas sehr Seltsames wird am nächsten Donnerstag
  geschehen.
Tomorrow **will be** warm and sunny.
  Morgen wird es warm und sonnig sein.
If you don't eat you**'ll die**.
  Wenn Du nicht ißt, stirbst Du.
Are you sure you**'ll be** all right?
  Bist Du sicher, daß Du zurechtkommst?

There will be und *it will be*

There will be + Hauptwort

There will be **snow**.
  Es wird Schnee geben.
There will be **a meeting** at eight o'clock this evening.
  Heute abend um acht findet ein Treffen statt.

It will be + Eigenschaftswort

It will be **cold**.
  Es wird kalt sein.
It won't be very **interesting**.
  Es wird nicht sehr interessant sein.

Die Unterschiede zwischen Verlaufsform der Gegenwart, *going to* und *will*

1. Pläne:
Die Verlaufsform der Gegenwart und *going to* werden
beide benutzt, um Pläne auszudrücken. Die Verlaufsform der Gegenwart wird besonders in Verbindung mit
Orts- und Zeitangaben benutzt. Vergleiche:

I'm going to travel round the world.
  Ich habe vor, eine Weltreise zu machen.
I'm travelling to France next week.
  Ich fahre nächste Woche nach Frankreich.

2. Voraussagen:
Going to und *will* werden beide benutzt, um Zukünfti-
ges vorauszusagen. *Going to* wird bevorzugt, wenn man
jetzt schon deutlich erkennen kann, was gleich oder
demnächst geschehen wird. Vergleiche:

Look! It's **going to rain**.
  Schau? Es wird gleich regnen.
Perhaps it **will snow** tomorrow.
  Vielleicht wird es morgen schneien.
She's **going to have** a baby.
  Sie bekommt ein Kind.
Do you think the baby **will have** blue eyes?
  Glaubst Du, das Kind wird blaue Augen haben?

Befehlsform, *-ing*-Form und Grundform

Die Befehlsform

Beispiele: *run; tell; don't run; don't tell*

Die Befehlsform im Englischen ist identisch mit der Grundform des Zeitworts (ohne *to*). Es gibt für jedes Zeitwort nur eine Befehlsform, ganz gleich, wer angesprochen wird. Die negative Form wird mit *don't* gebildet.

Run early in the morning – it's better.
  Laufen Sie/Laufe/Lauft früh am Morgen – es ist besser!
Come at seven o'clock.
  Komme um sieben Uhr!
Always wear comfortable clothing. (~~Wear always …~~)
  Tragen Sie immer bequeme Kleidung!
Never run in fog. (~~Run never …~~)
  Laufe nie im Nebel!
Don't run if you've got a cold.
  Laufen Sie nicht, wenn Sie erkältet sind!
Don't tell Carola.
  Sage es nicht der Carola!

Die *-ing*-Form

Beispiele: *seeing; going*

Die *-ing*-Form wird benutzt:
– nach bestimmten Zeitwörtern (z. B.: *like, love, hate*)

I **like speaking** French.
  Ich spreche gerne Französisch.
I **love going** to the theatre.
  Ich gehe sehr gerne ins Theater.

– für die Bildung der Verlaufsform

'What are you **doing**?' 'I'm **writing** letters.'
  „Was machst Du gerade?" „Ich schreibe Briefe."

– nach allen Verhältniswörtern

Thank you **for coming**.
  Danke, daß Du gekommen bist.
She's good **at swimming**.
  Sie ist eine gute Schwimmerin.

Die Grundform mit *to*

Beispiele: *to see; to go*

Die Grundform mit *to* wird benutzt:
– nach bestimmten Zeitwörtern (z. B.: *hope, want, have, would like*)

I **hope to see** you soon.
  Ich hoffe, Dich bald zu sehen.
I **don't want to go** home.
  Ich will nicht nach Hause gehen.
You **have to change** at Coventry.
  Du mußt in Coventry umsteigen.
Would you **like to dance**?
  Möchtest Du tanzen?

– nach *something, anything, nothing*

Would you like **something to eat**?
  Möchten Sie etwas zu essen haben?
Have you got **anything to drink**?
  Haben Sie etwas zu trinken?
There's **nothing to do**.
  Es gibt nichts zu tun.

– um den Zweck einer Handlung auszudrücken (deutsch: *um … zu*)

'Why did you come here?' '**To see** you.'
(~~For to see …~~) (~~For seeing …~~)
  „Warum bist Du hierher gekommen?"
  „Um Dich zu sehen."
You go to a supermarket **to buy** food.
  Man geht zum Supermarkt, um Lebensmittel zu kaufen.

Die Grundform ohne *to*

Beispiele: *see; go*

Die Grundform ohne *to* wird benutzt:
– nach den besonderen Zeitwörtern *can, could, will, would* und *do*

I **can speak** German. (~~I can to speak …~~)
  Ich kann Deutsch sprechen.
Could you **speak** more slowly?
  Könnten Sie etwas langsamer sprechen?
It **will rain** tomorrow.
  Es wird morgen regnen.
What **would** you **like**?
  Was hätten Sie gerne?
Does he **smoke**?
  Raucht er?
Don't stop.
  Höre nicht auf!

– nach *Let's*

Let's all **go** and see Ann.
  Laßt uns alle Ann besuchen gehen!

Hauptwörter und Artikel

Die Mehrzahl des Hauptworts

Die meisten Hauptwörter:	boy ⟶ boys
	girl ⟶ girls
	name ⟶ names
	parent ⟶ parents
Hauptwörter, die auf einem Mitlaut + -y enden:	family ⟶ families
	secretary ⟶ secretaries
Hauptwörter, die auf -ch, -sh, -s oder -x enden:	watch ⟶ watches
	crash ⟶ crashes
	address ⟶ addresses
	six ⟶ sixes
Unregelmäßige Mehrzahlformen:	child ⟶ children
	man ⟶ men
	woman ⟶ women
	life ⟶ lives
	wife ⟶ wives
	knife ⟶ knives
	foot ⟶ feet
	potato ⟶ potatoes
	tomato ⟶ tomatoes

Die Aussprache des Mehrzahl-*s*

1. /z/ nach Selbstlauten und den meisten stimmhaften Mitlauten (/b/, /d/, /g/, /v/, /ð/, /l/, /m/, /n/, /ŋ/)

   days /deɪz/   trees /triːz/   heads /hedz/
   wives /waɪvz/   miles /maɪlz/   pens /penz/

2. /s/ nach den meisten stimmlosen Mitlauten (/p/, /t/, /k/, /f/, /θ/)

   cups /kʌps/   plates /pleɪts/   books /bʊks/

3. /ɪz/ nach /s/, /z/, /ʃ/, /ʒ/, /tʃ/, /dʒ/

   buses /ˈbʌsɪz/   noses /ˈnəʊzɪz/   watches /ˈwɒtʃɪz/

4. **Ausnahme:** house /haʊs/ ⟶ houses /ˈhaʊzɪz/

Der Artikel

A und *an*; die Aussprache von *the*

An wird vor einem Selbstlaut (*a, e, i, o, u*) benutzt.

an artist   **an** engineer   **an** apple   **an** orange

A wird vor einem Mitlaut benutzt.

a doctor   **a** housewife   **a** banana   **a** tomato

Vor einem Selbstlaut wird *the* /ði/ ausgesprochen.

the egg /ði ˈeg/   the Italians /ði ɪˈtælɪənz/

Vor einem Mitlaut wird *the* /ðə/ ausgesprochen.

the book /ðə ˈbʊk/   the problem /ðə ˈprɒbləm/

Vorsicht! Es geht bei diesen Regeln um die **Aussprache** am Anfang des nachfolgenden Wortes, nicht notwendigerweise um den Anfangsbuchstaben. Das ist wichtig bei Wörtern, die mit den Buchstaben *h* und *u* anfangen und bei Abkürzungen.

a hospital   *ABER:* **an** hour /ən ˈaʊə/
an umbrella *ABER:* **a** uniform /ə ˈjuːnɪfɔːm/
the underground /ði ˈʌndəgraʊnd/ **aber** the university /ðə juːnəˈvɜːsəti/
the USA /ðə juːesˈeɪ/ the FBI /ði ef biːˈaɪ/

Der Gebrauch des Artikels

In der Regel werden *a/an* (*ein, eine,* usw.) und *the* (*der, die, das,* usw.) genauso angewendet wie im Deutschen. Es bestehen jedoch die folgenden Unterschiede:
Im Englischen steht *a/an* bei der Angabe des Berufs oder der gesellschaftlichen Stellung einer Person.

I'm **a student.**   (I'm student.)
   Ich bin Student.
She's **a millionaire.** (She's millionaire.)
   Sie ist Millionärin.
Are you **a doctor?** (Are you doctor?)
   Sind Sie Arzt?
He's **an engineer.** (He's engineer.)
   Er ist Ingenieur.

Weiterhin wird *a/an* in der Bedeutung von „pro" bzw. „je" bei Preis- und Maßangaben benutzt.

eighty pence **a** kilo   achtzig Pence pro/je Kilo
fifty kilometres **an** hour   fünfzig Kilometer pro Stunde

Wenn Wörter in einem sehr allgemeinen Sinne verwendet werden (z. B. *die Preise im großen und ganzen, alle Arten von Autos, das Leben im allgemeinen,* usw.), wird *the* nicht benutzt.

Prices are going up.   (The prices …)   Die Preise steigen.
Cars are very expensive these days.   (The cars …)
   (Die) Autos sind heutzutage sehr teuer.
Love is a beautiful thing.   (The love …)
   Die Liebe ist etwas Schönes.
That's **life.**   (… the life.)   So ist das Leben.

Bei Eigennamen wird *the* nie benutzt.

I'm Paul.   (I'm the Paul.)   Ich bin der Paul.
Ask Frank!   (Ask the Frank!)   Frage den Frank!

Bei der Bezeichnung von Sprachen wird *a* nie benutzt.

He speaks very good English.
   Er spricht ein sehr gutes Englisch.

Wortverbindungen, bei denen der Artikel fehlt:

in bed (~~in the bed~~)	im Bett
go to school (~~go to the school~~)	zur Schule gehen
at school (~~at the school~~)	in der Schule
at work (~~at the work~~)	bei der Arbeit
by train/bus/plane (~~by the train~~)	mit dem Zug/Bus/Flugzeug

---

Probleme bei zählbaren und nichtzählbaren Hauptwörtern, Einzahl- und Mehrzahlformen

Im Gegensatz zum Deutschen sind folgende Wörter im Englischen nichtzählbar (d. h. sie bilden keine Mehrzahlform und werden ohne *a/an* benutzt): *advice, information, hair, bread, news, furniture* und *toothache. Headache* hingegen ist zählbar.

Could you give me **some information**?
(~~… an information … some informations~~)
  Können Sie mir einige Informationen geben?
I'd like to give you **some advice**. (~~… an advice~~)
  Ich möchte Ihnen einen Rat geben.
She has long black **hair**. (~~… long black hairs~~)
  Sie hat lange, schwarze Haare.
Here **is** the **news**. (~~… are the news~~)
  Hier sind die Nachrichten.
Old English **furniture** is expensive.
  Alte englische Möbel sind teuer.
I've got **toothache**.
  Ich habe Zahnschmerzen.
ABER: I've got **a headache**.
  Ich habe Kopfschmerzen.

Die folgenden Wörter sind Mehrzahlformen im Englischen: *Trousers (eine Hose), jeans (eine Jeans), pyjamas (ein Schlafanzug), pants (ein Slip), glasses (eine Brille)* und *stairs (eine Treppe).*

Those trousers are too big for you.
  Diese Hose ist zu groß für Dich.
I need **some** new jeans. (~~… a new jeans~~)
  Ich brauche eine neue Jeans.
I wear **glasses** for reading.
  Ich trage eine Brille beim Lesen.
These **stairs** are dangerous. (~~This stair is…~~)
  Diese Treppe ist gefährlich.

Fürwörter, Begleitwörter und Fragewörter

Das Fürwort als Satzgegenstand oder als Ergänzung und das besitzanzeigende Fürwort

Satzgegenstand	Ergänzung	besitzanzeigendes Fürwort
I	me	my
you	you	your
he	him	his
she	her	her
it	it	its
we	us	our
you	you	your
they	them	their

He likes **me**, but **I** don't like **him**.
  Er mag mich, aber ich mag ihn nicht.
They've invited **us** to a party.
  Sie haben uns zu einer Party eingeladen.
Could **you** give **me** some water?
  Könntest Du mir etwas Wasser geben?
That's **my** bicycle.
  Das ist mein Fahrrad.
Ann and **her** husband work in Stoke.
  Ann und ihr Mann arbeiten in Stoke.
John and **his** wife both play tennis.
  John und seine Frau spielen alle beide Tennis.

Besitzanzeigendes 's

Zugehörigkeit wird im Englischen vorwiegend durch das besitzanzeigende -'s ausgedrückt. Die Formulierung *of* + Hauptwort (*from* + Hauptwort) wird seltener benutzt.

Sam is **Judy's** boyfriend.   (... the boyfriend from Judy.)
  Sam ist Judys Freund.   Sam ist der Freund von Judy.
Susan's surname is Perkins.
(The surname from Susan ...)   (... of Susan ...)
  Susans Familienname ist Perkins.
That's my **parents'** house.
(... the house from my parents.)
  Da steht das Haus meiner Eltern.

Aussprache des besitzanzeigenden 's

Judy's   Mary's   Joe's   Harry's   (/z/)
Sam's   Bob's   Anne's   Susan's   (/z/)
Eric's   Margaret's   Jeff's   Kate's   (/s/)
Alice's   Joyce's   George's   Des's   (/ɪz/)

Some, any und no

Some und any entsprechen dem deutschen *etwas, einige*.
No entspricht dem deutschen *kein/e/er*.

Some und any

Some wird gewöhnlich in bejahten Aussagesätzen, *any* in Fragen und verneinten Aussagesätzen benutzt. Im Deutschen wird oft auf ein solches Begleitwort verzichtet.

bejahte Aussagesätze	Fragen	verneinte Aussagesätze
There's **some** bread.	Is there **any** bread?	There isn't **any** bread.
I've got **some** eggs.	Have you got **any** eggs?	I haven't got **any** eggs.

Some in Fragen

Some wird gewöhnlich in Fragen benutzt, wenn wir um etwas bitten oder etwas anbieten.

Would you like **some** coffee?
  Möchtest Du Kaffee?
Could you lend **me** some sugar?
  Könnten Sie mir etwas Zucker leihen?

No (= not any)

No bzw. *not ... any* entsprechen dem deutschen *kein, keine*.

I'm sorry, there's **no more** roast beef.   (= ... there isn't any more ...)
  Leider gibt es kein Roastbeef mehr.

Somebody, anything, etc.

somebody	anybody	everybody	nobody
something	anything	everything	nothing
somewhere	anywhere	everywhere	nowhere

Somebody telephoned when you were out.
  Jemand hat angerufen, als Du weg warst.
Would you like **something** to drink?
  Möchtest Du etwas zu trinken haben?
Have you got **anything** to read?
  Hast Du etwas zu lesen?
Have you seen my glasses **anywhere**?
  Hast Du irgendwo meine Brille gesehen?
I didn't understand **anything**.
  Ich habe nichts verstanden.
Everybody was late.
  Alle waren verspätet.
She gave **everything** to her children.
  Sie hat alles ihren Kindern gegeben.
'What are you doing?'   **'Nothing.'**
  „Was machst Du?"   „Nichts."

Everybody wird als **Einzahl** verwendet.

Everybody knows him.
  Alle kennen ihn.   Jeder kennt ihn.

This, that, these und those

This cheese is terrible.
These tomatoes are very nice.
How much is **that** sweater over there?
I like **those** ear-rings that she's wearing.

Mengen- und Maßangaben bei zählbaren und nichtzählbaren Hauptwörtern

bei nichtzählbaren Hauptwörtern	bei der Mehrzahlform zählbarer Hauptwörter
(not) much	(not) many
how much?	how many?
too much	too many
more	more
enough	enough
a lot of	a lot of

There isn't **much** rain here in the summer.
   Es gibt hier nicht viel Regen im Sommer.
Are there **many** hotels in the town?
(Are there much hotels …?)
   Gibt es viele Hotels in der Stadt?
How much money do you want?
   Wieviel Geld möchten Sie?
How many states are there in the USA?
(How much states …?)
   Wie viele Staaten gibt es in den USA?
I've got **too much** work.
   Ich habe zu viel Arbeit.
You've given me **too many** chips. (… too much chips.)
   Du hast mir zu viele Pommes frites gegeben.
Could I have a little **more** bread?
   Könnte ich noch ein wenig Brot bekommen?
I'm afraid there are no **more** potatoes.
   Leider gibt es keine Kartoffeln mehr.
Have you got **enough** bread?
   Hast Du genug Brot?
There aren't **enough** buses from our village.
   Es fahren nicht genug Busse von unserem Dorf aus.
The children are making **a lot of** noise.
   Die Kinder machen viel Lärm.
She's got **a lot of** problems.
   Sie hat viele Probleme.

Diese Wörter und Ausdrücke können auch ohne Hauptwörter stehen.

How much does it cost?
   Wieviel kostet das?
'Do you like her?' 'Not **much**.'
   „Magst Du sie?" ' „Nicht besonders."
I think about you **a lot**. (… a lot of.) (… much.)
   Ich denke viel an Dich.

Much und *many* werden vorwiegend in Fragen und verneinten Aussagesätzen benutzt. In bejahten Aussagesätzen wird eher *a lot (of)* verwendet. Vergleiche:

Have you got **many** friends?
   Hast Du viele Freunde?
I have**n't** got **many** friends.
   Ich habe nicht viele Freunde.
She's got **a lot of** friends.
   Sie hat viele Freunde.

Das Fragewort

Vorsicht! Die englischen Fragewörter *who* und *where* lassen sich leicht mit ihren deutschen „falschen Freunden" verwechseln:
   Who = Wer (Wo)
   Where = Wo (Wer)

Who

'**Who**'s that?' 'It's my brother.'
   „Wer ist das?" „Es ist mein Bruder."
Who wrote *Gone with the wind*? (Who did write …?)
   Wer hat *Vom Winde verweht* geschrieben?
Who are you looking at? (Who you are …?)
   Wen schaust Du an?

124

Where

'**Where**'s my pen?'   'Under your book.'
  „Wo ist mein Stift?"   „Unter Deinem Buch."
'**Where** are you from?'   'Egypt.'
  „Wo kommst Du her?"   „Aus Ägypten."
Where was Jesus Christ born?   (~~Where was born …?~~)
  Wo ist Jesus Christus geboren worden?

Which

'**Which** platform for the 3.49 train?'   'Platform 6.'
  „Auf welchem Gleis fährt der Zug um 3.49 Uhr ab?"
  „Gleis 6."
Which of these singers was not a member of the Beatles?
  Welcher dieser Sänger war nicht bei den Beatles?

What

'**What**'s your name?'   'Miriam Jackson.'
  „Wie heißen Sie?"   „Miriam Jackson."
What does *coat* mean?   (~~What means *coat*?~~)
(~~What does mean *coat*?~~)
  Was heißt *coat*?
What time does the next train leave?
(normalerweise NICHT: At what time …?)
  Um wieviel Uhr fährt der nächste Zug?
What sort of music do you like?
  Welche Art von Musik gefällt Dir?
'**What** do you do?'   'I'm a student.'   (~~I'm student.~~)
  „Was machst Du?"   „Ich bin Student."
What a nice colour!   (~~What nice colour.~~)
(~~What for a nice colour.~~)
  Das ist aber eine schöne Farbe!

How

'My name's Ann Carter.'   '**How** do you do?'
'**How** do you do?'
  „Ich heiße Ann Carter."   „Guten Tag."   „Guten Tag."
'**How** are you?'   'Very well, thank you. And you?'
  „Wie geht es Dir/Ihnen?"   „Danke, sehr gut.
  Und Dir/Ihnen?"
'**How** old are you?'   'I'm 35.'
  „Wie alt bist Du?"   „Ich bin 35."
How did Louis Blériot travel from France to England?
(~~How travelled Louis …?~~)   (~~How did travel Louis …?~~)
  Wie ist Louis Blériot von Frankreich nach England
  gefahren?

When

When did the Second World War start?
(~~When started …~~)   (~~When did start …?~~)
  Wann hat der Zweite Weltkrieg begonnen?

Why

'**Why** did you come to Australia?'   'To learn English.'
(~~'For learning English.'~~)   (~~For to learn English.~~)
  „Warum bist Du nach Australien gekommen?"
  „Um Englisch zu lernen."

Das Fragewort als Satzgegenstand oder als Ergänzung

Wenn nach der Ergänzung gefragt wird, gelten die normalen Regeln zur Bildung von Fragen.

I saw **someone**.   (someone = Ergänzung)
Who did you see?   (Frage nach der Ergänzung)

Wenn nach dem Satzgegenstand gefragt wird, tritt das Fragewort an dessen Stelle. Bei der Bildung solcher Fragen bleibt die Satzstellung des bejahten Aussagesatzes unverändert.

Someone saw me.   (someone = Satzgegenstand)
Who saw you?   (Frage nach dem Satzgegenstand)

Das englische Fragewort *who* entspricht dem deutschen *wer, wen* und *wem. Whom* für *wen/wem* wird heutzutage nur in sehr formellem Englisch benutzt.

Who (Satzgegenstand) **wrote** the James Bond novels?
(~~Who did write …?~~)
  Wer hat die James Bond Romane geschrieben?
Who (Ergänzung) **do** you know well in the class?
(~~Who know you well …?~~)
  Wen kennst Du gut in der Klasse?
What (Satzgegenstand) **made** you angry?
(~~What did make …?~~)
  Was hat Dich wütend gemacht?
What (Ergänzung) **do** you want?   (~~What want you?~~)
  Was willst Du?
What animals (Satzgegenstand) **live** in trees?
(~~… do live …?~~)
  Welche Tiere leben auf Bäumen?
What animals (Ergänzung) **did** Hannibal take across the Alps?
(~~What animals took Hannibal …?~~)
  Welche Tiere nahm Hannibal mit über die Alpen?
How many children (Satzgegenstand) **came** to the party?
(~~… did come …?~~)
  Wie viele Kinder sind zu der Party gekommen?
How many children (Ergänzung) **did** you invite to the party?
(~~… invited you …~~)
  Wie viele Kinder hast Du zu der Party eingeladen?

Eigenschaftswörter

Steigerungsformen des Eigenschaftswortes

Einsilbige Eigenschaftswörter			
	Eigenschaftswort	*1. Steigerungsform*	*2. Steigerungsform*
Die meisten einsilbigen Eigenschaftswörter:	old	old**er**	old**est**
	short	short**er**	short**est**
	cheap	cheap**er**	cheap**est**
	young	young**er** (/ˈjʌŋgə(r)/)	young**est** (/ˈjʌŋgɪst/)
	long	long**er** (/ˈlɒŋgə(r)/)	long**est** (/ˈlɒŋgɪst/)
Eigenschaftswörter, die auf -*e* enden:	late	late**r**	lat**est**
	fine	fine**r**	fin**est**
Eigenschaftswörter, die auf einen Selbstlaut + einen Mitlaut enden:	fat	fa**tter**	fa**ttest**
	slim	sli**mmer**	sli**mmest**
	big	bi**gger**	bi**ggest**
Unregelmäßige Formen:	good	better	best
	bad	worse	worst
	far	farther	farthest

Zweisilbige Eigenschaftswörter			
	Eigenschaftswort	*1. Steigerungsform*	*2. Steigerungsform*
Eigenschaftswörter, die auf -*y* enden:	happy	happ**ier**	happ**iest**
	easy	eas**ier**	eas**iest**
Die meisten anderen Eigenschaftswörter:	complete	**more** complete	**most** complete
	famous	**more** famous	**most** famous

Längere Eigenschaftswörter			
	Eigenschaftswort	*1. Steigerungsform*	*2. Steigerungsform*
	interesting	**more** interesting	**most** interesting
	beautiful	**more** beautiful	**most** beautiful
	difficult	**more** difficult	**most** difficult

Die Anwendung der Steigerungsformen

1. Steigerungsform

I'm **taller than** my mother.   (... taller as ...)
  Ich bin größer als meine Mutter.
I'm **much** taller than my brother.
  Ich bin viel größer als mein Bruder.
She's **a bit** more intelligent than me.
  Sie ist etwas intelligenter als ich.

2. Steigerungsform

Who is **the oldest** person here?
  Wer ist hier der/die Älteste?
I'm **the tallest** in my family.
  Ich bin der Größte in meiner Familie.
It's **the most beautiful** place in the world.
(... of the world.)
  Das ist der schönste Ort auf der Welt.

(Not) as ... as

(Not) as ... as entspricht dem deutschen *(nicht) so ... wie* bei Vergleichen ohne Steigerungsformen.
Not as ... as und *not so ... as* sind austauschbar.

I'm **as good-looking as** a film star.
(I'm so good looking as ...)
  Ich sehe genauso gut aus wie ein Filmstar.
He's not **as tall as** me.
  Er ist nicht so groß wie ich.
A Volkswagen is not **as quiet as** a Rolls Royce.
  Ein Volkswagen ist nicht so leise wie ein Rolls Royce.

As und *than*

Die Ähnlichkeit zwischen dem englischen *as* und dem deutschen *als* führen oft zu Fehlern bei der Bildung von Vergleichen.

> *than = als*
> *as = so/wie*

faster **than** (faster as)   schneller als
more beautiful **than**   (more beautiful as)   schöner als
as fast **as**   (as fast than)   so schnell wie

Beachten Sie auch:

the same **as**   (the same than)
Peking is **the same as** Beijing.
   Peking ist dasselbe wie Beijing.
different **from**   (different as)   (different than)
A pen is **different from** a pencil.
   Ein Füller ist etwas anderes als ein Bleistift.

Umstandswörter

Das Eigenschaftswort und das Umstandswort

Das Eigenschaftswort beschreibt ein Hauptwort und steht entweder vor dem Hauptwort oder nach *be*. Das Umstandswort gibt weitere Informationen zu einem Zeitwort (Art und Weise, Häufigkeit, usw.) oder zu einem Eigenschaftswort (Grad).

Vergleiche:
   You've got a **nice face**. (Eigenschaftswort)
      Du hast ein schönes Gesicht.
   You **sing nicely**. (Umstandswort)
      Du singst schön.

   I'm **angry** with you. (Eigenschaftswort)
      Ich bin wütend auf Dich.
   She **spoke** to me **angrily**. (Umstandswort)
      Sie sprach mich wütend an.

It's **terrible**. (Eigenschaftswort)
   Es ist schrecklich.
It's **terribly cold**. (Umstandswort)
   Es ist schrecklich kalt.

You speak **good English**. (Eigenschaftswort)
   Du sprichst ein gutes Englisch.
You **speak** English **well**. (Umstandswort)
(You speak English good.)
   Du sprichst gut Englisch.

Die Rechtschreibung von Umstandswörtern mit *-ly*

	Eigenschaftswort	Umstandswort
Die meisten Wörter:	kind	kind**ly**
	careful	careful**ly** (carefuly)
	extreme	extreme**ly** (extremly)
Eigenschaftswörter, die auf *-y* enden:	happ**y**	happ**ily**
	angr**y**	angr**ily**
Eigenschaftswörter, die auf *-ble* enden:	comforta**ble**	comforta**bly**

Ausnahmen:

Eigenschaftswort	Umstandswort		
good	well	gut	(goodly)
fast	fast	schnell	(fastly)
late	late	spät	(lately = kürzlich)
hard	hard	schwer	(hardly = kaum)

Die Stellung des Umstandswortes im Satz

Im Englischen stehen die Umstandswörter nicht zwischen
dem Zeitwort und der Ergänzung.

She speaks English **well**.   (She speaks well English.)
  Sie spricht gut Englisch.
I opened the letter **carefully**.   (I opened carefully the letter.)
  Ich habe den Brief vorsichtig geöffnet.
I **never** read science fiction.   (I read never science fiction.)
  Ich lese nie Science-fiction.

Umstandswörter der Häufigkeit: Gebrauch und Stellung

How often do you go to the cinema?   Wie oft gehst Du ins Kino?
Do you **ever** go to the opera?   Gehst Du schon mal in die Oper?

In Aussagesätzen stehen die weniger präzisen Umstandswörter der Häufigkeit
(*always, often, sometimes*, usw.) **vor** einem normalen Zeitwort bzw. **nach** einem
besonderen Zeitwort (*be, can*, usw.). Präzisere Beschreibungen der Häufigkeit
(*every day, once a week, twice a year*, usw.) stehen **am Ende** des Satzes.

I	**always** **very often** **quite often**	come here on Sunday mornings. (I come here always …)
Ich komme	immer sehr oft ganz oft	am Sonntagmorgen hierhin.

I am	**sometimes** **occasionally** **hardly ever** **never**	unhappy. (I sometimes am unhappy.)
Ich bin	manchmal gelegentlich sehr selten nie	unglücklich.

I come here	**every day.** **every three days.** **once a day.** **twice a week.** **three times a year.**	(I come every day here.)
Ich komme	jeden Tag alle drei Tage einmal am Tag zweimal pro Woche dreimal im Jahr	hierhin.

Umstandswörter des Grades

I'm	**not at all** **not very** **a bit** **quite** **very** **extremely**	tired.
Ich bin	überhaupt nicht nicht sehr etwas ziemlich sehr äußerst	müde.

Die Steigerungsformen des Umstandswortes

Die Steigerungsformen des Umstandswortes werden
gewöhnlich mit *more* und *most* gebildet.

Could you speak **more slowly**?
  Könnten Sie langsamer sprechen?
She sings **most beautifully**.
  Sie singt äußerst schön.
Ausnahmen: *faster, fastest; better, best.*
She can run *faster* than me.
  Sie kann schneller laufen als ich.
I speak English **better** than my brother.
  Ich spreche besser Englisch als mein Bruder.

128

Verhältniswörter

Zeit

I'll see you	at ten o'clock.
	in the afternoon.
	on Thursday.
	on June 22nd.
	at the weekend.
Wir sehen uns	um zehn Uhr.
	am Nachmittag.
	am Donnerstag.
	am 22. Juni.
	am Wochenende.

I don't work **on** Saturdays.
  Ich arbeite samstags nicht.
I'll see you **in** three days.
  Wir treffen uns in drei Tagen.
We go skiing every year **for** two weeks.
  Wir fahren jedes Jahr zwei Wochen in Skiurlaub.
I started this job three years **ago**.
(... ~~for three years~~.)
  Ich habe diesen Job vor drei Jahren begonnen.

(*Ago* ist zwar kein Verhältniswort, entspricht aber in diesem Zusammenhang dem deutschen Verhältniswort *vor*.)

I've been here	for six weeks. (~~since six weeks.~~)
	since Christmas.
Ich bin hier	seit sechs Wochen
	seit Weihnachten.

I work **from** nine **to/until** six.   Ich arbeite von neun bis sechs.
She only studies **before** exams.   Sie lernt nur vor Prüfungen.
I'm free **after** six o'clock.   Ich habe ab sechs Uhr Zeit.
half **past** nine   halb zehn
five **to** ten   fünf vor zehn

Kein Verhältniswort

What time do you get up?   (*NICHT üblich:* At what time ...?)
  Um wieviel Uhr stehst Du auf?
I'll see you **next month**.
  Wir sehen uns im nächsten Monat.
I saw her **last summer**.
  Ich habe sie im letzten Sommer gesehen.

Raum

```
            on
┌──────┐ ┌──────┐ ┌──in──┐ ┌──────┐
│under │ │      │ │      │ │      │ near
```

It's	on the table.
	under your chair.
	in the fridge.
	near the door. (... in the near of ...)
	(... ~~nearby the door.~~)
Es ist	auf dem Tisch.
	unter Deinem Stuhl.
	im Kühlschrank.
	in der Nähe der Tür.

in the living room   im Wohnzimmer
in a small flat   in einer kleinen Wohnung
on the second floor   auf der zweiten Etage
at 53 Park Street   Park Street 53
in Park Street   in der Park Street
in London   in London
in England   in England
He **lived in** Saigon.   Er hat in Saigon gewohnt.
He **studied at** Saigon University.
  Er hat an der Universität in Saigon studiert.
I'm going **to** Edinburgh tomorrow.
  Ich fahre morgen nach Edinburg.
I'll **arrive at** Waverley Station at 9.15.
  Ich komme um 9.15 Uhr am Bahnhof in Waverley an.
'Where are you **from**?'   'I'm **from** Ireland.'
  „Wo kommst Du her?"   „Ich komme aus Irland."
Our bedroom is **over** the living room.
  Unser Schlafzimmer ist über dem Wohnzimmer.

She was the first woman to fly	across the Atlantic.	
	round the world.	
Sie war die erste Frau, die	über den Atlantik	geflogen ist.
	um die Welt	

He's	at the disco.	Er ist	in der Disko.
	at the supermarket.		im Supermarkt.
	at the doctor's		beim Arzt.
	at the bus stop.		an der Haltestelle.
	at the station.		am/im Bahnhof.
	at home.		zu Hause.
	at work.		bei der Arbeit.
	at school.		in der Schule.
	at lunch.		beim Mittagessen.
	in bed.		im Bett.
	on his way to work.		auf dem Weg zur Arbeit.

It's	by the reception desk.	Es ist	neben der Rezeption.
	near the stairs.		in der Nähe der Treppe.
	next to the post office.		neben der Post.
	opposite the station.		gegenüber vom Bahnhof.
	outside the window.		draußen vor dem Fenster.
	behind the tree.		hinter dem Baum.
	in front of the tree.		vor dem Baum.
	between those two trees.		zwischen den beiden Bäumen dort.

Go straight on **for** 300 metres and it's **on** the right.
  Gehen Sie 300 Meter geradeaus. Es ist auf der rechten Seite.
He got **into** his car and drove away.
  Er stieg in sein Auto ein und fuhr weg.
She got **out of** the car and went **into** the house.
  Sie stieg aus dem Auto aus und ging ins Haus.

Kein Verhältniswort

I want to go **home**.   (~~... to home.~~)
Ich möchte nach Hause gehen.

Andere Anwendungsbereiche von Verhältniswörtern

Here's a letter **for** you.
Hier ist ein Brief für Dich.
the girl **in** jeans
das Mädchen mit der Jeans
the man **with** the beard
der Mann mit dem Bart
My sister looks **like** me.
Meine Schwester sieht aus wie ich.
We're all slim **except** Joe.
Wir sind alle schlank außer Joe.
'How old is she?'   '**Over** twenty.'   '**Under thirty.**'
"Wie alt ist sie?"   „Über zwanzig."   „Unter dreißig."
good **at** maths   (~~good in ...~~)
gut in Mathe
good **at** running
ein guter Läufer
the most beautiful place **in** the world
der schönste Ort auf der Welt
We went to Spain **on** holiday.
Wir sind nach Spanien in Urlaub gefahren.

We went there **by** bus/car/train/air.
Wir sind mit dem Bus/Auto/Zug/Flugzeug dahin gefahren.
I often think **about** you.
Ich denke oft an Dich.
We were talking **about** money.
Wir sprachen über Geld.
The film is **about** love.
Der Film handelt von der Liebe.
I can't go **without** sleep for very long.
Ich komme nicht sehr lange ohne Schlaf aus.
Look at my new dress.   (~~Look to my new dress.~~)
Sieh Dir mein neues Kleid an.
Would you like to **listen to** some music?
(~~... to listen some music.~~)
Würdest Du gerne etwas Musik hören?
I'm **looking for** a sweater.   (~~I'm looking after a sweater.~~)
Ich suche einen Pullover.

Wie man verschiedene Satzelemente bzw. Sätze miteinander verknüpft

Die Verknüpfung von Satzgegenständen

Both Al **and** Jake robbed the bank.
  Al und Jake haben (beide) die Bank ausgeraubt.
Neither Al **nor** Jake went to bed early.
  Weder Al noch Jake sind früh zu Bett gegangen.

Bindewörter: Die Verknüpfung von Haupt- und Nebensätzen

And und *but*

The British sailors woke up **and** started fighting, **but** they could not stop Jones and his men.
  Die britischen Seeleute wachten auf und begannen zu kämpfen, aber sie konnten Jones und seine Männer nicht aufhalten.

That

One American captain wanted to show the British **that** size was not everything.
  Einer der amerikanischen Kapitäne wollte den Briten zeigen, daß Größe nicht alles ausmacht.
We both agree **that** I'm more optimistic than her.
  Wir sind uns beide einig, daß ich optimistischer bin als sie.
He told the policeman (**that**) he got up at eight o'clock.
(He told to the policeman …)
(He told that he got up …)
  Er sagte dem Polizisten, daß er um acht Uhr aufgestanden sei.
He said (**that**) they went to an art gallery.
(He said the policeman that …)
  Er sagte, daß sie zu einer Kunstgallerie gegangen seien.

Who

Galileo was the man **who** discovered sunspots.
  Galileo war der Mann, der die Sonnenflecken entdeckt hat.
They laughed at the small navy of the Americans, **who** were fighting to be free of Britain.
  Sie lachten über die kleine Flotte der Amerikaner, die um ihre Freiheit von Großbritannien kämpften.

Where

The Americans left Whitehaven and sailed to Scotland, **where** they carried out more attacks.
  Die Amerikaner verließen Whitehaven und segelten nach Schottland, wo sie weitere Überfälle verübten.

As soon as

As soon as he arrived, he took a group of his men to an inn.
  Sobald er angekommen war, führte er eine Gruppe seiner Leute zu einem Gasthaus.

Because

Amelia Earhart stopped studying **because** she wanted to learn to fly.
  Amelia Earhart hörte auf zu studieren, weil sie fliegen lernen wollte.

Before und *after*

Always warm up **before** you run.
  Wärmen Sie sich immer auf, bevor Sie laufen.
Rest for a few minutes **after** you finish.
  Ruhen Sie sich ein paar Minuten aus, nachdem Sie gelaufen sind.

If und *when*

> *If* und *when* entsprechen beide dem deutschen *wenn*:
>   *if* = *wenn/falls* (etwas ist möglicherweise der Fall oder wird eventuell passieren)
>   *when* = *wenn* (etwas ist normalerweise der Fall oder wird auf jeden Fall passieren)

If you are rich you can buy anything you want.
  Wenn man reich ist, kann man sich alles kaufen.
If I have time, I'll come and see you.
(If I will have time …)
  Wenn ich Zeit habe, werde ich Dich besuchen.
When Fred's hungry he goes to a restaurant.
  Wenn Fred Hunger hat, geht er in ein Restaurant.
I'll phone you **when** I get home.
(… when I will get home.)
  Ich rufe Dich an, wenn ich nach Hause komme.

Logische Beziehung zwischen Sätzen

Then they started work. **First of all** they went to the fort and destroyed the guns. **Next,** they began burning British ships … **Finally,** the Americans left Whitehaven …
  Dann gingen sie ans Werk. Zuerst gingen sie zur Festung und zerstörten die Kanonen. Als nächstes begannen sie, die britischen Schiffe in Brand zu stecken … Schließlich verließen die Amerikaner Whitehaven …

Einige problematische Wörter

Lend und *borrow*

Im Englischen gibt es zwei Wörter für das deutsche *leihen*: *lend* = etwas verleihen; *borrow* = sich etwas ausleihen

Could you **lend** me some sugar?
(Could you borrow me ..?)
   Könnten Sie mir etwas Zucker leihen?
Could I **borrow** some sugar (from you)?
(Could I lend some sugar ..?)
   Könnte ich mir etwas Zucker von Ihnen leihen?

Say und *tell*

Say und *tell* bei indirekter Rede werden unterschiedlich benutzt. Bei *tell* steht immer, **wem** etwas gesagt wurde (ohne das Verhältniswort *to*). Bei *say* kann stehen, **wem** etwas gesagt wird, dann aber **mit** *to*.

What did he **tell you**?
What did he **say to you**?   (What did he say you?)
   Was hat er Dir gesagt?
He **told the policeman** (that) they had lunch in a pub.
(He told that they had lunch …)
   Er sagte dem Polizisten, daß sie in einem Pub gegessen hätten.
He **said** (that) they went for a walk.
(He said the policeman that …)
   Er sagte, daß sie spazierengegangen seien.

Like und *would like*

Like bedeutet **im allgemeinen** *etwas mögen*; *would like* bedeutet **im Augenblick** *etwas wollen*.

'**Do** you **like** dancing?'
'Yes, I do. I go dancing every weekend.'
   „Tanzt Du gerne?"
   „Ja. Ich gehe jedes Wochenende tanzen."
'**Would** you **like** to dance?'   'No, thanks. I'm tired.'
   „Möchtest Du tanzen?"   „Nein danke, ich bin müde."

Be like, look like, und *look*

'What **is** your new girlfriend **like**?'
'She's a bit shy, but very nice.'
(How is she?)   (What for a person is she?)
   „Wie ist Deine neue Freundin?"
   „Etwas schüchtern, aber sehr nett."
He **looks like** a footballer.
   Er sieht aus wie ein Fußballspieler.
I think he **looks** more **like** a businessman.
   Ich glaube, er sieht eher wie ein Geschäftsmann aus.
She **looks like** her mother.
   Sie sieht wie ihre Mutter aus.
She **looks** bad-tempered.
   Sie sieht schlecht gelaunt aus.
You **look** tired.
   Du siehst müde aus.

Get

1. *Get* + Ergänzung = *bekommen, holen, kaufen*

Where can I **get some stamps?**
(Where can I become some stamps?)
   Wo kann ich Briefmarken kaufen?
I **get a letter** from my mother every week.
   Ich bekomme jede Woche einen Brief von meiner Mutter.
Can you **get** me **some bread**, please?
   Kannst Du mir bitte etwas Brot holen?

2. *Get* + Eigenschaftswort = *werden*

It's **getting late**.
   Es wird spät.
If you work too hard you'll **get tired**.
   Wenn Du zu hart arbeitest, wirst Du müde werden.

3. *Get* + Verhältniswort = *Bewegung*

What time do you usually **get up?**
   Um wieviel Uhr stehst Du gewöhnlich auf?
It takes me an hour to **get to** work.
   Ich brauche eine Stunde, um zur Arbeit zu kommen.
I **got on** the wrong bus, so I **got off** at the next stop.
   Ich bin in den falschen Bus eingestiegen und an der nächsten Haltestelle wieder ausgestiegen.
Get out!!
   Raus hier!!

4. *Have got* = *haben, besitzen*

You'**ve got** beautiful eyes.
   Du hast schöne Augen.

5. *Get lost, married, killed = sich verlaufen, heiraten, ums Leben kommen*

We went for a walk and **got lost** in the woods.
   Wir sind spazierengegangen und haben uns im Wald verlaufen.
She's **getting married** next week.
   Sie heiratet nächste Woche.
He **got killed** in a car crash.
   Er ist bei einem Autounfall ums Leben gekommen.

Born

I **was born** in 1936.   (I am born …)
   Ich bin im Jahre 1936 geboren.
When **were** you **born?**   (When are you born?)
   Wann bist Du geboren?

Agree

I agree.   (I am agree.)
   Ich bin einverstanden. (Das stimmt.)
I don't agree.   (I am not agree.)
   Ich bin nicht damit einverstanden. (Das stimmt nicht.)

Grammatische Strukturen in Gesprächen

Wie man Interesse bekundet: verkürzte Fragesätze

'I'm Pisces.' 'Are you?'
  „Ich bin Fische." „Tatsächlich?" / „Wirklich?" / „Ehrlich?"
'I've got a cold.' 'Oh, have you?'
  „Ich bin erkältet." „Tatsächlich?" / „Wirklich?" / „Ehrlich?"
'My father can speak five languages.' 'Can he?'
  „Mein Vater spricht fünf Sprachen." „Tatsächlich?"
'I love skiing.' 'Do you?'
  „Ich fahre gerne Ski." „Wirklich?"
'I slept badly last night.' 'Oh, did you?'
  „Ich habe letzte Nacht schlecht geschlafen." „Ehrlich?"

So am I usw.

'I've got a pink Rolls-Royce.' 'So have I.' 'I haven't.'
  „Ich habe einen rosa Rolls-Royce." „Ich auch." „Ich nicht."
'I'm tired.' 'So am I.' 'I'm not.'
  „Ich bin müde." „Ich auch." „Ich nicht."
'Mary can swim.' 'So can Alice.' 'Louise can't.'
  „Mary kann schwimmen." „Alice auch."
  „Louise nicht."
'I go skiing twice a year.' 'So do I.' 'I don't.'
  „Ich fahre zweimal im Jahr in Skiurlaub." „Ich auch."
  „Ich nicht."
'John phoned last night.' 'So did your mother.'
  „John hat gestern abend angerufen."
  „Deine Mutter auch."

Die Formulierung von Sprechabsichten

Jemanden kennenlernen und begrüßen

Jemanden vorstellen

☐ 'Joe, this is Pat.'   ☐ „Joe, das ist Pat."
△ 'How do you do?'   △ „Guten Tag."
○ 'How do you do?' ('I'm fine.')   ○ „Guten Tag."

Formelle Begrüßungen

Good morning/afternoon/evening.
  Guten Morgen/Tag (am Nachmittag)/Abend.
Goodbye/Good night.
  Auf Wiedersehen/Gute Nacht.

Informelle Begrüßungen

Hi/Hello.
  Hallo.
Bye/Goodbye/See you.
  Tschüs/Auf Wiedersehen/Bis dann.

Sich nach der Gesundheit erkundigen

'How are you?' 'Very well, thanks.' ('Thanks.')
                'Fine, thanks. And you?' ('Thanks fine.')
                'Not too bad.'
„Wie geht's?"   „Danke, sehr gut."
                „Danke, gut. Und Dir/Ihnen?"
                „Nicht schlecht."/„Ganz gut."

Fragen zur Person

'Where are you from?' 'Scotland.'
  „Wo kommen Sie/kommst Du her?" „Aus Schottland."
'Where do you live?' 'In Edinburgh.'
  „Wo wohnst Du?" „In Edinburg."
'Where do you work?' 'In a small shop in George Street.'
  „Wo arbeitest Du?" „In einem kleinen Geschäft in der
  George Street."
'What's your phone number?' '7623305.' (Seven six two,
double three oh five.)
  „Welche Telefonnummer haben Sie?" „7623305."
'What newspaper do you read?' *'The Independent.'*
  „Welche Zeitung lesen Sie?" „Den *Independent*."
'How do you travel to work?' 'By bus.'
  „Wie fahren Sie zur Arbeit?" „Mit dem Bus."
'What sort of books do you like?' 'Science Fiction.'
  „Welche Art von Büchern mögen Sie?"
  „Science-fiction-Romane."
'Are you interested in politics?' 'Yes, I am.'
  „Interessieren Sie sich für Politik?" „Ja."

Um Verzeihung bitten, sich entschuldigen

'Excuse me, is your name Fred Andrews?'
  „Verzeihung, heißen Sie Fred Andrews?"
'No, I'm sorry, it's not. It's Jake Barker.'
  „Nein, tut mir leid. Ich heiße Jake Barker."
'Pardon?'
  „Bitte?"
'It's Jake Barker.'
  „Ich heiße Jake Barker."
'Oh, I'm sorry.'
  „Oh, entschuldigen Sie bitte."
'That's all right.'
  „Das macht nichts."

Persönliche Meinung, Zu- und Abneigung ausdrücken

'How do you like this place?'
'Great / Not bad / Not much / Terrible.'
  „Wie finden Sie / findest Du diesen Ort /
  diese Wohnung / usw.?"
  „Großartig / Nicht schlecht / Nicht besonders gut /
  Schrecklich."
Do you like modern jazz?
  Mögen Sie modernen Jazz?
What do you think of the government?
  Was halten Sie von der Regierung?
What's your favourite food?
  Was essen Sie am liebsten?

I like the Greek statue **very much**.
  Mir gefällt die griechische Statue sehr gut.
I **quite** like the mask.
  Die Maske gefällt mir ganz gut.
It's **OK**.
  Er / sie / es ist in Ordnung.
I like the Vermeer **best**.
  Mir gefällt der Vermeer am besten.
I **hate** shopping on Saturdays.
  Ich hasse es, samstags einzukaufen.
I **don't** like classical music **at all**.
  Ich mag klassische Musik überhaupt nicht.
'Do you like travelling?' **'It depends.'**
  „Reisen Sie gerne?"   „Es kommt darauf an."

Etwas vorschlagen; eine Einladung aussprechen; auf eine Einladung reagieren

'Are you doing anything this evening?
Would you like to see a film?'
  „Hast Du heute abend etwas vor?
  Möchtest Du ins Kino gehen?"
'**I don't know**. I'm a bit tired. **I don't really want** to do anything tonight.'
  „Ich weiß nicht. Ich bin etwas müde. Eigentlich möchte
  ich heute abend gar nichts machen."
'Well, **what about** tomorrow?'
  „Wie wär's denn mit morgen?"
'**I'd love to**, but **I'm afraid** I'm not free. I'm going to a concert in London.
  „Sehr gerne. Aber leider bin ich schon verabredet.
  Ich fahre nach London zu einem Konzert."
'**Let's** do something at the weekend. Are you free?'
  „Laß uns am Wochenende etwas zusammen machen.
  Hast Du Zeit?"
'Perhaps. Yes, **why not**?'
  „Vielleicht. Ja, warum nicht?"
'**How about** Saturday? **Shall we** have dinner?'
  „Wie wär's mit Samstag? Sollen wir zusammen essen?"
'**What a** nice idea!'
  „Das ist eine gute Idee!"
'OK. **See you** about eight o'clock.'
  „OK. Dann sehen wir uns gegen acht."
'Right, see you then.'
  „In Ordnung. Bis dann."

Über das persönliche Befinden sprechen

I feel ill.
  Ich fühle mich krank.
What's the matter?
  Was ist los? / Was fehlt Ihnen / Dir?
My eyes hurt.   My arm hurts.
  Meine Augen tun weh.   Ich habe Schmerzen im Arm.
Do they hurt / Does it hurt very badly?
  Tun sie / Tut er sehr weh? / Ist es sehr schlimm?
I've got a (bad) cold / a (bad) headache / (bad) toothache / flu / a temperature. (Im Amerikanischen: a toothache; the flu)
  Ich habe eine (starke) Erkältung / (starke) Kopf-
  schmerzen / (starke) Zahnschmerzen / die Grippe /
  Fieber.
Why don't you see the doctor/dentist?
  Warum gehst Du nicht zum Arzt/Zahnarzt?

Um Erlaubnis bitten; Erlaubnis erteilen

Do you mind if I	sit here?
	open the window?
	smoke?
	look at your paper?
Macht es Ihnen etwas aus, wenn ich	mich hierhin setze?
	das Fenster öffne?
	rauche?
	Ihre Zeitung lese?

Not at all.
  Keineswegs. Überhaupt nicht.
No, please do.
  Nein, Bitteschön.
Go ahead.
  Bitte. / Nur zu!
I'm sorry, it's not free.
  Dieser Platz ist leider besetzt.
Well, it's a bit cold.
  Hm, eigentlich ist mir ein bißchen kalt.
Well, I'd rather you didn't.
  Lieber nicht.
Well, I'm reading it myself, actually.
  Na ja, eigentlich lese ich sie/es gerade selbst.

Etwas ausleihen

I'm sorry to trouble you, but could you lend me some sugar?
  Entschuldigen Sie die Störung, aber könnten Sie mir etwas
  Zucker leihen?
Could you possibly lend me your car?
  Könntest Du mir vielleicht Dein Auto leihen?
Could I borrow your keys **for a moment**?
  Könnte ich mir für einen Augenblick Deine Schlüssel
  leihen?
Yes, **here you are**.
  Ja, Bitteschön.
Yes, **of course**.
  Ja, natürlich.
I'm sorry, **I need it/them**.
  Tut mir leid. Ich brauche es/sie selbst.
I'm afraid I haven't got one/any.
  Leider habe ich keinen/keine.
I'm sorry, **I'm afraid** I can't.
  Tut mir leid, aber es geht nicht.

Anweisungen geben

Please hurry?
  Beeile Dich bitte!
Take your time.
  Laß Dir Zeit!
Don't worry.
  Keine Angst!
Look.
  Schau!
Come in.
  Kommen Sie/Komm herein!
Wait here, please.
  Warten Sie bitte hier!
Be careful.
  Seien Sie/Sei vorsichtig!
Follow me, please.
  Folgen Sie mir, bitte!
Look out!
  Achtung! / Paß auf!

Etwas bestellen und Wünsche äußern

I'll start with soup, please, and then **I'll have** roast beef.
  Ich hätte gerne zuerst eine Suppe und danach nehme ich
  das Roastbeef, bitte.
Chicken **for me**, please.
  Hähnchen für mich, bitte.
Could you bring me a beer, please?
  Können Sie mir bitte ein Bier bringen?
Just some water, please.
  Nur Wasser, bitte.
a little more coffee
  noch etwas Kaffee
Could you bring us **the bill**, please?
  Könnten Sie uns bitte die Rechnung bringen?
Is service **included**?
  Ist die Bedienung inbegriffen?

Nach dem Weg fragen; einen Weg beschreiben

Excuse me. Where's the nearest post office, please?
  Verzeihung. Wo ist bitte das nächste Postamt?
Excuse me. Is there a post office near here, please?
  Verzeihung. Gibt es hier in der Nähe ein Postamt?
It's over there by the police station.
  Dort drüben, neben dem Polizeirevier.
First on the right, then second on the left.
  Erste Straße rechts, dann die zweite Straße links.
Take the first right, second left, then straight on.
  Nehmen Sie die erste Straße rechts, dann die zweite links
  und dann geradeaus.
How far is it?
  Wie weit ist es?
About a hundred metres.
  Etwa hundert Meter.
About a hundred yards.
  Etwa hundert Yards.
Thank you very much.
  Vielen Dank.
Not at all.
  Bitteschön.
I'm sorry. I don't know.
  Es tut mir leid. Ich weiß es nicht.
Thank you anyway.
  Trotzdem vielen Dank.

Beim Einkaufen

'Can I help you?'   'I'm just looking.'
  „Kann ich Ihnen helfen?"   „Ich möchte mich nur etwas
  umschauen."
'I'm looking for a sweater.'   'Here's a lovely one.'
  „Ich suche einen Pullover."   'Hier ist ein schöner.'
What a lovely sweater!   (What lovely sweater!)
  Was für ein schöner Pullover!
What nice shoes!
  Was für schöne Schuhe!
Those aren't very nice.   I don't like that very much.
  Diese sind nicht sehr schön.   Mir gefällt das nicht
  besonders gut.
Can I look round?
  Darf ich mich umschauen?
Can I try them on?
  Kann ich sie anprobieren?
'Have you got anything in black?'   'I'll just see.'
  „Haben Sie etwas in Schwarz?"   „Ich schau mal nach."
'No, I'm afraid I haven't. Would you like to try these?'
  (Would you like try these?)
  Nein, leider nicht. Möchten Sie diese hier anprobieren?"
How much are they?   How much is it?
  Wie teuer sind sie?   Wie teuer ist das?
I'll take them, please.
  Ich nehme sie.
I'd like a red one.
  Ich hätte gerne ein rotes/eine rote/einen roten.
I'd like to look at some watches.
  (I'd like look at some watches.)
  Ich würde mir gerne einige Uhren anschauen.

Am Telefon

Can/Could I speak to …?
  Kann/Könnte ich (mit) … sprechen?
This is …
  Hier ist …
Is that …?
  Spreche ich mit …?
He/She's not in.
  Er/Sie ist nicht da.
Can I take a message?
  Soll ich ihm/ihr etwas ausrichten?

Fragen zur englischen Sprache

What's this?   What's this called in English, please?
  Wie heißt dies?   Wie heißt dies auf englisch?
What are these?
  Wie heißen diese?
Is this a pen or a pencil?   Is this a lighter?
  Ist dies *a pen* oder *a pencil*?   Ist dies *a lighter*?
How do you say *Fahrrad* in English?
  Was heißt *Fahrrad* auf englisch?
What does *shy* mean?   (What means shy.)
  Was bedeutet *shy*?
How do you pronounce k-n-e-w?
  Wie wird *k-n-e-w* ausgesprochen?
How do you spell that word?
  Wie wird dieses Wort buchstabiert?
Could you speak more slowly, please?
  Könnten Sie bitte langsamer sprechen?

Alters-, Größen- und Gewichtsangaben

The Great Pyramid is 4,500 years old.
  Die große Pyramide ist 4.500 Jahre alt.
It is 135 metres high.
  Es ist 135 Meter hoch.
The car is 4 metres long.
  Das Auto ist 4 Meter lang.
The statue weighs three kilos.
  Die Statue wiegt drei Kilo.
Lucy is four months old.
  Lucy ist vier Monate alt.
Her mother is 40 (years old).
  Ihre Mutter ist 40 (Jahre alt).
I am 1 metre 91.
  Ich bin 1 Meter 91 (groß).
I weigh 85 kilos.
  Ich wiege 85 Kilo.
She's over 21 and under 30.
  Sie ist über 21 und unter 30 (Jahre alt).
How old/tall are you?
  Wie alt/groß sind Sie/bist Du?
How much do you weigh?
  Wieviel wiegen Sie/wiegst Du?

Das Datum

Man schreibt	Man sagt
14 Jan(uary) 1990 14. 1. 90 (BE) 1. 14. 90 (AE)	January the fourteenth, nineteen ninety (BE) January fourteenth ... (AE)
5 Apr(il) 1892	April the fifth, eighteen ninety-two
9 Dec(ember) 1600	December the ninth, sixteen hundred
14 May 1906	May the fourteenth, nineteen hundred and six OR: ... nineteen oh six

Das Abfassen formeller Briefe

Flat 6
Monument House
Castle Street
Newcastle NE1 2HH

12 September 1990

Dear Mr Bell,

I am arriving at Waverley Station, Edinburgh ...

...

I look forward to seeing you.

Yours sincerely,

Paul Sanders

Key to Exercises (Lösungsschlüssel)

Unit 1, Lesson A

1 2. Carmen. What's *your name?*
3. Is *your name* Joe?
4. No, *it isn't.* It's (first name).
5. *Is your name* Lucy?
6. Yes, it *is.*
7. Is *your name* Sally?
8. Yes, *it is.*
9. Hello. *My name's* Anne.
10. *What's your name?*

2 2. *What is* your name?
3. My *name is* Judy.
4. *It is* Mary.

3 2. one
3. three
4. two
5. three

Unit 1, Lesson B

1 1. your
2. My
3. your
4. Your

2 1. Her
2. His
3. her
4. His

3 2. Gavin: first name
3. Quinton: surname
4. Wharton: surname
5. Dorrington: surname
6. Gillian: first name
7. Jowitt: surname
8. James: first name

5

Unit 1, Lesson C

1 2. 'Fine, thanks.' / 'I'm fine.'
3. (First name and surname.)
4. 'How do you do?'

2 'Excuse *me.* Is *your* name Alice Stevens?'
'No, *I'm* sorry. *It's* Alice Carter.'

　　　*　　*　　*

'*Excuse* me. *Are* you Bill Wallace?'
'Yes. I *am.*'
'Hello, Bill. *My* name's Jane Marks.'

3 2. three　　7. four
3. five　　　8. three
4. four　　　9. one
5. two　　 . 10. six
6. five

4 1. Excuse me.
2. I'm sorry.
3. I'm sorry.
4. Excuse me.
5. Excuse me.

Unit 1, Lesson D

2 2. No, it *is not.*
3. *He is* from Tanzania.
4. *She is* American.
5. *I am* from Oxford.
6. *Where is* she from?

3 2. Thai
3. Egyptian
4. Japanese
5. Greek
6. German
7. British
8. French
9. Cuban
10. Chinese

6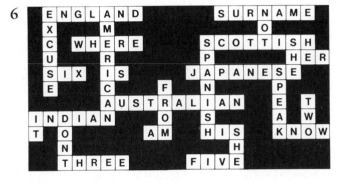

Unit 2, Lesson A

1 1. you; I
2. Her
3. He
4. you
5. it
6. My

3 (Mögliche Antworten)
A: a dentist, a student, a secretary, a housewife, a shop assistant
AN: an engineer, an architect, an artist

4 (Mögliche Antworten)

A: *What's your first name,* Mr Smith?
B: James.
A: *What do you do?*
B: I'm an electrician.

　　　*　　*　　*

A: *Are you a* photographer?
B: No, *I'm an* accountant.
A: Oh!

　　　*　　*　　*

A: *Is she a* doctor?
B: No, *she's an* actress.

　　　*　　*　　*

A: *Is he a* pilot?
B: Yes, *he is.*

Unit 2, Lesson B

1 1. are
2. is
3. am
4. 's; isn't
5. 'm not

2 2. afternoon
3. morning
4. night
5. morning or afternoon
6. morning

3 (Mögliche Antworten)

Dialogue 1
A: *Hi, Tom. How are you?*
B: Not bad. And you?
A: *Fine, thanks.*

Dialogue 2
A: *Good afternoon, Dr Smith. How are you?*
B: Good afternoon, Mr Kowalski. I'm fine, thank you. And you?
A: *I'm very well, thank you.*

Dialogue 3
A: Hello. I'm Polly. What's your name?
B: *I'm Dan. Are you from Canada?*
A: No, I'm Australian. And you?
B: *I'm from Scotland. Are you a teacher?*
A: Yes, I am. Oh, dear! It's 10.45! I must go. Bye!
B: *Bye.*

4

WOMAN	MAN	WOMAN OR MAN
her	he	Chinese
housewife	his	doctor
she	Tom	electrician
Susan		engineer
		Italian
		photographer
		secretary
		shop assistant
		Spanish
		student

5

| I am (*I'm*) |
| you *are* (*you're*) |
| he/*she*/it is (*he's, she's, it's*) |

| *am* I? |
| are you? |
| *is he/she/it?* |

| I am not (*I'm not*) |
| you *are not* (*you aren't*) |
| he/she/it *is not* (*isn't*) |

Unit 2, Lesson C

1
1. He
2. she
3. am
4. you; I
5. Are; am
6. 's
7. Is; is(n't)
8. She is

2
1. 'Are you married?'
3. 'Where are you from?'
4. 'What's your name?'
5. 'Is your name Alice?' (Mögliche Antwort)

3
1. from
2. speak
3. first name; surname
4. me
5. How; thanks

4

FIRST NAME	SURNAME
Anne	Jackson
Bill	Jennings
Catherine	Manning
Dan	Perkins
James	Wagner
Jane	Watson
John	Webber
Mary	Wharton
Miriam	
Peter	
Philip	
Susan	
Steve	
Susan	
Tom	

7 Alice is sixteen. She is a student from Aberdeen, in Scotland. Her surname is MacAllen. MacAllen is a Scottish name, not an English name. Alice lives at 6, Menzies Way. She is not very well today.

Steve is twenty. His surname is Berczuk; it's a Ukrainian name. He's an artist, so his job is interesting. He is from Australia, but now he is both British and Australian. He is from Sydney. His address in London is 113 Beech Road, NW2.

Unit 2, Lesson D

1
2. How old are you?
3. I'm an engineer.
4. Suzanne is French.
5. Are you an architect?
6. John isn't in England.
7. She's twenty-seven.

2

55	five	6	sixty-six	99	ninety
15	fifty-five	16	six	90	nineteen
50	fifty	60	sixteen	19	nine
5	fifteen	66	sixty	9	ninety-nine

3

82	eighty-two	47	forty-seven
23	twenty-three	88	eighty-eight
14	fourteen	17	seventeen
30	thirty	54	fifty-four
61	sixty-one	12	twelve

4
2. Hi (Alle anderen sind Fragewörter.)
3. Japan (Alle anderen sind Nationalitäten.)
4. Thanks (Alle anderen sind Begrüßungen.)
5. good (Dies kann nicht als Antwort auf *'How are you?'* benutzt werden.)
6. seven (Alle anderen sind gerade Zahlen.)
7. eighty-two (Diese Zahl läßt sich nicht durch fünf teilen.)

5 (Mögliche Antwort)
'Good morning. I'm Ms Wharton. Do sit down. Now what's your name, please?'
'Bill Jackson.'
'And your address?'
'80 Winstanley Road.'
'Is that a London address?'
'Yes, it is.'
'I see. Now, how old are you, please?'
'33.'
'And what's your job?'
'I'm an accountant.'
'Fine. Now, how are you today?'
'Not bad, thanks.'
'OK. Please read this . . .'

Unit 3, Lesson A

1
3. Ann *is* married.
4. *His* bag is under the table.
5. Is *her* book French?
6. *His* pen isn't on the table.
7. *His* coat *is* on the chair.
8. Mary *is* single.
9. Where *is her* pen?
10. Dan *is* Italian.

2 (Mögliche Antworten)
3. How do you do?
4. What do you do?
5. Where is the pen?
6. Is he a doctor?
7. Is the bag under the table?
8. How are you?
9. Are you married?
10. How is she?
11. What's your address?
12. How do you spell your surname?
13. Where are you from?

3
1. a doctor's bag
2. a housewife's bag
3. a dentist's coat
4. an electrician's bag
5. a pilot's coat
6. an architect's book
7. an artist's bag

Unit 3, Lesson B

1

> *I am*
> you *are*
> he/she/it *is*
> we *are*
> you *are*
> *they* are

2
2. They are very good-looking.
3. She is a doctor.
4. We are fair.
5. They are quite intelligent.
6. He is very slim.
7. He is not very tall.
8. They are tall and dark.
9. They are American.
10. We are quite good-looking.
11. You are engineers, aren't you?

3
2. Are they American?
3. Is his father English?
4. Is Alice married?
5. Are you and your wife British?
6. Are John and Polly doctors?
7. Is Susan pretty?
8. Is Eric's girlfriend tall?
9. Is your secretary good-looking?
10. Are Ingrid and Christiane German?
11. Is your name Sam Lewis?
12. Is your boyfriend's name Peter?

Unit 3, Lesson C

1
2. is
3. is, her, is
4. are, are
5. is, her
6. is; Her
7. are, their, is
8. are, their
9. is
10. are; is, their

2
/z/: John's, Ann's, Alan's, Ronald's
/s/: Mark's, an artist's, my parents'
/ɪz/: Joyce's, Greece's, Alice's, Mr Nash's

3
1. Peter's sister is very pretty.
2. My mother's brother is a doctor.
3. Anne's boyfriend is tall and good-looking.
4. Robert's girlfriend is not very pretty.
5. Mrs Lewis's children are students.

5
2. boyfriends
3. artists
4. secretaries
5. women
6. doctors
7. children
8. countries
9. daughters
10. men

Unit 3, Lesson D

1
1. got
2. have
3. has
4. got
5. Have you got

2 (Mögliche Antworten)
A: Good morning, Mrs Martin.
B: *Good morning, Mr Brown.*
A: Please sit down.
B: *Thank you.*
A: *How old are you, Mrs Martin?*
B: Thirty-three.
A: *Are you married?*
B: Yes, I *am.*
A: What is *your husband*'s name?
B: Alex.
A: And *his age?*
B: Thirty-two.
A: Have you got any *children?*
B: Yes, *two.* A boy and a *girl.*
(Phone rings)
A: *Excuse* me, Mrs Martin. Hello? Yes. Yes. I'm *sorry, I don't* know. No. Goodbye. I'm *sorry,* Mrs Martin. Now, you want to borrow some money.
B: Yes.

6

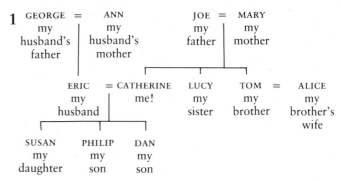

Unit 4, Lesson A

1

GEORGE	=	ANN		JOE	=	MARY
my		my		my		my
husband's		husband's		father		mother
father		mother				

		ERIC	= CATHERINE	LUCY		TOM	=	ALICE
		my	me!	my		my		my
		husband		sister		brother		brother's
								wife

SUSAN	PHILIP	DAN
my	my	my
daughter	son	son

2
1. How
2. What
3. Where
4. How
5. Who
6. How; How
7. How
8. What
9. Where
10. What

3
1. Pardon?
2. Excuse me.
3. Excuse me.
4. I'm sorry.
5. Pardon?
6. I'm sorry.

4
2. ages
3. widows
4. men
5. women
6. boyfriends
7. children
8. families
9. parents
10. sisters
11. wives
12. addresses
13. housewives
14. secretaries

5
100 a hundred
83 eighty-three
17 seventeen
70 seventy
12 twelve
32 thirty-two
14 fourteen
40 forty
58 fifty-eight
10 ten
2 two
61 sixty-one
95 ninety-five
76 seventy-six
29 twenty-nine
11 eleven

6

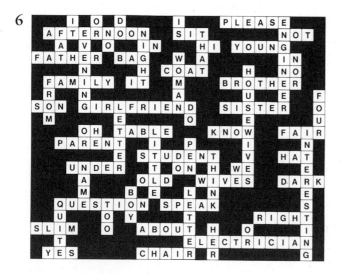

Unit 4, Lesson B

1   2. Where is it?
     3. How are you?
     4. What do you do?
     5. How do you spell your surname?
     6. What's your surname?
     7. What's your first name?
     8. How old is she? (Mögliche Antwort)
     9. Is your name Joe White? (Mögliche Antwort)
    10. How do you do?
    11. Good night.
    12. Have you got any children? (Mögliche Antwort)
    13. Are they doctors? (Mögliche Antwort)

2   1. I'm
     2. I am
     3. he is
     4. My/His/Her/Our/Their
     5. I'm/He's/She's/(Fred)'s a
     6. good-looking/rich/. . .
     7. about
     8. or
     9. too
    10. double L

3 ☐☐   ☐☐   ☐☐☐   ☐☐☐
double   excuse   secretary   engineer
evening   goodbye
housewife   hello
husband
letter
little
married
morning
number
question
single
sister
sorry
student
surname
table
teacher
widow
woman

4   1. quite tall
     2. tall
     3. very tall
     4. intelligent
     5. quite intelligent
     6. very intelligent
     7. Good night.
     8. Hi.
     9. Good evening.
    10. It's Italy.
    11. It's Italian.
    12. on
    13. in
    14. near
    15. under
    16. slim, dark
    17. fat, fair

5 (Mögliche Antwort)
My friend Solange is from Paris. She's a dark, slim, pretty woman, and very intelligent. She speaks English, German, Spanish and a little Italian. She's a journalist for the international page of a daily newspaper.

Solange is divorced; she and her ex-husband have got one son, Julien. He is fifteen. He is quite tall and fair, and a good swimmer. Solange is a good swimmer, too, and a good tennis player. Her holiday home has got a swimming pool, and it is near a tennis court.

Unit 4, Lesson C

1

I	my	I am	I'm	I am not	I'm not	am I?
you	your	you are	you're	you are not	you aren't	are you?
he	his	he is	he's	he is not	he isn't	is he?
she	her	she is	she's	she is not	she isn't	is she?
it	(its)	it is	it's	it is not	it isn't	is it?
we	our	we are	we're	we are not	we aren't	are we?
you	your	you are	you're	you are not	you aren't	are you?
they	their	they are	they're	they are not	they aren't	are they?

2   2. They are   7. How is
     3. I have   8. John is
     4. are not   9. What is
     5. have not   10. I am
     6. He is

3   4. her bag   8. his mother
     5. his books   9. her coat
     6. Ann is   10. she is
     7. Tom is

4   3. Eric's son is fourteen.
     4. My daughters' teacher is Canadian.
     5. My father's sister is an artist.
     6. Alice's doctor is not very intelligent.
     7. My students' books are on the table.
     8. Dr Wagner's two brothers are doctors too.

5   1. do you spell
     2. or
     3. pretty (Mögliche Antwort)
     4. Her (Mögliche Antwort)
     5. He is an (Mögliche Antwort)
     6. about
     7. too
     8. she is
     9. She's
    10. I am

6 There are two doctors, and only one of the children is a doctor, so one of the parents is a doctor. The two doctors are fair, and the father and the daughter are dark; so the mother, Mary, is a doctor. Elizabeth is the only daughter, so she is the actress. Tom is an architect, so he isn't one of the children: he's the father. Harry is dark, so he isn't a doctor, he's an artist. John is a doctor.

7 A: Hello, Dan. How are you?
   D: Oh, hi, Andrew. Not bad, not bad.
   A: And how's your mother?
   D: Oh, very well now, thanks. And you, Andrew? How are you?
   A: Fine, thanks. Yes, very fine: I've got a new girlfriend.
   D: Have you? I've got a new girlfriend, too.
   A: Oh? Is she pretty?
   D: Pretty, *and* intelligent.
   A: What does she do?
   D: She's a student, a business student.
   A: Yeah? My girlfriend's a business student, too. She's very pretty: tall, and fair . . .
   D: Er, is she English?
   A: English? Oh, no, she's Swedish, in fact.
   D: Swedish? From Stockholm?
   A: No, from Malmö.
   D: Oh. And her name is Kirsten, isn't it?
   A: Well, yes, it is. Do you mean . . . ?
   D: Yeah, I think Kirsten has got two new boyfriends.

Unit 5, Lesson A

1 4. Yes, there are two (women).
   5. No, there isn't. There's a chair near the table.
      (Mögliche Antwort)
   6. Yes, there are two (windows).
   7. Yes, there are.
   8. Yes, there is.
   9. Yes, there is.
   10. Yes, there is.
   11. No, there aren't.
   12. Yes, there are two (coats).

3 2. There's a table in the living room.
   3. There are three armchairs in the living room.
   4. There's a woman on the sofa.
   5. There are two children in the room.

4 1. the   5. a, the
   2. the   6. a
   3. an, the   7. a
   4. a

5 Sally's flat:
   There *are* four *rooms* in Sally's flat: a living room, two *bedrooms* and a big *kitchen*. *There* is *a* bathroom too, and a separate *toilet*. In the kitchen *there is* a big *fridge* and a dishwasher. *There is* a colour *TV* in the *living room*.

   Jenny's flat:
   There are two rooms in Jenny's flat: a bed-sitting room and a very small kitchen. There is a small bathroom too, with a shower and a toilet. In the kitchen there is a small fridge. There is a black and white TV in the bed-sitting room.

Unit 5, Lesson B

1 1. at   5. On
   2. in, in   6. at
   3. on   7. in
   4. in   8. in

2 1. lives
   2. live
   3. live
   4. lives
   5. lives

4 If the photographer and the doctor are women, the architect is a man. If Philip is not an artist, he is an architect; and he lives on the ground floor. Jane lives on the first floor, and Susan is not a doctor, so Jane is a doctor. If Jane is a doctor, Susan is a photographer. If Susan lives under Dan, she lives on the second floor, and Dan lives on the third floor (he is an artist).

NAME	JOB	FLOOR
Dan	artist	third
Susan	photographer	second
Jane	doctor	first
Philip	architect	ground

5 LESLIE: Excuse me, John. What's your address?
   JOHN: A hundred and sixteen Market Street.
   LESLIE: Thanks. And your phone number?
   JOHN: What?
   LESLIE: Your phone number.
   JOHN: Oh, er, 314 6829.

Unit 5, Lesson C

1 (Mögliche Antworten)
   A: *Excuse me. Where's the reception desk, please?*
   B: Over there by the stairs.
   A: *Oh, thank you very much.*

   * * *

   A: Excuse me. Where's Room 8, please?
   B: *Upstairs on the first floor.*
   A: *Oh, thank you very much.*

   * * *

   A: Excuse me. Where's the nearest *car park?*
   B: *I'm sorry, I don't know.*
   A: *Thank you anyway.*

3 1. True (between Alaska and Siberia)
   2. False (but in 1610 it was true)
   3. False (4,807 metres)
   4. False (100 pence)
   5. True
   6. False (1.6 kilometres)
   7. True
   8. False (There are penguins in the Antarctic.)

4 2. Is there an armchair in your bathroom?
   3. Is there a hotel in your street?
   4. Is there a bank at the station?
   5. Are there (any) camels in Argentina?
   6. Is there a bus stop in this street?
   7. Is there a fridge in your kitchen?
   8. Are there (any) crocodiles in Texas?

5 A: *Excuse me. Where's the manager's office, please?*
   B: *It's over there* by the reception desk.
   A: *Thank you.*

   * * *

   A: *Excuse me. Where are the toilets, please?*
   B: Upstairs *on* the first floor, first door *on the* left.
   A: *Thank you* very much.

Unit 5, Lesson D

2 1. from   6. on/under
   2. at   7. at
   3. for   8. in
   4. on   9. of
   5. in   10. on/under

4 (Mögliche Antworten)
   1. . . . table, cupboard, fridge, *etc.*
   2. . . . engineer, photographer, housewife, *etc.*
   3. . . . station, police station, car park, *etc.*
   4. . . . kitchen, bathroom, hall, *etc.*

6 You are at A. Go straight on, take the second street on the left and the first on the right. Where are you?

Unit 6, Lesson A

1 1. 'Do you like Mozart?' 'No, I *don't.*'
   2. 'I *like* orange juice, but I *don't like* apple juice at all.' 'Don't you?'
   3. 'I like Picasso very much.' '*Do you?*' 'Yes, I *do.*'
   4. What sort of books *do you like?*
   5. Everybody *likes* Sally. Nobody *likes* Ann.
   6. 'Do *you like* big dogs?' 'No, I *don't.*'
   7. 'Only two people in my family *like* dancing.'

2 1. They   7. they
   2. him   8. he
   3. them   9. it
   4. she; her   10. them
   5. them   11. it
   6. her   12. him

141

4 Lösung: Catherine

Peter likes Anne. John likes two people; one of them can't be Catherine, because only one person likes her, and that is Anne. So John likes Anne and Peter, and the person who doesn't like Anne is Catherine.

Unit 6, Lesson B

2 B. a quarter past nine
C. five past eleven
D. twenty-five to seven
E. ten to eight
F. twenty past four
G. half past ten
H. half past two

3

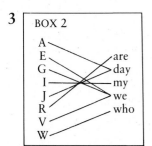

BOX 2

A
E
G ——— are
I ——— day
J ——— my
R ——— we
V ——— who
W

4 A, B, D

5

O	C	L	O	C	K		E	I	G	H	T	Y			E	I	G	H	T
F		I	N	N			N		O		E		O	F		I		H	
	O	K		N	O		G	R	O	U	N	D	F	L	O	O	R		A
O	N	E		W			L		D			O		O		F	L	A	T
	L			S	I	X			O			O				O			F
M	Y			T	H	I	S		O		Q	U	A	R	T	E	R		N
U		O		T	H	E	R	E				I				I			I
C	A	T	S							T	H	I	R	T	E	E	N		E
H		W		I		O	N	E			E				N				E
	M	O	R	N	I	N	G		O		M	A	R	R	I	E	D		

Unit 6, Lesson C

1 1. Does
2. do
3. does
4. Do
5. do
6. Does
7. does

2 1. start
2. have
3. lives
4. opens
5. sells
6. have
7. repairs

3 (Mögliche Antworten)
Where do you live?
Does your sister live in London?
What time does Dr Wagner start work?
Does Jane start work early?
Do you work in a garage?
What time do her children have lunch?
Does your mother live in London?
Where does Mr Carter live?

5 A. She is an air hostess.
B. She is a doctor.
C. He is a bank manager.
D. He is an artist.
E. She is a singer.
F. He is a lorry driver.

Unit 6, Lesson D

1 1. has   6. like
2. have   7. gets up
3. go   8. work
4. goes   9. live
5. works   10. do

2 2. I hate *it*.
3. Alice loves *them*.
4. Children love *her*.
5. I don't like *it*.
6. Can I speak to *him*, please?
7. Do you like *it*?
8. She loves *them*.
9. I don't like *her* very much.
10. I hate *it*.
11. You can't speak to *him*. He isn't here.
12. Do you like *them*?

3 (Mögliche Antworten)
1. I *sometimes* eat bananas.
2. I *never* go to the cinema.
3. I *often* drink coffee.
4. I *never* speak French.
5. I *usually* work at home.
6. I *always* get up before six o'clock.
7. I *never* eat fish.
8. I *often* go dancing.
9. I *always* drink tea.
10. I *never* read poetry.
11. I *often* watch TV on Sundays.
12. I *sometimes* play tennis.

5 Hello. How are you?
What's your name?
Where are you from?
What do you do?
Are you married?
Have you got any brothers or sisters?
Where do you live?
What's your address?
What's your phone number?
How old are you?
Pardon?
Do you speak English?
What newspapers do you read?
Do you like music?
What sort of music do you like?
Do you play football?

Unit 7, Lesson A

1 haven't – have not
doesn't – does not
don't – do not
I'm – I am
we're – we are
you're – you are
they're – they are

2 1. Our
2. She
3. they; Their
4. her
5. We
6. his

4 like – likes   finish – finishes
watch – watches   have – has
get – gets   sell – sells
go – goes   study – studies

5 1. do   5. do
2. do   6. does
3. Does   7. does
4. Do   8. do

6
2. eighth
3. tenth
4. ninth
5. first
6. fifth
7. third
8. second
9. fourth
10. seventh

7 980 calories

Unit 7, Lesson B

1
1. the
2. –
3. –
4. the
5. –, –
6. the, the
7. –, –
8. –

2
1. am
2. was
3. was, was
4. is
5. Are
6. were
7. Were
8. Is

4
1. No, I'm not.
2. No, I don't.
3. No, he isn't.
4. No, she doesn't.
5. No, we aren't.
6. No, you aren't.
7. No, they don't.
8. No, he doesn't.
9. No, they aren't.

6 girl's bicycle: £40
winter coat: £20
12lbs of apples: £1
two Alsatian puppies: £90
Renault 12TL: £650
violin: £125
three ducks: £5.25

Total cost: £931.25

Unit 7, Lesson C

1

U	C
butter	£5 note
wool	sheep
beer	banana
rain	tomato
bread	bank
music	
wine	
money	

2
1 – a potato
2 – a paper
3 – some chicken
4 – a glass
5 – some potato
6 – some melon
7 – a chicken
8 – some glass
9 – some paper
10 – a melon

3
1. some
2. any
3. some
4. any
5. any
6. any
7. any
8. any
9. some
10. some

5
3. Where *does* your mother *live*?
4. What time *do* you *start* work?
5. Lucy *does not work* on Friday afternoons.
6. *Does* Cathy *like* reading?
7. *Do* they *speak* German in Switzerland?
8. I watch football, but I *do not play* it.
9. Robert *likes* dancing and tennis.
10. Alexandra *plays* the violin very well.

6 Is there any water in this room?
Is there any cheese in your house?
Are there any doctors in the class?
Is there any money on your table?
Is there any apple juice in your fridge?
Are there any eggs in your fridge?
Are there any chairs in your bedroom?
Are there any horses near your home?
Is there any bread in your kitchen?

Unit 7, Lesson D

1
1. How many
2. How much
3. How many
4. How many
5. How much
6. How much
7. How many
8. How many

2 (Mögliche Antworten)
I haven't got enough money.
I've got too many clothes.
I haven't got a lot of free time.

5 (Mögliche Antwort)
Dear Mary,
Well, here we are at last. Our hotel is very nice. We're on the 14th floor with a good view of the sea. The room's small, but it's clean and quiet. The food's good and there's always enough. Sometimes there's too much! There aren't many English people here, but there's a nice couple from Manchester in the next room.
Love,
Carol and Jim

Unit 8, Lesson A

1
1. in
2. on
3. in
4. in
5. near
6. to
7. by
8. at
9. on
10. to
11. opposite / next to / near
12. of
13. next to / opposite / near
14. outside
15. from
16. until
17. at
18. at
19. from
20. at
21. in
22. on
23. in
24. at
25. in
26. On
27. in
28. On
29. On

2 (Mögliche Antworten)
2. Is there any butter in the fridge?
3. What time is your train?
4. Do you go by train?
5. Are there any apples in the fridge?
6. Where do you live?
7. Were you at home?
8. Excuse me. Where's the bank?
9. How far is the post office?
10. Where do you work?
11. What is your telephone number?
12. How do you get to work?
13. What sort of books do you like?
14. Do you like Mozart?

3
1. There *are some* apples in the cupboard.
2. *Is* there *any* ice cream in the fridge?
3. How *many* students *are* there in your class?
4. *A lot of* my friends play tennis, but not many of them play badminton.
5. How *much* milk have we got?
6. There are too *many* chairs in here.
7. *There is* too *much* coffee in this cup.
8. There *isn't any* cheese in the fridge, but there *are some* eggs.
9. There *are* seven people, but only five books – that's not *enough*.
10. Are there *any* fair people in your family?

4 (Mögliche Antworten)

Ann sometimes watches TV. She sometimes plays tennis. She never plays football. She often goes dancing. She never goes to work by bus, but she often goes to work by taxi or by train. She sometimes travels by air. She never works on Saturdays, but she often works at night. She sometimes falls in love.

Joe never goes to the theatre. He often goes to the cinema. He sometimes watches TV. He often plays tennis, and he often plays football. He never goes dancing. He always goes to work by bus; he never goes to work by taxi or by train. He sometimes travels by air. He very often works on Saturdays, but he never works at night. He very often falls in love.

6

Unit 8, Lesson B

1
1. Where *do you live*?
2. How *do Miriam and Stephen travel* to work?
3. My sister *lives* in a large flat in London.
4. *Does she work* in London?
5. Everybody in my class *speaks* Japanese.
6. My brother *doesn't live* in Britain.
7. I *speak* some Spanish, but I *don't understand* much.
8. What sort of food *do they like*?
9. *Do Teresa and Patricio live* near their parents?
10. 'Do you know Shelagh Anderson?' 'No, I don't.'
11. 'Do you read a newspaper on Sundays?' 'Yes, I read The Observer.'
12. What time *do your children go* to bed?
13. My sister and her husband haven't got a car; *they go* to work by bus.
14. My sister and I *dislike* shopping, but my brother *loves* it.
15. 'Does your brother play tennis?' 'No, but my sister plays very well.'

3

dislikes	plays
gets	reads
goes	starts
hates	stops
likes	travels
listens to	tries
lives	watches
loves	works

4
1. And is it a house or a flat?
2. How many bedrooms has it got?
3. ✓
4. ✓
5. Do you listen to music?

5 On Mondays she plays the violin and goes swimming.
On Tuesdays she reads or watches television.
On Wednesdays she plays the violin and plays basketball.
On Thursdays she goes shopping.
On Fridays she plays the violin and goes to an English class.
On Saturdays she reads or watches television or goes to the cinema.

Unit 8, Lesson C

2
1. There are/He's got too many books.
2. I've got enough.
3. There are some children.
4. There are a lot of children.
5. There are too many children.
6. There is a lot of snow.
7. There is not enough snow.
8. There is some water on the street.
9. There is too much water.
10. There are not enough chairs.

3

1.	an	11.	–
2.	–	12.	–
3.	–	13.	a
4.	–	14.	the
5.	some	15.	the, the
6.	–	16.	a
7.	–	17.	some
8.	a	18.	–
9.	a, –	19.	–
10.	the	20.	an

4

2.	police station	6.	post office
3.	bank	7.	supermarket
4.	car park	8.	bus stop
5.	station	9.	swimming pool

5 (Mögliche Antworten)
1. Go straight up Stratton Way and take the second street on the left. Go straight on and take the second right (Boxhill Walk). Then take the first left.
2. Go straight up Stratton Way and on up Vineyard. Take the second left after The Holt, and The Siger Road is the first left.
3. Go along Stratton Way and turn left into Bath Street. Take the first right and go along Letcombe Avenue. At the end turn left into Fitzharry's Road. Turn right at the end and then first left.

6 Well, erm, go straight on up Stratton Way, and take the first, no, not the first, the second left. That's Bath Street. Keep straight on to Letcombe Avenue, and turn right, I think that's the first right. Then take the second right, and the first left. It's on the right.

Er, let's see, go straight on here up Stratton Way, second left, first right, second right, first left. It's on the right.

ÜBUNGEN ZU LESSON 8D ENTFALLEN.

Unit 9, Lesson A

1 (Mögliche Antworten)
1. Mrs Calloway's flat *has got* a big kitchen.
2. You*'ve got* pretty eyes, Mary.
3. We*'ve got* four bedrooms in our house.
4. Some Eskimo languages *have got* no word for 'snow'.
5. I*'ve got* a very good dentist.
6. My sister *has got* three boyfriends.
7. My father*'s got* double nationality.
8. Sam *has got* enough money.
9. The President*'s got* a TV in his bathroom.

2 3. and 7. and
4. – 8. –
5. – 9. –
6. and 10. –, –

3 1. What 6. Where
2. Where 7. How
3. Who 8. Who
4. What 9. How
5. What

4 3. Yes, I have. / No, I haven't.
4. Yes, I do. / No, I don't.
5. Yes, I am. / No, I'm not.
6. Yes, I do. / No, I don't.
7. Yes, I have. / No, I haven't.
8. Yes, I do. / No, I don't.
9. Yes, she/he has. / No, she/he hasn't.

Unit 9, Lesson B

1 1. yellow 6. grey
2. black and white 7. blue
3. red 8. green
4. green 9. white
5. orange

3 1. have got 7. has got
2. is, has got 8. is
3. are 9. is
4. is 10. Are
5. has got 11. has got; are, are
6. have got 12. has got

4 1. We have got a small blue car.
2. I am wearing a green and yellow dress.
3. Jane has got long dark hair.
4. Elephants have got big grey ears.
5. There are two dark green chairs and a colour TV in my living room.
6. Sally has got long hair, green eyes and small ears.

5

Satzgegenstand	Ergänzung	Besitzanzeigendes Fürwort
I	me	my
you	you	*your*
he	him	*his*
she	her	her
we	us	*our*
they	them	their

6 Are you wearing a sweater?
Who's wearing brown shoes?
Are you wearing jeans?
Are you wearing a skirt?
Are you wearing glasses?
Are you wearing blue socks?
Who's wearing boots?

Unit 9, Lesson C

1 we are – we're
you have got – you've got
we have not got – we haven't got
it is not – it isn't
John is – John's
John has got – John's got
John has not got – John hasn't got
they have – they've
you are – you're
it is – it's

2 2. Has she got a sister?
3. Have your parents got a nice house?
4. Have you got any coffee?
5. Has Mrs Hawkins got any children?
6. Has your house got a dining room?
7. Have you got a TV?

3 4. My parents haven't got a very nice house.
5. I haven't got any bread in my bag.
6. Peter and Ellen haven't got a Rolls-Royce.
7. Sally hasn't got long hair.
8. Robert hasn't got his father's nose.
9. I haven't got my mother's personality.

5 STEVE: 'She's about 5ft 8, about 9 stone, fair hair and a fairly thin face, slender figure, a slightly turned-up nose and a little double chin. And that's about it. And that's my wife. I don't know the colour of her eyes.'

LORNA: 'I'm going to describe my mum. She's 5ft 5, long wavy dark brown hair, dark brown eyes, fairly pretty – wearing well, I think – fairly slim, fairly pale complexion. That's about it.'

Unit 9, Lesson D

1 2. What newspaper do you read?
3. How do you travel to work?
4. Do you play tennis?
5. Do you speak Chinese?
6. Where do you live?
7. Where do you work?

2 (Mögliche Antworten)
2. What newspaper does she read?
3. How does she travel to work?
4. Does she play tennis?
5. Does she speak Chinese?
6. Where does she live?
7. Where does she work?

3 (Mögliche Antwort)
A: Mr *Sanders?*
B: *Yes.*
A: I'm *John Bell. Did you have a good* journey?
B: *Not bad, thanks.*
A: *My* car's *outside.* Let's *go.*

Unit 10, Lesson A

1 1. have
2. have, has
3. Are
4. is
5. am, have
6. is
7. has
8. is

2 2. When Mary is tired she has a bath.
3. When I am bored I go shopping.
4. When Fred is hot he has a shower.
5. When Judy is unhappy she goes to the cinema.
6. When Sam is hungry he goes to a restaurant.
7. When Ann is bored she telephones friends.
8. When Lucy is happy she goes to a disco.

4 2. swimming pool
3. bathroom
4. doctor
5. dentist
6. supermarket
7. school
8. disco

5

B	O	R	E	D		B	A	T	H
Y		O		I		U		A	
		C	O	L	D		S	H	O	P
E		M		T		A		P	
N			U	N	H	A	P	P	Y
G	O	T		I		P			
L		D	I	R	T	Y		R	
I	L	L		S			M	E	
S				T	I	R	E	D	
H	U	N	G	R	Y			N	

Unit 10, Lesson B

1 A: Can I *help* you?
B: I'm looking *for* a blouse.
A: What *size*?
B: 14.
A: Here's a lovely *blue one*.
B: Well, blue doesn't really suit *me*. Have you got anything *in* yellow?
A: Yes. Here's a nice *one* in yellow.
B: Can I try *it* on?
A: *Of* course.

      *   *   *

B: How much *is* it?
A: £19.95.
B: All right. I'll *take* it.

2 (Mögliche Antworten)
1. A red one.
2. An old one.
3. A green one.
4. An expensive one.
5. A large one.
6. A round one.
7. A small one.

3 1. He, him
2. it
3. She, her
4. them
5. It
6. They; them
7. him

4 1. –
2. a
3. the; the, –
4. –
5. – , a
6. the

Unit 10, Lesson C

2 2. Can I help you?
3. Can I look at those shoes?
4. What a nice shirt!
5. I'm looking for a French dictionary.
6. I'd like to try it on.
7. Have you got anything in blue?

3 1. at, at   6. on
2. Until   7. in; in, of
3. On   8. in
4. to   9. with
5. at   10. on

4 1. many   6. much
2. much   7. many
3. much   8. many
4. much   9. many
5. many   10. much

5 1. Park Lane
2. 350
3. *5 minutes*
4. *2*
5. nothing

Unit 10, Lesson D

1 1. too many   6. How many
2. Not many   7. not much
3. how much   8. too many
4. not much   9. How many
5. too much   10. not many

6 A: What time is the next train to York, please?
B: There's one at 4.45, change at Birmingham.
A: Is there a direct one?
B: There's a direct one at 5.52, arriving at 8.28.
A: Which platform for the 5.52?
B: Platform 6.

A: Can I help you?
B: Yes, I'd like a room, please.
A: Single or double?
B: Double, please.
A: For one night?
B: No, two nights.
A: With bath or with shower?
B: With bath, please. How much is the room?
A: £75 a night, including breakfast.
B: Can I pay by credit card?
A: Yes, of course. Could you fill in the form, please?

Unit 11, Lesson A

1 arrive – arrived   pronounce – pronounced
change – changed   remember – remembered
help – helped   start – started
live – lived   stay – stayed
look – looked   try – tried
love – loved   watch – watched
marry – married   work – worked

3 9.20 twenty past nine   7.40 twenty to eight
9.25 twenty-five past nine   5.30 half past five
10.45 a quarter to eleven   1.50 ten to two
5.15 a quarter past five   11.55 five to twelve
3.35 twenty-five to four   7.05 five past seven
6.10 ten past six

4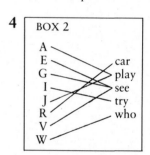

Unit 11, Lesson B

1 3. . . . were you sometimes hungry?
4. . . . were you at home a lot?
5. . . . were your parents happy?
6. . . . was your family rich?
7. . . . was your house big enough?
8. . . . was your father out all day?
9. . . . was your grandmother pretty?
10. . . . was your mother very young?

2 2. milk (not furniture)
3. eye (not hair)
4. hand (not on the face)
5. long (not a colour)
6. shoes (not clothes)
7. mouth (not an adjective)
8. tie (others are all women's clothes)
9. restaurant (not an adjective)
10. breakfast (not a place)

5 I was born in a small flat in Berlin. My parents were poor. My father was a shop assistant and my mother was a housewife. Sometimes we were hungry. My parents were very good to me and I was nearly always happy.

Unit 11, Lesson C

2 2. She did not live in London.
3. She did not play basketball.
4. She did not study languages.
5. She did not marry a doctor.
6. She did not work in an office.
7. She did not often travel to Africa.

3 2. Where did she live?
3. What did she play?
4. What did she study?
5. Who did she marry?
6. Where did she work?
7. Where did she travel?

4 (Mögliche Antwort)
Philip Hallow was born in London in 1967. His father
was a bus driver and his mother was a librarian. They
didn't have much money, but Philip and his two sisters,
Jane and Sarah, were very happy children. In 1984 Philip's
father died, so Philip didn't go to university. He started
working in a bank but didn't like it so he changed to an
import-export firm. Now he's the Assistant Manager and
he's very happy.

Unit 11, Lesson D

1

want – wanted	hate – hated
study – studied	help – helped
have – had	get – got
know – knew	tell – told
come – came	shop – shopped
stop – stopped	

2

woke – wake	could – can
worked – work	finished – finish
called – call	did – do
died – die	liked – like
said – say	went – go

3 (Mögliche Antworten)

THEN	NOW
He started work at 7.30.	*He starts work at 9.30.*
He worked ten hours a day.	He works five hours a day.
He ate cheap food.	*He eats expensive food.*
He never went to restaurants.	He often goes to restaurants.
He did not travel much.	*He travels a lot.*
He played football on Saturday afternoons.	*He plays golf on Saturday afternoons.*
He had a lot of girlfriends.	He still has a lot of girlfriends.
He wanted to be an artist.	He doesn't want to be an artist.
His mother worked in a shop.	*His mother doesn't work in a shop.*
He didn't have a car.	He's got three cars.

7 1. What time did you *come home* last night, then, June?
2. About half past *twelve*, I think.
3. I didn't want to wake *you* up.
4. You know I *don't like* loud music.
5. Why did you come *back* so late?
6. No, but we went to Alice's place and *had coffee.*

Unit 12, Lesson A

1

1. was	12. wanted	22. started
2. lived	13. got	23. was not
3. went	14. read	24. was
4. bought	15. tried	25. had
5. travelled	16. looked	26. were
6. walked	17. tried	27. saw
7. was	18. went	28. heard
8. loved	19. talked	29. thought
9. were	20. met	30. loved
10. met	21. had	31. came
11. spoke		

2 (Mögliche Antworten)
2. Did you like school?
3. How did you come to work?
4. Were you happy or unhappy when you were a child?
5. Did you like Mozart when you were young?
6. What time was it?
7. Where were your parents born?
8. Where did you live?

3

1. am, have	9. am; have got
2. has got	10. have got
3. are	11. are
4. have	12. are
5. have got	13. have
6. (I')m	14. have got
7. is	15. (I')m
8. are	

4 (Mögliche Antworten)
1. 'What's this called in English?'
2. 'Who do you look like?'
3. 'I'm just looking.'
4. 'Have you got this in red?'
5. 'How much are these?'
6. 'How was your journey?'

6 1. 13.10
2. £7.50
3. No.
4. No.

7

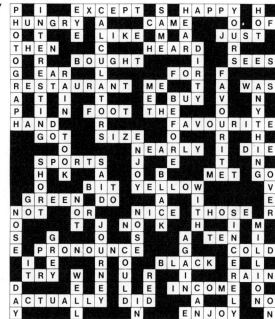

Unit 12, Lesson B

1 (Mögliche Antworten)
1. ... table, fridge
2. ... bread, butter
3. ... station, supermarket
4. ... American, German
5. ... he, it
6. ... on, next to
7. ... tired, happy

2 1. came
2. that
3. those
4. this; here
5. These
6. that
7. go

3
1. ten
2. all
3. bank
4. home
5. cost
6. ear
7. here
8. live
9. feet
10. who

4
5. Where do your sister and her husband live?
6. Is there any butter in the fridge?
7. Have you got any American friends?
8. Where does your aunt Helen work?
9. When does the 9.25 train arrive?
10. How many children have Fred and Catherine got?
11. How many chairs are there in the kitchen?
12. How many wives did Henry VII have?

5 Indira Gandhi was the first woman Prime Minister of India.
Van Gogh painted pictures.
Agatha Christie wrote detective stories.
Shakespeare wrote *Hamlet.*
Karl Marx wrote *Das Kapital.*
Hitchcock made many famous films.
Columbus discovered America in 1492.

6 (Mögliche Antwort)
Ernest Hemingway was born in Illinois in 1899 and died in Idaho in 1961. His father was a doctor and his mother was a musician and a painter. Hemingway drove an ambulance in Italy during the First World War. After the war he was a journalist in Paris for several years. He wrote many well-known novels, including *The Sun Also Rises, Farewell to Arms, For Whom the Bell Tolls* and *The Old Man and the Sea.* He won the Nobel Prize for literature in 1954.

Unit 12, Lesson C

1
1. pants
2. bra
3. socks
4. jeans
5. jacket
6. dress
7. tights
8. shirt
9. blouse
10. skirt
11. trousers
12. sweater
13. boots
14. shoes
15. glasses
16. tie
17. ear-rings

2
2. hotel
3. income
4. eleven
5. good-looking
6. Chinese
7. again

3
2. 'When did she arrive?'
3. 'What time did you get up?'
4. 'How many French people were there?'
5. 'When did he die?'
6. 'How old are you?'
7. 'What sort of music do you like?'

4
3. –
4. s
5. –
6. –, –
7. s, –
8. –, –
9. –, –, –

5
1. some
2. any
3. any
4. some
5. any
6. any
7. some
8. any

6 – . . . and can you describe the man, Mr Harris?
– Yes. He's quite tall, about 25 or 30, with long fair hair, big ears, and a scar under his left eye. Oh, and he's got a big nose.
– Colour of eyes?
– I've no idea.
– What was he wearing?
– A blue jacket and brown trousers . . .

7 Grace Kelly: 1, 5, 7, 8, 10, 13
Queen Elizabeth I: 2, 3, 4, 6, 9, 11, 12

> ÜBUNGEN ZU LESSON 12D ENTFALLEN.

Unit 13, Lesson B

1
1. My aunt can play tennis better than Steffi Graf.
2. I can ski better now than I could when I was younger.
3. I was good at football when I was younger.

3
2. Can your brother cook quite well?
3. Can you swim 200 metres?
4. Did she come by car?
5. Was your mother a dancer (too)?
6. Were they unhappy?
7. How many words a minute can he type?
8. How many keys has your piano got?

5 Valerie is not the organist, so put *no* in that column.
Lorna cannot speak German, so put *no* in that column.
Mary cannot speak Italian, so put *no* in that column.
Anthea cannot play the violin, so put *no* in that column.
Anthea cannot speak Spanish, so put *no* in that column.
Valerie can't speak French, so put *no* in that column.
Lorna doesn't play the harp, so put *no* in that column.
The girl who plays the violin speaks French, so Valerie (who doesn't speak French) cannot play the violin. Put *no* in that column.
This puts three *nos* in the violin column; so Lorna is the one who can play the violin, and since the girl who plays the violin speaks French, that is Lorna, too. Put *yes* in those two columns and *no* in all Lorna's other columns.
This puts three *nos* in the organ column. Put *yes* in Anthea's organ column and *no* in her other instrument columns.
The organist can't speak Italian, so put *no* in Anthea's Italian column.
This leaves Valerie who can speak Italian; put *yes* there and *no* in the other language columns.
This means Mary can speak Spanish, which means Anthea can speak German.
The only harp column now free is Valerie's. Valerie can speak Italian and play the harp.

Unit 13, Lesson C

1
pretty	prettier	prettiest
cold	colder	coldest
young	younger	youngest
rude	ruder	rudest
red	redder	reddest
talkative	more talkative	most talkative
cheerful	more cheerful	most cheerful
terrible	more terrible	most terrible
thirsty	thirstier	thirstiest
large	larger	largest
tall	taller	tallest
warm	warmer	warmest
hot	hotter	hottest
long	longer	longest

2
funnier – funny
nicest – nice
worse – bad
oldest – old
noisiest – noisy
later – late
cheaper – cheap
bigger – big
thinner – thin
smaller – small

3 2. She's shorter than me.
3. I'm smaller than her.
4. She's lighter than him.
5. I'm fairer than her.
6. We're taller than them.
7. Italian is easier than Chinese.

4 The highest mountain in the world is K2, not Everest.
The smallest continent in the world is Australia.
The largest ocean in the world is the Pacific.
The largest sea in the world is the South China Sea.
The farthest spot from land in the world is in the South Pacific.
The longest river in the world is the Nile or the Amazon. (It depends on how you measure.)
The highest lake in the world is Titicaca, in Peru.
The largest active volcano in the world is Mauna Loa, in Hawaii.

Unit 13, Lesson D

4 1. good-looking
2. expensive
3. understand

Unit 14, Lesson A

1 DOCTOR: *How tall are you*, Mr Rannoch?
PATIENT: 1 metre 76, doctor.
DOCTOR: Yes, I see. And *how much do you weigh*?
PATIENT: About 80 kilos.
DOCTOR: Yes, right. *How old are you?*
PATIENT: 32.

2 Oscar Duke is thirty-seven. He is one metre eighty-three, and weighs eighty-six kilos.
Tony Lands is fourteen. He is one metre fifty-five, and weighs forty-seven kilos.
Amelia Barry is sixty-eight. She is one metre sixty, and weighs forty-five kilos.
Oliver Ashe is thirty-three. He is one metre seventy-five, and weighs a hundred and four kilos.

3 two hundred and seventy-nine
four hundred and sixty-six
one thousand five hundred
one thousand seven hundred and ninety-nine
four thousand three hundred and twenty-eight
seventeen thousand six hundred
ninety-five thousand, seven hundred and sixty-seven
four million

5 2. four o'clock
3. half past seven
4. a quarter to twelve
5. twenty-five past four
6. ten past five
7. a quarter past eleven
8. twenty to three
9. five past two
10. twenty to six

6

Unit 14, Lesson B

1 1. looks like   5. looks like, like
2. look   6. looks like
3. like   7. look
4. look   8. like

2 1. the   6. –
2. an   7. the
3. – , –   8. a
4. a, the, an   9. a, –
5. –

4 1. than   5. than
2. than   6. as, as
3. as, as   7. than
4. as   8. as

6 The first picture.

Unit 14, Lesson C

1 8 May 1986 – 'May the eighth, nineteen eighty-six'
17 July 1600 – 'July the seventeenth, sixteen hundred'
12 December 1945 – 'December the twelfth, nineteen forty-five'
3 October 1844 – 'October the third, eighteen forty-four'
11 March 1011 – 'March the eleventh, ten eleven'
20 November 1907 – 'November the twentieth, nineteen hundred and seven' (OR: ' . . . nineteen oh seven')

2 1. bis 6. Verschiedene mögliche Antworten.
7. March 1, 1992
8. Sunday; Wednesday
9. yes
10. Verschiedene mögliche Antworten.
11. July
12. June
13. week
14. year

5 This is a picture of a *large light room*. There are fourteen *pieces of furniture: nine chairs, three tables* and *two cupboards*. There are *ten people* in the room – a woman *and nine men*. The *woman is* talking *to the men*, who *are listening*.

Unit 14, Lesson D

1 1. What sort of music do you like?
2. How many children have you got?
3. How many days are there in a year?
4. How many rooms are there in the flat? (Mögliche Antwort)
5. What sort of books do you like?
6. What sort of sweater have you got? (Mögliche Antwort)
7. How many students are there in your class? (Mögliche Antwort)
8. How many litres of milk have we got? (Mögliche Antwort)

2 ANN: Cambridge 342266.
BOB: Hi. *This* is Bob. Is *that* Ann?
ANN: Yes. Hi, Bob.
BOB: *Can* I speak to Jill?
ANN: I'm afraid she's not *in* at the moment. Can I *take a message*?
BOB: Yes, could you *ask* her to phone me when she gets home?
ANN: OK. I'll tell her.
BOB: Thanks a lot.
ANN: You're *welcome*. Bye.
BOB: *Bye.*

3	Einzahl zählbar	Mehrzahl zählbar	Nichtzählbar
	eye	ear-rings	water
	watch	jeans	beer
	apple	glasses	snow
	foot	feet	money
	bank	pounds	news
		people	
		trousers	

Unit 15, Lesson A

4 (Verschiedene mögliche Antworten, einschließlich:)
Grandmother is sleeping.
Some children are playing outside.
Father is sitting in an armchair.
Mother is cooking in the kitchen.

Unit 15, Lesson B

1 drive – driving
get – getting
go – going
lie – lying
live – living
make – making
play – playing
run – running
shop – shopping
smoke – smoking
start – starting
stop – stopping
think – thinking
wear – wearing
work – working

2 (Mögliche Antworten)

A: Hello. Cardiff 945 5928.
B: Hello, Jenny. *This* is Owen. *Could I speak to* Mike, please?
A: I'm sorry, he can't come to the phone just now, Owen. He's *cooking*.
B: OK, I'll ring back later.
A: I'll tell *him* you called. Bye.
B: Bye.

* * *

A: What *are you eat*ing?
B: Chocolate. *Would you* like some?
A: No, thanks. *I don't* like chocolate.

4 1. It is *rain*ing.
2. It is *snow*ing.
3. The *sun* is shining.
4. The weather is *terrible*.
5. The *weather* is fine.

Unit 15, Lesson C

1 (Mögliche Antworten)
PAT: Hello, Waterford 31868.
MARY: *Is Pat there, please?*
PAT: This is Pat. Who's *speaking, please?*
MARY: Oh, hello, Pat. It's Mary. *Are you free this evening?*
PAT: No, I'm sorry. I'm not. My uncle's *coming* to dinner with us.
MARY: Well, are you *free* on Thursday?
PAT: *Yes, I am.*
MARY: *Would you like to go to a jazz concert?*
PAT: I'd love to. What time?
MARY: Let's meet at eight at *the station.*
PAT: OK. *See you on Thursday at eight at the station.*
MARY: *Fine. Bye.*

3 1. taller
2. tallest
3. older
4. easier
5. largest
6. More
7. better
8. worse
9. most, nicest
10. more

4 BILL: Hello, Jane. Are you doing anything this evening?
JANE: Oh, hello, Bill. I'm not sure. Perhaps. What's today? Monday. I don't know. Why?
BILL: Well, Michael Bentley's singing at the Palace. Would you like to come?
JANE: I don't know, I'm a bit tired. I don't really want to go out tonight.
BILL: What about tomorrow, then? Would you like to see a film, have something to eat?
JANE: Oh, dear. I'd love to, but I'm going to a concert in London. What about Wednesday? Can we do something on Wednesday?
BILL: No, I'm working on Wednesday evening. What about Thursday?
JANE: No, I'm working on Thursday, and my granny's probably coming on Friday.
BILL: Well, let's do something at the weekend. City are playing at home on Saturday. Would you like to go?
JANE: Perhaps. Yes, why not?
BILL: OK. See you outside the ground about two o'clock, OK?
JANE: Right, see you then. Bye.
BILL: Bye.

5 A: Manchester are playing against Arsenal on the 12th and Tottenham on the 19th. So on the 26th Manchester are playing against Liverpool, which means that Arsenal are playing against Tottenham.

B: O'Connor is performing on September 19th or 21st before he leaves Fantasia, which means that he is either doing folk songs in the Jazz Cellar or acting *Hamlet*. But Ducarme is the actor, so Ducarme is doing *Hamlet*, and O'Connor is doing the folk songs. Haas is talking about butterflies (he isn't musical); so Carlotti is playing the violin.

Unit 15, Lesson D

1 1. hour
2. hours, day
3. days, week
4. days, month
5. months, year

3 1. on
2. at
3. in
4. for
5. in
6. –
7. for *or* in

Unit 16, Lesson A

1
comfortable	more comfortable	most comfortable
economical	more economical	most economical
funny	funnier	funniest
heavy	heavier	heaviest
high	higher	highest
late	later	latest
long	longer	longest
noisy	noisier	noisiest
quiet	quieter	quietest
slim	slimmer	slimmest
warm	warmer	warmest

2 1. My boyfriend is the same age as me.
2. He is much taller than me.
3. Who is the best footballer in the world?
4. I speak English a bit better than my father.
5. I think I am as good-looking as a film star.
6. England is very different from the United States.
7. Do you think you are stronger than me?

150

3 17.10.88 – the seventeenth of October, nineteen eighty-eight
5.3.69 – the fifth of March, nineteen sixty-nine
1.12.97 – the first of December, nineteen ninety-seven
3.6.99 – the third of June, nineteen ninety-nine
18.4.1900 – the eighteenth of April, nineteen hundred
21.1.94 – the twenty-first of January, nineteen ninety-four
2.3.36 – the second of March, nineteen thirty-six
20.5.1908 – the twentieth of May, nineteen hundred and
  eight (OR: . . . nineteen oh eight)

4 ALEX: Are you doing anything this evening?
  Well, what about tomorrow?
  Are you free on Thursday?
  What about Friday?
  What about the weekend?

5 Hello, Mary. Yes, I'm sorry. I know, I *wanted* to phone you yesterday but I *didn't have* time. It's crazy here. We *leave* the day *after* tomorrow, and there's too much to do. Yes, China. We *are going for* six weeks. Jim *is working* with some engineers on a big housing development in Beijing and I *am giving* six concerts. Excuse me a minute – the children are very quiet, and I don't like it when I don't know what they *are doing.*

* * *

Sorry about that, Mary. I'm back. It's OK. Sally *is watching* TV and Peter *is making* a cake. Yes, I know. He's a terrible cook, but if that's what he wants to do. No, they *are not coming* with us – they're staying with Granny *for* three weeks, and then Sally *is going* to Louise for the rest of the time, and Peter *is staying* with his friends in Durham. *What* about you? What *is happening* with you and John? Really? So he *is changing* his job to be near you? I say, Mary! Perhaps this is the real thing after all these years.

Oh dear, Sally *is asking* for *something* to eat again. Look, I can't *talk* any more now, but let's meet when we're back. Middle of August, OK? Thanks for phoning. Bye, Mary.

6

F	O	O	T	B	A	L	L	M	A	T	C	H	
A		C		E		A		E		O		A	T
S	A	T		A	N	S	W	E	R		N	O	
T		O		U		T		T	E	N		D	O
	B	O	T	H		D		D	O	E	S		
	H	E		I		O	R		U		O	F	
E	A	R		F	O	R	E	I	G	N		M	E
	P		S	U	N		W			F	E	B	
A	P	R	I	L			S	E	A				
M	Y		T		T	A	L	K	A	T	I	V	E
	H		O		O		I	T		M			
P	R	O	B	A	B	L	Y		S	O	N		
	T		T	E	A		Y	O	U		E		
M	E			T	O	M	O	R	R	O	W		
W	E	L	C	O	M	E		U		E	S		

Unit 16, Lesson B

1 1. is getting
2. are you drinking
3. 's having
4. do you like
5. I don't
6. do you usually go
7. 'm just cooking
8. 'm just practising
9. Are you working
10. don't work

4 Reihenfolge: 17, 4, 13, 16, 9, 2, 8, 14, 12, 6, 1, 15, 10, 5, 3, 7, 11

One day a man was walking in the park when he met a penguin. So he took it to a policeman and asked what to do.

'Take it to the zoo,' answered the policeman. Next day the policeman saw the man again. He still had the penguin.

'Didn't I tell you to take that penguin to the zoo?' he asked.

'I did', said the man, 'and he liked it very much. Now I'm taking him to the cinema.'

Unit 16, Lesson C

1 1. Where does Mrs Wagner work?
2. Does George like fast cars?
3. What is that girl eating?
4. How often does your boss go on holiday?
5. What are you doing this evening?
6. Are Mr and Mrs Smith coming to dinner with us?
7. What does your wife usually have for breakfast?
8. Is Dr Harris working today?

2 (Mögliche Antworten)
1. a city
2. the sea
3. a car
4. a child
5. life
6. a car
7. work
8. a mountain
9. love
10. a month

4 1. looks like
2. look
3. like
4. looks . . . like
5. like
6. look like
7. looks

7 This is a picture of a bank – Barclay's Bank. There are four people in the bank: the cashier, another man, a woman and a small child. The cashier is dark. The other man, who is tall and fair, is taking money from the cashier. The woman is neither tall nor short; she's dark and very pretty. She is on the man's right. She has got two dogs with her. The child is sitting in a chair by the window. There are three doors in the picture. The time is twenty to three in the afternoon; it is Tuesday March 18th.

ÜBUNGEN ZU LESSON 16D ENTFALLEN.

Unit 17, Lesson A

1 1. There aren't any more potatoes.
2. There's no tea in the pot.
3. I spent no money yesterday.
4. Fifty million years ago there weren't any people.
5. There are no good films on TV this evening.
6. We've got no food in the house.

2 CUSTOMER 1: *Have you got a* table *for* four?
WAITER: Yes, just over here, madam.

* * *

C1: *I'll start with* tomato salad, please, and then *I'll have* fish.
W: *And what would you like*, sir?
C2: *I'll start with* soup, and *then I'll have* roast beef with a green salad.

* * *

W: *Would you like something to* drink?
C1: *I'll have a* lager, please.
C2: *Would you give me a* lager, *please*?
W: *Of* course, sir.

* * *

C1: *How's the* beef?
C2: *Not too bad. How about the* fish?
C1: Very good. *The* potatoes aren't very nice, *though*.

* * *

W: *Is everything all right*?
C1: Yes, fine, thank you.

* * *

W: *Can I offer you* a little more coffee?
C1: No, *thank you*.
C2: Yes, *please*.

* * *

C1: *Can you give us the* bill, please?
W: *Certainly, madam*.
C1: *Is* service *included*?
W: Yes, madam.

4
1. 'And for you, sir?' 'Chicken for me, please.'
2. 'Vegetables, sir?' 'Mushrooms and a green salad, please.'
3. 'Would you like something to drink?' 'Just some water, please.'
4. 'How's the chicken?' 'Not too bad.'
5. 'What about the steak?' 'A bit tough.'
6. 'Is everything all right?' 'Oh, yes, excellent, thank you.' 'Very good.'
7. 'Can I give you a little more coffee?' 'No, thank you.' 'Yes, please.'

Unit 17, Lesson B

1 (Mögliche Antworten)
1. 'Sorry to trouble you. Could you lend me some tea?'
'Yes, of course.'
2. 'Excuse me. Have you got a light, please?'
'Just a minute.'
3. 'Have you got a cigarette?'
'Sorry, I don't smoke.'
4. 'Could you lend me your dictionary?'
'I'm afraid I haven't got one.'

2 (Mögliche Antworten)
1. Could you possibly lend me your car for the weekend? (Polite)
2. Could I borrow a pound, please? (Casual)
3. Could you possibly lend me your jacket? (Polite)
4. Excuse me, have you got a cigarette? (Polite)
5. Have you got a cigarette? (Casual)
6. I'm sorry, I'm afraid I'm using it myself this weekend.
7. I'm sorry, I need it myself.
8. I'm sorry, I'm afraid I haven't got any.

3
1. lend
2. borrowed
3. borrow
4. lends
5. borrow

4
1. e
2. d
3. a
4. b
5. f
6. c

You can cook in the kitchen.
You can sleep in the bedroom.
You can wash in the bathroom.
You can sit and watch television in the living room.
You can eat in the dining room.

6

Unit 17, Lesson C

1 (Mögliche Antworten)
A: Excuse me. Where can I buy a colour film near here?
B: I'm sorry. I'm afraid I don't know.
A: Thanks anyway.

     *   *   *

A: Excuse me. Do you know where I can buy some bread?
B: At the supermarket.
A: Could you possibly tell me where it is?
B: First right, second left.
A: Is it far?
B: About two hundred yards.
A: Thank you very much.
B: You're welcome.

     *   *   *

SALLY: Hello. Cambridge 83105.
BRUCE: Hello. Could I speak to Lorna, please?
SALLY: I'm afraid she's out. Can I take a message?
BRUCE: No, it's all right. I'll ring back later.
SALLY: OK. Bye.
BRUCE: Bye.

     *   *   *

A: Let's go to the cinema tonight.
B: No, let's go to the theatre.
A: No, it's too far.
B: OK. Why don't we go and see Mother?
A: No. Look, why don't we stay at home and watch TV?
B: Good idea. OK.

2
1. in
2. on
3. from, to/until
4. on
5. in
6. at
7. to
8. for
9. by
10. of

3
SARAH: Why don't we go to Turkey for our holiday this year?
FATHER: Yeah, OK, why not?
MOTHER: Hey, wait a minute. Let's think about this. Turkey will be much more expensive than France. We can't really drive there – we haven't got the time.
SARAH: Yes, but we can get package holidays to Turkey. Ted went last year, and he said it was great, and really cheap. I can phone about it.

Unit 17, Lesson D

4 A DREAM
Last night I dreamt that I was in a very fast car, driving along a road in Ireland. It was raining, and I couldn't see very well. Then suddenly I saw a woman standing in the middle of the road. When I stopped, she got into the car and told me to drive to Dublin. It was difficult to understand her, because she had a strange accent. She started to sing, and then she looked at me and smiled. I asked her name, but she didn't answer. She smiled again, and kissed me on the cheek. Then I woke up.

Unit 18, Lesson A

1
2. When did he discover them?
3. When was she born?
4. How did he go there?
5. Where did she work?
6. Why were they famous?
7. What was her name? / What did she do?

2
2. Dickens did not paint pictures.
3. Van Gogh did not play football.
4. Maradona did not live in London.
5. Karl Marx did not live in New York.
6. John Lennon did not travel to the moon.
7. Neil Armstrong did not write plays.

3 Amelia Earhart was a famous aeroplane pilot. She was born in Atchison, Kansas in 1898. When she was 22, she stopped her studies at Columbia University, New York, to learn to pilot a plane. Flying lessons were expensive and she took several jobs to pay for them: once she worked as a lorry driver because the pay was good. In 1932 she was the first woman to fly her own plane across the Atlantic, from Newfoundland to Ireland.

4 (Mögliche Antwort)
Marco Polo
– Venice 1254–1324
– to China with father, uncle 1275 (first Europeans)
– ambassador for Chinese emperor
– back to Venice 1295, rich
– wrote book; people did not believe

Unit 18, Lesson B

1
began – begin	left – leave
bought – buy	saw – see
broke – break	thought – think
brought – bring	told – tell
fought – fight	took – take
knew – know	woke – wake

2 (Mögliche Antworten)
1. went	6. took
2. got/came	7. broke
3. had	8. began
4. brought	9. ate/made
5. said, knew/thought	

3
1. then	8. where
2. finally	9. First of all, then, next, finally
3. as soon as	10. and
4. First of all	11. but
5. because	12. that
6. why	13. who
7. so	

6 Florence Nightingale came from a rich family and was very pretty. In her family, young girls usually spent their time going to parties until they married rich young men. But Florence found parties boring; she wanted to be a nurse. Finally, in 1850, when she was 30, her parents accepted her decision. So she went to study in a hospital in Germany. Then she was in charge of a nursing-home for women in London. Soon she was asked to go to the Crimea to take charge of the wounded soldiers.

The conditions in the Crimean hospital were terrible. Forty per cent of the patients died. Certain beds seemed fatal: soldiers died in them after two days. Nightingale decided that this was because of bad drains, and insisted that the government do something about it. Workmen put in a proper drainage system and supplied pure drinking water. The death rate dropped to two per cent. On her return to England people greeted Florence Nightingale as a heroine. She was an important force in the movement to reform hospitals and nursing in England. By 1900 unsafe hospitals and ignorant nurses were things of the past.

Unit 18, Lesson C

3
1. the, the	6. the, the
2. a, –	7. the, The
3. the, –	8. –
4. the, –	9. –
5. an, a	

5
1. How did Blériot travel to England?
2. When did the war start?
3. Why did she leave?
4. Where did you go?
5. What did your mother want?
6. When was Shakespeare born?
7. Who wrote *Hamlet*?
8. What happened yesterday?

6

Unit 18, Lesson D

1
1. I asked for orange juice, not tomato juice.
2. 'Is that Peter?' 'No, this is John.'
3. I don't like yellow. Have you got anything in red?
4. Tuesdays's no good. Can we meet on Thursday?
5. French bread is much nicer than English bread.
6. French bread is nice, but French milk isn't always very good.

3
1. told
2. said
3. tell
4. said
5. says
6. tells
7. told
8. said
9. say

6 Yeah, well, I got up about eight o'clock, didn't I? Washed and shaved, had breakfast. Wrote a letter to my old mother. Went out of the house about, say, 11.30. Met my friend Jake outside the Super Cinema at about twelve. We went for a drink, then we went for a walk in the park. Talked about music and books, things like that. Then we had lunch in a pub somewhere – sandwiches and a glass of orange juice. Then we went to a flower shop to buy some flowers to give to the hospital. After that we went to the art gallery for an hour or two – 'cos old Jake's very interested in pictures. Then I went home, and spent the evening listening to the radio and reading philosophy.

Rolls-Royce? Yes, my Aunt Lucy gave it to me. That's right. Kind of her, wasn't it? Yes, she really loves me, Aunt Lucy does.

Unit 19, Lesson A

1 A: *Excuse me. Is this seat free?*
B: No, *I'm afraid* it *isn't*.

      *   *   *

A: *Could I borrow your* car?
B: Sorry, *I need* it.

      *   *   *

A: *Do you* mind *if I* look at *your* newspaper?
B: *Not at* all.

      *   *   *

A: *Can I* borrow *your* pen?
B: *Yes, of* course.

2
GROUP 1 (like *eat*)	GROUP 2 (like *it*)	GROUP 3 (other)
ski	sing	fine
these	sister	bread
people	this	steak
jeans	him	
meat	England	
meet	pretty	
feel	fridge	
speak		
cheap		

3 (Mögliche Antworten)
I have got some bread.
I have not got enough milk.
My boss has got a lot of houses.
My mother has not got any friends.
My brother has got too many hobbies.

153

4 (Bitten – mit möglichen Antworten)

'Do you mind if I sit here?'
  – 'I'm sorry. It's not free.'
  – 'Go ahead.'
'Do you mind if I smoke?'
  – 'Well, I'd rather you didn't.'
  – 'No, please do.'
'Do you mind if I use your dictionary?'
  – 'I'm sorry. I'm using it myself, actually.'
  – 'Not at all.'
'Do you mind if I ask you a question?'
  – 'I'm sorry. I'm busy at the moment, actually.'
  – 'No, please do.'
'Can I look at your newspaper?'
  – 'Well, I'm reading it myself, actually.'
  – 'Go ahead.'
'Could I open the window?'
  – 'Well, I'd rather you didn't.'
  – 'Please do.'

Unit 19, Lesson B

1 (Mögliche Antworten)

1. often	7. occasionally
2. sometimes	8. never
3. hardly ever	9. hardly ever
4. quite often	10. sometimes
5. occasionally	11. very often
6. hardly ever	

3
1. Do you?
2. Does she?
3. Do you?
4. Does he?
5. Has he?
6. Have you?
7. Did he?
8. Does she?
9. Am I?

4
1. do
2. can't
3. have I
4. am I
5. I'm
6. can
7. do
8. don't

5 'It's three o'clock.' *Is it?*
'I'm hungry.' *Are you?*
'We live in a very small house.' *Do you?*
'I like dancing.' *Do you?*
'Mary telephoned yesterday.' *Did she?*
'Mr and Mrs Harris are coming tomorrow.' *Are they?*
'I forgot to buy bread.' *Did you?*
'We're going on holiday next week.' *Are you?*
'It's snowing.' *Is it?*
'You're late.' *Am I?*
'John's here.' *Is he?*
'My sister works in a cinema.' *Does she?*

Unit 19, Lesson C

2 (Mögliche Antworten)
1. Yes, I do.
2. I like it.
3. Yes, I do.
4. No, I don't.
5. Yes, I do.
6. Yes, I have.
7. No, I haven't.
8. Yes, I have.
9. Yes, I have.
10. No, I haven't.

3
2. Have you always lived in Tokyo?
3. Have you been to Rome before?
4. Have you ever seen any Russian films?
5. Have you ever tried to write a novel?
6. Have you ever been on a plane?
7. Have you ever driven a bus before?

4 ▢▢▢▢   ▢▢▢▢
First on the left.   Buy a large steak.
English and French.   Not the green one.
What do you want?   Thirty-five days.

▢▢▢▢
There were two cars.
Do you live here?
In a red car.
Do you like fish?

Unit 19, Lesson D

1

Grundform	Vergangenheitsform	Dritte Form
Regelmäßige Zeitwörter		
start	*started*	*started*
stop	*stopped*	*stopped*
play	*played*	*played*
change	*changed*	*changed*
Unregelmäßige Zeitwörter		
be	*was*	been
know	*knew*	known
have	*had*	had
see	*saw*	seen
read (/riːd/)	*read* (/red/)	read (/red/)
write	wrote	written
hear (/hɪə(r)/)	heard (/hɜːd/)	heard (/hɜːd/)

2
1. seen
2. been
3. known
4. had
5. been
6. read
7. heard
8. written

3
1. Where *do* you *live*?
2. How long *have* you *lived* there?
3. *Do* you *know* my friend Alison Haynes?
4. How long *have* you *known* her?
5. How long *have* you *had* that watch?
6. *Have* you *read* today's newspaper?
7. *Have* you *seen* Mary today?
8. What *do* you *think* of your new boss?
9. How long *have* you *been* learning English?
10. Why *are* you learning English?

Unit 20, Lesson A

1
1. I am neither fair nor dark.
2. She is neither at home nor in her office.
3. John is neither fat nor slim.
4. It is neither true nor false.
5. I speak neither French nor German.
6. Our village has got neither a bank nor a post office.
7. Neither John nor Peter is married.
8. Neither my mother nor my father smokes.

154

3
1. am
2. was
3. have been
4. can
5. does
6. do
7. Did
8. don't

4

Hauptwort	Eigenschaftswort
Asia	*Asian*
Africa	African
Australia	*Australian*
England	English
Ireland	*Irish*
Scotland	Scottish
Wales	*Welsh*
France	*French*
Germany	*German*
Spain	Spanish
Italy	Italian
Poland	*Polish*
Turkey	*Turkish*
Greece	Greek
Brazil	Brazilian
Mexico	Mexican
Egypt	*Egyptian*
Israel	Israeli
Nigeria	*Nigerian*
Japan	*Japanese*
China	Chinese

5 (Mögliche Antworten)
2. Would you like a drink?
3. Would you like something to do?
4. Would you like to go to bed?
5. Why?
6. Not very often.
7. I am sorry.
8. Oh, really? Which languages?
9. I'm sorry. I need it myself.
10. That's a good idea.
11. Yes, I'd like that.
12. Not at all. Here you are.
13. I don't like it at all.
14. Yes, I do.

Unit 20, Lesson B

1 (Mögliche Antworten)
tea – make, drink
tennis – play, watch
steak – cook, eat
music – play, listen to
TV – watch
a car – buy, drive, wash
a door – open
a train – catch
money – pay, spend
dirty clothes – wash
a book – read, write
a song – sing, listen to
a piano – play
a house – live in

3

10 Bound Road
Wood Park
London SW17 6OJ
16.6.90.

Dear Susan,

Thanks so much for your letter. It was lovely to hear from you again and to get all your news.

Things *are starting* to go very well. I *came* to London in the first week of June, and *found* a room the first day I was here. That was really lucky – some people *spend* ages looking for somewhere to live. It's a nice place in a big house. The landlady's really friendly, and there are a lot of other students. They *come* from all over the world, but most of them *speak* good English, so it's easy to talk to them.

College is OK, but I think I*'m going to change* from Design to Engineering – I*'ve been* interested in Engineering for a long time, and I really think it's the right thing for me. I*'ve talked* to two or three of the teachers about it, and I *saw* the Principal yesterday, and they all say it's OK to change.

Social life is great! I*'ve been* out every night this week, and tomorrow I*'m having* a party in my room for my new friends. Next weekend some of us *are going* to Wales – let's hope the weather's OK. I *play* tennis two or three times a week, too. The only problem is finding time to work!

When *are you going to come* over? It would be lovely to see you, and I'd really like you to meet some of my friends.

Tell Joe I *haven't forgotten* him, and I*'ll write* as soon as I can. And give my love to Alice and Ted and the others. And a big kiss to you. Write again soon.

Love,

Karen

5

Unit 20, Lesson C

1

Grundform	Vergangenheitsform	Dritte Form
spend	*spent*	*spent*
show	*showed*	*shown*
find	*found*	*found*
catch	*caught*	*caught*
learn	*learnt*	*learnt*
pay	*paid*	*paid*
build	*built*	*built*
lead	*led*	*led*
feel	*felt*	*felt*

2 (Mögliche Antworten)
1. any more
2. some more
3. any more
4. some more
5. no more
6. any more
7. a little more
8. some more

4
1. Nobody
2. Everybody
3. get
4. want
5. Behind
6. heard
7. standing
8. looking
9. across
10. lying
11. Tell
12. send
zusätzliches Wort – say

> ÜBUNGEN ZU LESSON 20D ENTFALLEN.

Unit 21, Lesson A

3
1. haven't seen
2. knows
3. has known
4. have you been learning
5. saw
6. 's coming
7. are you doing
8. rains
9. are getting married

4
MAN: I'm taking a year off next year.
WOMAN: Yes? Lucky you. Can you afford it?
MAN: Well, one of my uncles died last year and left me some money. So I'm going to buy some free time.
WOMAN: Great. What are you going to do?
MAN: Oh, lots of things. First of all I'm going to take a big rest. Read my books, listen to music, watch some of my videos, that sort of thing. Then I'm going to do all the things I've always wanted to do. I'm going to learn Chinese, study astronomy, start playing the violin again, walk right across Scotland, take up skiing, write a novel, play some football.
WOMAN: Yes, well, I hope you have a good time. One year, you said?
MAN: No, that's just the spring. Then in summer I'm going to travel round the world, learn karate, . . .

5 RUTH'S PLANS
Ruth *is going* to leave school next summer. She *is going* to *study* engineering at Brunel University, *in* London, but before going there she wants to *spend* a year working. She says '*I want to get* some work experience *before I start studying*.' She *is going to* spend six months in Italy and six *months* in Britain, working in car *factories* where her teacher has got *contacts*.

Unit 21, Lesson B

1
2. When are your parents going to move to London?
3. Why is your son going to study engineering?
4. How are we all going to travel to Scotland?
5. Where is Alice going to buy her new car?
6. Who is going to cook supper?

2 Louise is going to be the lorry driver because her job begins with the same letter as her name. Kate is going to be the tennis player because she is not going to study after leaving school. Mark is going to be the teacher since he is not going to be the doctor or the engineer. This means that George is going to be the doctor, since he cannot become the teacher. Phil is going to be the engineer.

5
A. plane
B. train
C. bus
D. car
E. van
F. motorbike
G. bicycle
H. lorry

Unit 21, Lesson C

1
1. He is going to open the door.
2. She is going to sit down.
3. They are going to have a drink.
4. They are going to see a film.
5. He is going to get into the car.
6. She is going to read a book.
7. The tree is going to fall.

4
1. head
2. ear
3. mouth
4. hair
5. eye
6. nose
7. beard
8. arm
9. hand
10. leg
11. foot

Unit 22, Lesson A

1 (Mögliche Antworten)

A: I've got a cold.
B: *Why don't you take some medicine?*

*   *   *

A: How are you?
B: *I feel* ill.
A: *Why don't you go to the doctor's?*

*   *   *

A: I've got *a bad headache.*
B: *Why don't you take an aspirin?*

*   *   *

A: What's the problem?
B: *My eyes hurt.*

*   *   *

A: Why don't you go to bed?
B: *That's a good idea.*

*   *   *

A: *Have you got a* temperature?
B: I don't think so.

3
1. our
2. their
3. she, she
4. him
5. me
6. we
7. they
8. my
9. us
10. his

5 1c, 2b, 3d, 4e, 5a

Unit 22, Lesson B

1 1. Always
2. Never/Don't
3. Don't/Never
4. Don't
5. Always
6. Never/Don't
7. Never/Don't
8. Never/Don't
9. Don't/Never
10. Don't

2
Grundform	Vergangenheitsform	Dritte Form
cost	cost	*cost*
draw	*drew*	drawn
drink	*drank*	*drunk*
eat	ate	*eaten*
forget	*forgot*	forgotten
get	*got*	*got*
give	gave	*given*
go	*went*	gone/been
leave	*left*	*left*

3 Erm, I think it's bad advice not to run if you feel tired; erm, bad advice not to drink water when you're running. Erm, I think don't run till two hours after eating is good advice. Erm, I don't think it matters if you run when you've got a cold or not. I think it's good advice not to run fast downhill. I think it's bad advice not to run if you're over fifty; and I think it's good advice not to run in fog.

4 C, B, A

Unit 22, Lesson C

1 1g, 2e, 3f, 4a, 5d, 6h, 7b, 8c

3 2. Don't worry
3. Come in
4. Please hurry
5. Follow me
6. Look
7. Look out
8. wait here
9. Take your time

4
Grundform	Vergangenheitsform	Dritte Form
lend	*lent*	*lent*
lie	lay	*lain*
make	*made*	made
mean	*meant*	meant
meet	*met*	*met*
run	ran	*run*
say	*said*	said
send	*sent*	*sent*
show	showed	*shown*
sing	*sang*	sung

6 Sit down, children. Time for your story. Are you all sitting comfortably? Good. Then I'll begin. Once upon a time, long long ago, there was a beautiful girl who lived with her mother and father in a small village. She – don't do that, George – she worked very hard on her father's farm looking after the cows – George, stop that!

7

Unit 22, Lesson D

1 easy – easily
last – lastly
sensitive – sensitively
possible – possibly
probable – probably
certain – certainly
careful – carefully
different – differently
quick – quickly
heavy – heavily

2 1. She opened every book carefully.
2. I like British television very much.
3. She read the newspaper quickly.
4. He said 'No' angrily and walked away fast.
5. He answered the phone sleepily.
6. Please say your name and age clearly.

3 1. saw
2. got
3. built
4. felt, went
5. was, came
6. bought
7. fell
8. flew

5 1. If you take my records again, there's going to be trouble.
2. Good morning. Are there any letters for me?
3. I'm sorry. I can't help you.
4. Don't play with those!
5. What a lovely surprise! Flowers – that *is* nice.
6. All right, Mary, just wait there for a minute and I'll see what I can do for you.

Unit 23, Lesson A

4
Grundform	Vergangenheitsform	Dritte Form
say	*said*	said
take	took	*taken*
buy	*bought*	bought
speak	*spoke*	spoken
leave	left	*left*
understand	*understood*	*understood*
give	*gave*	given
know	knew	*known*
write	*wrote*	*written*
read	read	read
come	came	*come*

Unit 23, Lesson B

1 1. born, on, at, in; baby
2. dream; to, driving, lights; saw, in, of; woke
3. spoke, hear
4. out of, happening
zusätzliche Wörter – again, long, shop

4 1. 263 km/h
2. 34.58 km/h
3. 1001.473 km/h
4. 206.25 km/h
5. 15.121 km/h

Unit 23, Lesson C

1 2. had
3. will go
4. went
5. will come
6. spent
7. will meet
8. met
9. will be
10. was
11. will be
12. was

2 (Mögliche Antworten)
1. . . . green, yellow, pink, *etc.*
2. . . . skirt, shirt, blouse, *etc.*
3. . . . armchair, fridge, cupboard, *etc.*
4. . . . banana, bread, milk, *etc.*
5. . . . engineer, teacher, doctor, *etc.*
6. . . . angry, unhappy, *etc.*
7. . . . quiet, impatient, self-confident, *etc.*
8. . . . bank, shop, restaurant, *etc.*

Unit 23, Lesson D

3 1. next to / by / opposite
2. in
3. after
4. at
5. for
6. before
7. under/near/by/opposite
8. at, at
9. next to
10. on

Unit 24, Lesson A

1 hungry – hungrily
beautiful – beautifully
free – freely
economical – economically
noisy – noisily
quiet – quietly
warm – warmly
sure – surely
real – really
comfortable – comfortably

2 1. She speaks Chinese very well.
2. Please write your address clearly.
3. He wrote my name slowly without looking at me.
4. He closed the door angrily.
5. Please read this paper carefully.

3 (Mögliche Antworten)
2. If you *don't sleep*, you'll get tired.
3. If you *don't drink*, you'll get thirsty.
4. If you *go out in the rain*, you'll get wet.
5. If I *meet her again*, I'll be very happy.
6. If *I don't get a place at university*, I'll be very unhappy.
7. If *the President dies*, it will be very bad for the country.
8. If *there is a revolution*, it will be very good for the country.

4 1c, 2a, 3c, 4b, 5b, 6c, 7a, 8b

5

Unit 24, Lesson B

3 1. woke up
2. saw
3. knew/saw
4. bought
5. took
6. put
7. said, had
8. came
9. could
10. went
11. told
12. began
13. heard

5 1. First of all
2. because
3. When
4. how
5. who
6. Then
7. because
8. Then
9. Finally
10. because
11. so
12. but
13. because
14. I'm afraid
15. So
16. when
17. so
18. what

ÜBUNGEN ZU LESSON 24D ENTFALLEN.

Key to Translations (Lösungen zu den Übersetzungsaufgaben)

Unit 1, Lesson A

5
1. Hallo. Mein Name ist Mary Lake.
2. Hallo. Ja. Raum drei eins zwei (dreihundertzwölf), Mrs. Lake.
3. Danke.
4. Wie heißt du?
5. Catherine.
6. Wie heißt du?
7. John.
8. Heißt du Mary Perkins?
9. Nein. Ich heiße Harry Brown.

Unit 1, Lesson B

4
1. Ihr Name.
2. Sein Name.
3. Ihr Nachname ist Quinton.
4. Sein Vorname ist James.
5. Ich weiß nicht.
6. Ja, das stimmt.
7. Nein, das stimmt nicht.

Unit 1, Lesson C

5
1. Hallo.
2. Wie geht es dir / Ihnen?
3. (bei Vorstellung mit Handschlag) Guten Tag / Abend, angenehm (formell)
4. Danke, gut.
5. Entschuldigung, entschuldigen Sie.
6. Es tut mir leid, Entschuldigung.

Unit 1, Lesson D

4
1. Woher kommst du / kommen Sie?
2. Sie kommt aus Indien.
3. Er ist Chinese.
4. Helena ist aus Griechenland.
5. Andrew ist Schotte.

Unit 2, Lesson A

5
1. Was machst du / machen Sie? (beruflich)
2. (bei Vorstellung mit Handschlag) Guten Tag / Abend, angenehm (formell)
3. Wie geht es dir / Ihnen?
4. Ich bin Ingenieur(in).
5. Sie ist Ingenieurin.
6. Er ist Ingenieur.
7. Ist sie Ärztin?
8. Ja.
9. Nein.

Unit 2, Lesson B

6
1. Guten Morgen.
2. Hallo.
3. Guten Tag. (nur nachmittags anzuwenden)
4. Guten Abend.
5. Mir geht es sehr gut, danke.
6. Danke, gut.
7. Mir geht es heute nicht gut.
8. Oh, es tut mit leid, das zu hören.

Unit 2, Lesson C

5
1. elf
2. zwölf
3. dreizehn
4. neunzehn
5. Sie ist verheiratet.
6. Er ist alleinstehend, unverheiratet.
7. Das ist interessant.

Unit 2, Lesson D

6
1. Wie alt bist du / sind Sie?
2. Wie geht es dir / Ihnen?
3. Er lebt getrennt.
4. Sie ist geschieden.
5. Sie ist Witwe.
6. (ein)hundert
7. Herr Jackson
8. Frau Jackson
9. Fräulein Jackson
10. Dr Jackson

Unit 3, Lesson A

5
1. Johns Mantel liegt auf dem Tisch.
2. Wo ist Pollys Tasche?
3. Liegt Anns Mantel auf dem Stuhl?
4. Anns Stift liegt auf Johns Buch.

Unit 3, Lesson B

4
1. Sie ist hübsch.
2. Er sieht ganz gut aus.
3. Dies ist Sams Freund, Eric.
4. Dies ist Sams Freundin, Judy.
5. Sie ist Engländerin. Nein, sie ist Französin.

Unit 3, Lesson C

6
1. Joe und Ann haben drei Kinder.
2. Ich habe zwei Töchter und einen Sohn.
3. Wie heißen sie?
4. Mein Sohn heißt Fred.
5. Meine Töchter heißen Alice und Lucy.
6. Wer ist Johns Tochter?

Unit 3, Lesson D

3
1. Setze dich / Setzen Sie sich, bitte.
2. Du bist / Sie sind Kanadier(in), oder?
3. Entschuldigen Sie mich einen Augenblick.
4. Wie viele Kinder hast du / haben Sie?
5. Wie bitte?

Unit 5, Lesson D

5
1. Es gibt zwei Schlafzimmer im Haus.
2. Es gibt eine Couch / ein Sofa im Wohnzimmer.
3. Meine Schwester arbeitet in Edinburgh.

4. Ich wohne in der Valley Road 37.
5. Meine Schwester wohnt im Erdgeschoß und mein Bruder wohnt in einer kleinen Wohnung im dritten Stock.
6. Entschuldige / Entschuldigen Sie, wo ist die nächste Post?
7. Dort drüben, rechts.
8. „Vielen Dank". Keine Ursache.
9. Es tut mir leid, ich weiß es nicht.
10. Trotzdem, vielen Dank.
11. Gehe / Gehen Sie ungefähr 300 Meter geradeaus.
12. (Die) erste rechts, dann (die) zweite links.
13. Wie weit ist es / das?

Unit 6, Lesson D

4
1. Ich mag keine Katzen, aber mein Bruder mag sie sehr.
2. „Hast du / Haben Sie Hunde gern," „Ja." / „Nein."
3. Je nachdem. / Es kommt darauf an.
4. Wie spät ist es?
5. Zehn nach drei; halb vier; (ein) Viertel vor vier; fünf (Minuten) vor vier
6. Sie ist zu Hause.
7. Er ist in der Schule.
8. Stan steht um sieben (Uhr) auf.
9. Nach dem Frühstück fährt er mit dem Bus zur Arbeit.
10. Wann steht Karen auf?
11. Welche Zeitung liest du / lesen Sie?
12. Was für Musik magst du / mögen Sie?

Unit 7, Lesson D

4
1. Weißt du / Wissen Sie, daß Kartoffeln achtzig *pence* das Kilo kosten?
2. Alles ist so teuer.
3. Das ist schrecklich.
4. Es liegen keine Bücher auf dem Tisch.
5. Es liegt kein Schnee im Garten.
6. „Gibt es auch Blonde in deiner / Ihrer Familie?" „Ja." „Nein."
7. Ich verstehe nicht.
8. Wie viele Staaten gibt es in den USA?
9. Es sind nicht viele Leute hier.
10. Es gibt nicht genügend Licht in diesem Zimmer.
11. Ich habe zu viel Arbeit.

Unit 9, Lesson D

6
1. Ich habe lange dunkle Haare und mein Bruder auch.
2. Meine Schwester hat braune Augen und graue Haare.
3. Pat trägt einen weißen Pullover, eine grüne Bluse und einen grünschwarzen Rock.
4. Ich kann mich nicht an ihre Augenfarbe erinnern.

5. Wie heißen die (hier)?
   Wie nennt man die (hier)?
6. Wie sprichst du / sprechen Sie dieses Wort aus?
7. Hattest du / Hatten Sie eine angenehme Reise?
8. Nicht schlecht, danke.
9. Mein Auto steht draußen.
10. Mit freundlichen Grüßen (Briefschluß)

Unit 10, Lesson D

4 1. Ich habe Hunger und bin ziemlich müde.
2. Den Kindern ist kalt.
3. Sie hat überhaupt keinen Durst.
4. Wenn ich mich langweile, gehe ich ins Kino.
5. Kann ich dir / Ihnen helfen?
6. Ich schaue mich nur um.
7. Ich suche einen Pullover.
8. Gelb steht mir nicht.
9. Welche Größe?
10. Kann ich es anprobieren?
11. Was kostet das?
12. Ich hätte gerne ein Zimmer.
13. Können Sie bitte etwas langsamer sprechen?

Unit 11, Lesson D

6 1. Als ich jünger war, haßte ich die Schule.
2. Ich habe fünfmal die Schule gewechselt.
3. Ich bin in einem Dorf in Südafrika geboren.
4. Meine Eltern waren sehr arm.
5. Mein Vater war Bauer.
6. Wir waren nicht sehr glücklich.
7. Ich bin wieder um drei (Uhr) morgens nach Hause gekommen.
8. Ich konnte meinen Schlüssel nicht finden; also bin ich durch ein Fenster gestiegen.

Unit 13, Lesson D

5 1. Ich kann singen, aber ich kann nicht zeichnen.
2. Ich war gut in Mathematik als ich jünger war, aber jetzt bin ich es nicht mehr.
3. Ich bin viel größer als meine Mutter.
4. Mario ist etwas älter als sein Bruder.
5. Ein Volkswagen fährt nicht so leise wie ein Rolls-Royce.
6. Sie sieht so gut aus wie eine Filmschauspielerin.

Unit 14, Lesson D

5 1. Das Auto ist etwa 4 Meter lang.
2. Ich bin über zwanzig und unter dreißig.
3. Meine Mutter ist 66, aber sie sieht älter aus.
4. Wie groß bist du / sind Sie?
5. „Was ist heute?" „Dienstag."
6. „Welches Datum ist heute?" „Der siebzehnte."
7. übermorgen; vorgestern
8. Ist das Mary? Das ist Peter.
9. Könnte ich Ann sprechen?

10. Einen Augenblick.
11. Es tut mir leid, sie ist nicht da. Kann ich etwas ausrichten?

Unit 15, Lesson D

6 1. Was ist los?
2. Was machst du / machen Sie?
3. Meine Mutter kauft wahrscheinlich gerade ein.
4. Die Sonne scheint.
5. Wir haben viel Spaß.
6. Morgen fahren wir nach London.
7. Hast du / Haben Sie heute abend etwas vor?
8. „Möchtest du dir / Möchten Sie sich mit mir einen Film anschauen?" „Es tut mir leid, ich habe keine Zeit."
9. Sie ist der intelligenteste Mensch, den ich kenne.
10. „Ich gehe im April nach Amerika." Das ist schön. Für wie lange?"

Unit 16, Lesson C

6 1. Du siehst / Sie sehen glücklich aus.
2. Sie sieht ihrer Mutter etwas ähnlich.
3. Wie ist dein / Ihr neuer Chef?
4. Bist du / Sind Sie wie dein / Ihr Bruder?
5. Magst du deinen Bruder?

Unit 17, Lesson D

3 1. Haben Sie einen Tisch für zwei (Personen)?
2. Ich fange mit Suppe an.
3. Ist alles in Ordnung?
4. Möchtest du / Möchten Sie noch etwas Kaffee?
5. Könnten Sie uns bitte die Rechnung bringen?
6. Inklusive Bedienung?
7. Entschuldigen Sie die Störung, könnten Sie mir etwas Brot (aus-)leihen?
8. Könntest du / Könnten Sie mir vielleicht für eine halbe Stunde das Auto (aus-)leihen?
9. Könnte ich mir deinen / Ihren Regenschirm leihen?
10. Warum fahren wir dieses Jahr nicht nach Kalifornien in Urlaub?
11. Eh, warte mal eine Minute. Laß(t) uns darüber nachdenken.
12. Ich denke, das ist eine gute Idee.
13. Laß(t) uns ein Flugzeug nach Spanien nehmen.

Unit 18, Lesson D

5 1. Galileo ist im 16. Jahrhundert geboren.
2. Sie war die erste Frau, die ein Flugzeug über den Atlantik flog.
3. Wie heißt der Mann, der das Penizillin entdeckte?
4. Die Studenten kamen aus ganz Europa, um seine Vorlesungen zu hören.

5. Für welche Sportart war Pele bekannt?
6. Ich bin aufgestanden, habe mich rasiert und habe gefrühstückt.
7. Er sagte dem Polizisten, daß er um 8 Uhr aufgestanden sei; tatsächlich ist er aber um 10 Uhr aufgestanden.
8. Das stimmt nicht.
9. Beide, Al und Jake sind spät ins Bett gegangen.
10. Weder Al noch Jake sind zum Fußballspiel gegangen.

Unit 19, Lesson D

4 1. Ist dieser Platz frei?
2. „Macht es dir / Ihnen etwas aus, wenn ich mich hierhin setze?" „Nein, überhaupt nicht."
3. Lieber, nicht!
4. Ich komme immer am Sonntagmorgen hierher.
5. Oh, wirklich? Ich auch.
6. Ich gehe alle sechs Wochen ins Theater.
7. Sie geht zweimal im Jahr Skifahren.
8. Was hältst du / halten Sie von der Regierung?
9. Hast du / Haben Sie schon immer in London gelebt?
10. Bist du / Sind Sie schon mal in Afrika gewesen?
11. seit 24 Stunden; seit gestern
12. Wie lange wohnst du / wohnen Sie hier?
13. Wie lange lernst du / lernen Sie schon Englisch?

Unit 21, Lesson D

5 1. Peter und Ann werden heiraten.
2. Dies wird das Kinderzimmer sein.
3. Das Badezimmer wird im Erdgeschoß sein.
4. Sie bekommt ein Kind.
5. Ich ging in die Bücherei, um ein Buch auszuleihen.
6. Ich ging in den Buchladen, um ein Buch zu kaufen.
7. Auf der ganzen Welt lernen Menschen Englisch.
8. Ich lerne Englisch, um Geschäfte in englischsprechenden Ländern zu machen.

Unit 22, Lesson D

4 1. Was ist los?
2. Ich fühle mich krank.
3. Ich habe eine Erkältung.
4. Ich habe Zahnschmerzen.
5. Mein Bein tut weh.
6. Laufe nicht, wenn du dich müde fühlst.
7. Beeile dich bitte, Liebling.
8. Laß dir / Lassen Sie sich Zeit.
9. Sei / Seien Sie vorsichtig.
10. Vorsicht!
11. Folgen Sie mir.
12. Ich bin sehr ärgerlich auf dich.
13. Sie sprach mich wütend an.
14. Du sprichst / Sie sprechen gut Englisch.